# THE MUSICAL WESLEYS

# STUDIES IN CHURCH MUSIC

*General Editor:* ERIK ROUTLEY, B.D., D.Phil., F.R.S.C.M.

*Volumes in this series*

MUSIC AND THE REFORMATION IN ENGLAND, 1549–1660
by Peter Le Huray, Ph.D., Mus.B.

TWENTIETH CENTURY CHURCH MUSIC
by Erik Routley

CHURCH MUSIC IN THE NINETEENTH CENTURY
by Arthur Hutchings, Mus.D.

ENGLISH CHURCH MUSIC 1625–1750
by Christopher Dearnley, Mus.B.

THE MUSICAL WESLEYS
by Erik Routley

# THE
# MUSICAL WESLEYS

By

ERIK ROUTLEY

*New York*
OXFORD UNIVERSITY PRESS
1968

© Erik Routley 1968

Library of Congress Catalogue Card Number: 68-55307

Printed in Great Britain

# Contents

|  | page |
| --- | --- |
| PREFACE | vii |
| ACKNOWLEDGEMENTS | xii |

1. THOSE REMARKABLE WESLEYS    1
   Some account of the peculiar tendency of the Wesley family towards the achievement of eminence.

2. JOHN WESLEY, MUSIC CRITIC    6
   Some musical references in the *Journal* of John Wesley, together with the treatise *The Power of Music* [1779] with some notes and glosses.

3. CHARLES WESLEY AND METHODIST MUSIC    28
   A discussion of the special ministry of Charles Wesley in hymns, and of the origins of the music to which hymns were first sung in evangelical circles.

4. "THE REV. CHARLES WESLEY'S ACCOUNT OF HIS TWO SONS"    43
   Transcribed from the *Journal*, with historical notes.

5. THE PROGRESS OF THE TWO SONS    58
   An account of the external events in the lives of Charles junior and of Samuel.

6. THE MUSIC OF THE TWO SONS    76
   Charles's music. Samuel's encounter with the music of J. S. Bach. Samuel as a musician.

7. SAMUEL SEBASTIAN, HIS LIFE AND ADVENTURES    102
   Introductory matter on the life of S. S. Wesley (1810–76).

8. THE CONDITION OF CHURCH MUSIC IN THE EARLY NINETEENTH CENTURY    109
   Evidence chiefly from J. A. Latrobe's *The Music of the Church* (1831) and, at a later stage, from the history of the Three Choirs' Festival.

9. SAMUEL SEBASTIAN ON CATHEDRAL MUSIC    127
   Light on S. S. Wesley's musicianship and methods from his own tract, *A Few Words on Cathedral Music*.

10. S. S. WESLEY'S CHORAL WORKS    138
    A critique of the chief choral works and of the Service in E.

v

*page*

11. THE ORGAN AND THE WESLEYS                                177
An interpolation on the condition of the English organ during
the first part of the nineteenth century, and its effect on the
texture of church music composition.

12. SAMUEL SEBASTIAN AND THE ENGLISH HYMN
TUNE                                                         195
A discussion chiefly of the contents of the *European Psalmist*
(1872).

13. A POSTSCRIPT AND A CONCLUSION                            233
On Anglican chants: the musicianship of the Wesleys.

APPENDIX I. Hymn tunes by Samuel Sebastian Wesley surviving in
the leading hymnals current in 1967                          246

IA. Hymn tunes by Samuel Sebastian Wesley appearing in
three English hymnals published 1904–14                      248

Symbols used in Appendixes I and IA                          249

II. The Handel-Wesley hymn tunes                             250

III. Extracts from a letter from Christian Ignatius Latrobe to
Joseph Foster Barham, M.P.                                   254

IV. A summary of the works of the musical Wesleys            256

V. On Samuel Wesley's *Original Hymn Tunes*, 1828            258

SELECTIVE BIBLIOGRAPHY                                       264

INDEXES

Index to the Principal Members of the Wesley Family          266

General Index                                                269

# Preface

It is now nearly ten years since it was suggested that I might write a study of the Wesley family in relation to their music. Many interruptions have held up the work, and now that I venture to present it, I feel that some explanation of its form is called for.

It has proved to be a fascinating subject, yet in some ways an exasperating one. It is difficult to resist the magic of the Wesley family; and yet, concerning the Wesley musicians, the amount of "hard" information available is tantalizingly small. The subject has engaged the attention of several authors, and there are one or two whom it seems to have defeated. For one of my difficulties has been that while this work was in its earlier stages I found that certain writings on the musical Wesleys were announced, for which I thought I had better wait. At least two of these works never did appear, and I have been given to understand that they have been abandoned.

Then, further, I found at a late stage that a close study of the music of Samuel Sebastian Wesley had been made by an American scholar; I am glad to be able to refer to this in the bibliography, and also to another American Wesley study, but neither of these has, as I write, found its way to publication.

Leaving aside the mountain of theological work that has been done on John Wesley and the smaller quantity written on his brother Charles, I find that the existing literature on the subject I have here attempted is small and somewhat patchy.

The classic source for the childhood of Charles junior and of his brother Samuel is, obviously, the *Journal* of Charles

Wesley senior. This is not a systematic and extensive work like that of the great John. The published *Journal* runs only from 1736 to 1756; to it are added other autobiographical papers and (in the standard two-volume edition) a selection of poems. It is from these additional papers that we get our accounts of the remarkable childhood years of Charles junior and Samuel.

There are a number of letters to be found in the Wesley archives, as well as a sketchy autobiography by Samuel (British Museum Add. Mss. 27,593), and on the whole they are remarkably unrevealing. Two later authors have done their best to gather material for biographies; they are W. Winters and J. T. Lightwood.

W. Winters, who seems to have been a priest at Waltham Abbey, published his *Account . . . of the Wesley Family* in 1874. The little ninety-page paperback is marked at one shilling: my copy, bought ninety years after its publication cost me half a guinea. It was, in its day, a valuable little work. It reprints the relevant parts of Charles senior's *Account of His Two Sons*, and, what is more valuable, a good deal of the autobiography of Samuel. It also sets out the whole of John Wesley's *On the Power of Music*, and it gives some other matter by way of gloss and comment, including that which appears in my Appendix II. But it has only half a page on Samuel Sebastian, who was still alive when it was written and deserved better; and there are many things it does not mention, especially Samuel's advocacy of J. S. Bach. Indeed, apart from its useful quotations from primary sources, it does little more than give a slightly romantic account of two young musical prodigies whose subsequent careers provided relatively little fulfilment of their early promise. Oddly enough, it does not mention the famous "accident" to Samuel—of which more in a moment. Since the date of the standard edition of Charles Wesley's *Journal* is 1849, one wonders why Winters went to the trouble of copying out the paper from the British Museum manuscript, as he claimed to have done.

Lightwood's biography of Samuel, the only full-scale ac-

count that exists, is a much more informative work. It is somewhat disorganized (but having been over this rough country
myself, I should be the last to blame Lightwood for that). It is
very short on musical criticism, and it relies at one or two
points on tradition which I think is unverifiable. In the matter
of Samuel Wesley's famous accident, which was first high-
lighted by Winters, Lightwood accepts the story that it was
responsible for all Samuel's eccentricities and failures in his
later years. I have been unable to find any serious medical
evidence about this business, and I am myself disposed to be a
good deal more cautious about this story. I am sure he had an
accident, and I am sure that he was ill after it. But when I look
at the marked depressive characteristics that are evident in both
his brother and his son, I am disposed to think that had there
been no accident, we still should not have had a Mozart in
Samuel Wesley. I have ventured to argue on these lines in the
course of this work.

And when you have mentioned these two sources, together
with the very useful scraps of scholarly conjecture that we find
in the introductions to the Hinrichsen edition of some of the
Wesleys' organ music (for which we have to thank Stainton
de B. Taylor, Gordon Phillips, and Peter Williams), we come
to the end of the serious literature about the Wesley trio. We
have very little from the men themselves that throws light on
their lives. Our account of their adventures has to be episodic
and incomplete; and where we are guessing, we have to say so.

But for me, and for the reader of a book in this series, it is
the music that matters. Very well then; what is the music like?
I must say at once that, for a reader who may be accustomed
to studying large works on the music of the great composers
in sacred or secular music, the music discussed here is a very
minor subject. The two senior musicians, Charles and Samuel,
were on the whole not very interesting composers. The
romance surrounding Samuel's "accident" has led to what I
regard as somewhat nostalgic speculations about what Samuel
might have written had he remained whole and sane. He was

1*

capable, on his best days, of really first-class work, but on that reckoning, his best days would add up to about a week. As for Charles, he has left nothing that appeals to anybody but an historian. Even his hymn tunes are preserved only because he has an illustrious name. If they had appeared anonymously in, say, Rippon's *Selection* they would have died generations ago. Samuel Sebastian is a more interesting but more limited composer, since he confined himself to church music. He was sometimes a remarkably bad composer, and sometimes looked like a really good one. His level was not quite low enough to have made him (had he been so inclined) a successful composer of secular music in the age of the Victorian bourgeoisie, but it was not high enough to get him clear of the swamp into which church music had fallen. He made some attempt to raise himself by his own bootstraps, but the bootstraps broke.

These three men were not great musicians. Their music is not rewarding to close study. I have studied it here as closely as I think it right to do short of boring my reader to rebellion. I have devoted a good deal of space to Samuel Sebastian because his music is more familiar than that of the other two, and because, from one angle, it is more interesting. Some may feel that I have given disproportionate attention to his hymn tunes.

But that brings me to the heart of my apologia. Hymn tunes are, rightly viewed by an historian, a very good clue to social history. They show a congregation behaving musically, and because people's musicianship in singing a hymn is unconscious, they betray certain values which in more censored moments they would rationalize or hide. Those who criticize hymn tunes directly (people like Martin Shaw and Percy Dearmer in later generations) are usually making social judgments as much as musical ones. And what applies to Samuel Sebastian's hymns applies in a more general way to all the music in this study. Their music may be uninteresting in itself, but these three Wesleys have a good deal to tell us about what music meant to the people of their time. You cannot talk this way about Mozart or Beethoven; there the music is all that really matters, but when music is made which on the whole doesn't matter as much as that, then other thoughts come into the mind. What did these men think they were doing when they made music? Now in Charles we have a musical journeyman who just wrote—for reasons we shall try to ascertain. In Samuel senior we have a similar journeyman, whose musical biography was punctuated by two massive crises—his contact with the Portuguese Embassy and his discovery of Bach. In Samuel Sebastian we have a musician who worked under protest at the conditions that surrounded him, who, in a less philistine society, and given a less anxious temperament, might have come to something. I cannot feel that Samuel or Charles would ever have made Mozarts, but I do feel that just possibly in other circumstances Samuel Sebastian might have made at least a Mendelssohn or a Gounod (and these two I regard as at least successful musicians, even if they were disastrous in that small part of their output that happened to fall in the ecclesiastical field).

So I am telling the story as I find it. I am convinced that these three musicians form a chapter in music, and especially in church music, which is worth reading.

E.R.
Edinburgh
June 1967

# *Acknowledgements*

I wish to thank several people who have helped me in this work: Mr Robert L. Arrowsmith, formerly Classics master at Charterhouse, for identifying a Latin quotation; Sir John Dykes Bower, formerly of St Paul's Cathedral, for giving me the evidence on the anthem which John Wesley heard there on the day of his conversion and much other help; my son Patrick Routley for copying out the music examples and doing other research; and my publisher for being so patient.

E.R.

JOHN WESLEY 1703–1791

CHARLES WESLEY 1707–1788

CHARLES WESLEY II 1757–1834

SAMUEL WESLEY 1766–1837

SAMUEL SEBASTIAN WESLEY 1810–1876

# I

# *Those Remarkable Wesleys*

The subject of luxury having been introduced, Dr Johnson defended it. "We have now", said he, "a splendid dinner before us; which of all these dishes is unwholesome?" The duke asserted, that he had observed the grandees of Spain diminished in their size by luxury. Dr Johnson politely refrained from opposing directly an observation which the duke himself had made; but said, "Man must be very different from other animals, if he is diminished by good living; for the size of all other animals is increased by it." I made some remark that seemed to imply a belief in *second sight*. The duchess said, "I fancy you will be a Methodist".—This was the only sentence her grace deigned to utter to me; and I take it for granted, she thought it a good hit on my *credulity* in the Douglas cause.

That evening of Monday, 25 October, 1773, cannot have been a comfortable occasion for James Boswell; but he writes of it, in his *Journal of a Tour to the Hebrides* (1785) with the air of one who, come what might, did his duty. He had called at Inveraray Castle, whose lady was not on speaking terms with him; he had introduced the name of the Doctor; he had procured a mighty civil invitation from the Duke of Argyll that they should both dine; and he had sat through a long evening under the chandeliers of Inveraray, during which the Duchess offered him but one observation: "I fancy you will be a *Methodist*."

She meant no compliment. There was an accent in which, even when John Wesley had passed his seventieth birthday, one could refer to "a *Methodist*", which we may be sure that the noble lady used. It implied, in him to whom such a comment was addressed, a religious association which set him apart from gracious company, and put him with "persons in trade" and other undesirables. There are still pockets of culture in which this accent survives, though it is nowadays rarely heard. When heard, it is more likely to be applied to an active member of the Campaign for Nuclear Disarmament, and with different, though no less pejorative, social overtones.

There is, however, a sign by which you may know whether your interlocutor is a true follower of John Wesley. It is not the sign of social dissent or of religious credulity. Should you hear him pronounce one of the six most famous names in English history to rhyme with "expressly", you may, without fear of its being taken as Boswell took the Duchess's words, fancy him to be, if not a Methodist, at least no disparager of Methodism; or perhaps an historian with a decent ear.

Such facts as that "Wesley" was before the eighteenth century "Westley", and that the Wesleys were kinsmen of the Wellesleys, the most eminent of whom, Arthur, first Duke of Wellington, spelt his name Wesley until he was twenty-eight, may be found in any biography of John Wesley. To the number of books specifically written about this staggering pioneer of modern evangelical religion, I am not here attempting to add. It is hardly too much to say that John Wesley was the most distinguished figure in English church history since King Henry VIII; others have said it with greater competence than I can here command. We are concerned with the Wesleys as musicians; and in this story, John Wesley (1703–91) must be introduced in the somewhat unfamiliar status of the hero of a prologue. With the best will in the world, we shall not be able to call John a musician; but of him and his brother Charles we may say something, for this John adds to his other distinctions those of being the uncle, twice over and also the great uncle, of a singular succession of English musicians, of all of whom it may be said that what they lack in absolute eminence in the history of European music at large, they compensate in being historical focuses of the social development of music in England.

Our chief business, then, is with Charles Wesley (1757–1834), Samuel Wesley (1766–1837) and Samuel Sebastian Wesley (1810–76). We introduce them by offering first some observations about the musical connections of the two best-known members of the senior generation.

There were, according to Eric Blom's (Everyman) *Dictionary of Music*, fifty-three Bachs eminent in music; Karl Geiringer's ampler list in *The Bach Family* (1957) mentions ninety-seven. How many Wesleys, Westleys or Wellesleys were famous in English history generally we will not stay to compute. It will not be so fabulous a number as that of the Bachs. But it cannot be overlooked that, apart from the first Duke of Wellington, our *Dictionary of National Biography* mentions Garrett Wellesley (or Wesley), first Earl of Mornington (1735–81), an able aristocratic musician remembered in those places where his Anglican chants in D and E flat are sung, and of whom it is told that he was the first English member of the aristocracy to allow himself to be seen carrying a violin case through the streets of London; then there is his son, Richard Colley, Marquis Wellesley (1760–1842), Governor-General of India; there is Henry Wellesley D.D., antiquary (1791–1866), natural son of this Richard Colley; Henry Wellesley, first Baron Cowley, third son of the first Earl (1773–1847), M.P., and diplomatist. There is his son, Henry Richard Charles, first Earl Cowley (1804–84), another diplomatist. Baron Cowley's third son, Gerald Valerian Wellesley (1809–92), became Dean of Windsor. William Wellesley-Pole, third Earl of Mornington in the Irish peerage and first Baron Maryborough in the United Kingdom (1763–1845), became a cabinet minister under Lord Liverpool's ministry; William Pole Tylney Long-Wellesley, fourth Earl of Mornington and second Baron Maryborough

(1788–1857), became an M.P., but developed a somewhat discreditable record. All these could call the evangelical Wesleys "cousin". All go back in their ancestry to that Puritan stock which produced the real vitality of England from the time of Cromwell to that of Gladstone.

Going back in history, it seems that the name "Wesley" came from an estate in Somerset called Welslegh, to which, according to tradition, the widow of the head of the family fled after the battle of Hastings in which her husband and all her sons over sixteen were killed. Thereafter, the Wesleys (Welswes, Welsleghs, Wellesleys, Wellesleighs) are Somerset people, maintaining connexions with a branch of the family which moved early to Ireland. Hence the Irish strain which turns up constantly in the family tree. Bartholomew Wesley, born about 1600, had for his father Sir Herbert Wesley, and for his mother the Irish Elizabeth Wellesley. The eighteenth-century distinction of the Morningtons, Irish peers, we have already noted. Bartholomew Wesley became a dissenting minister in Dorset and lost his living for espousing the Cromwellian cause at Worcester (1651).

The lustrous honours which gather round the name when it is spelt with three l's contrast oddly and instructively with the kind of life which the seventeenth-century Wesleys lived. Both John's grandfathers were ministers of the Puritan persuasion who, like his paternal great-grandfather Bartholomew, lost their livings at the Great Ejectment of 1662. His father, Samuel Wesley (1662–1735), born in the very year of that Ejectment, born to the name spelt Westley, was, by all accounts, a pious, scholarly and undistinguished minister of the Church of England, who in his personal life suffered his share of ill fortune, but who lived to a decent seventy-three. This was not precisely lustre. But with the new generation, there arises this John, who, had he not been a religious leader, would surely have competed with Arthur Wellesley himself in political and even possibly in military distinction.

Enough has been said to remind the reader that this is one of

England's most illustrious families; not of the ancient, but of the more recent, Puritan-based, aristocracy; not of those who have held title or influence from the Middle Ages, but rather, Cecil-wise, of those who through several generations have built themselves into the country's culture, and defied all dislodgement. Genius of a kind—of various kinds—was never far from a Wesley. The special genius of John was a quality which, in some ways, his distinguished relatives must all have shared; his precise, observant and eager mind.

This is, I think, prior to, and not a consequence of, his celebrated capacity for organization. No really brilliant administrator can manage without a certain kind of alertness and a good memory skilfully used. As one reads his *Journal*, one is impressed on every page by the fact that nothing lay outside his interest; nothing new could come into his sight but it would have, for the moment, his full attention, and elicit a characteristic and wise comment. It is this special faculty for observing what others merely see, for listening to what others passively hear, that would have made Wesley an outstanding politician had that been his destiny. Far from inerrant, far from uniformly patient, far from incapable of misjudgment, John would none the less never commit an error that was the direct result of ignorance or of inattention.

This happens to be important for our present enquiry. For John was not in any sense a musician. He may have been "naturally musical"; he may even have been a "music lover". But music is just one more of the thousand things which, when he notices them, are observed with a positive attention that many more naturally gifted might deny it. In the vast compass of his *Journal* there is not very much to be heard about music, but what he does say is not without historical and psychological interest, and it provides pegs on which to hang a few observations that will fill in a serviceable background for what is to come.

# John Wesley—Music Critic

### THE JOURNAL

The references to music in John Wesley's *Journal* fall into four groups: observations about music in general, about singing in church, about choirs, and about organs. Here is one which takes up the point we have just made; here is John Wesley, aged sixty-five, making a discovery.

[1] *22 October, 1768.* I was much surprised in reading an *Essay on Music*, wrote by one who is a thorough master of the subject, to find that the music of the ancients was as simple as that of the Methodists; that their music wholly consisted of melody, or the arrangement of single notes; that what is now called harmony, singing in parts, the whole of counterpoint and fugues, is quite novel, being never known in the world till the popedom of Leo the Tenth. He farther observes that, as the singing of different words by different persons at the very same time necessarily prevents attention to the sense, so it frequently destroys melody for the sake of harmony; meantime it destroys the very end of music, which is to affect the passions. [5. 290]

His author here is Charles Avison (d. 1770), who, in 1752, wrote a book called *Expression in Music*, from pages 49 and 63 of which John Wesley is here quoting. His attention may well

have been drawn to Avison by a hearing of his music a few
years before, of which he writes:

> [2] *13 February, 1765.* I heard *Ruth*, an oratorio, performed at Mr
> Madan's Chapel. The sense was admirable throughout; and
> much of the poetry not contemptible. This, joined with the
> exquisite music, might possibly make an impression even upon
> rich and honourable sinners.  [5. 106]

If Avison thought that there was no polyphony before the
pontificate of Leo X, which lasted from 1513 to 1521, then he
had yet to learn of the famous encyclical of Pope John XXII,
two hundred years earlier (1325) in which the dangerous effects
of polyphonic singing were set out in a solemn warning to the
faithful, and its extravagances were explicitly proscribed. But,
as we shall later see, this was an observation which chimed well
with Wesley's musical principles. He was never a lover of
polyphonic music.

There is another record of Wesley's talking music with a
musician, this time in personal encounter.

> [3] *13 June, 1748.* I spent an hour or two with Dr Pepusch. He
> asserted that the art of music is lost; that the ancients only
> understood it in its perfection; that it was revived a little in the
> reign of King Henry VIII by Tallis and his contemporaries; as
> also in the reign of Queen Elizabeth, who was a judge and a
> patroness of it; that, after her reign, it sunk for sixty or seventy
> years, till Purcell made some attempts to restore it; but that
> ever since the true, ancient art, depending on nature and
> mathematical principles, had gained no ground, the present
> masters having no fixed principles at all.  [3. 355]

This is Johann Christoph Pepusch (1667–1752), the German
composer and theorist, who like Handel settled in England in
the eighteenth century, and who arranged the music for *The
Beggar's Opera*. In 1748, Pepusch was a man of eighty-one, and
was talking like one. It is fascinating to contemplate the mind
of one who thought that Arne and Boyce were unprincipled
rascals. He is talking, of course, just as a convinced Elgarian

would talk of Poulenc, and what he says is very much to Wesley's taste.

It is important at this early stage to be clear that in music Wesley was a thoroughgoing conservative. Although he would no doubt accept Pepusch's opinion that the music of William Byrd was a very good kind of music (though not up to the standard of plainsong, which seems to be what the old man meant), it is hardly likely that if he heard Byrd's *Haec Dies* he would approve of it. For he hated music in which the words as well as the melodies were treated polyphonically. The exuberance of some of the later music associated with Methodism found no approval with John. We shall come to this in a moment.

Pepusch is, however, expressing a respectable eighteenth-century view of music. There was a tendency in those days for the serious-minded to philosophize everything; to form all concepts into groups comparable with an eighteenth-century terrace or garden. The "high" doctrine—which belongs all over Europe to the period around 1700, and which gave way to the "low" doctrine of a generation or two later—venerated Truth and Reality, and in that sense, Nature. That which was clearly compatible with a natural harmony of form was good, for Nature was good. Man constantly spoiled it, but it was created good, and if man would let it alone it would remain good. "Nature", in the "high" doctrine (for example, in Cambridge Platonism) is not so much physical nature as the sum of things, the transcendent reality.

It was along these lines that Pepusch theorized; and Wesley had a good deal of this in him too. The serenity of the new philosophy of nature sits uneasily alongside the dramatic and affective pattern of Wesleyan theology—conversion, sanctification and redemption. Wesley was very much at odds, theologically, with one distinguished representative of the mystical and philosophical school, William Law. But one's attitude to a subject in which one does not constantly exercise oneself is usually inconsistent with one's attitude in a field where one is constantly in debate; and Wesley had a Puritan background, and Puritanism in turn was deeply influenced by seventeenth-century philosophy. Wesley's musical conservatism was, clearly, not a matter of conviction so much as a matter of in-born intellectual instinct. He would listen quite reverently to his venerable senior saying that music was going to the dogs, even if that was not an attitude customary to him in religious concerns.

He is naturally more interested and involved by the music he hears in church.

[4] *9 August, 1768.* I took a full view of the castle [sc. of Llanelly], situate on the top of a steep hill, and commanding a various and extensive prospect, by sea and land. The building itself is far the loftiest which I have seen in Wales. What a taste had they who removed from hence, to bury themselves in the hole at Margam!

When we came to Neath I was a little surprised to hear I was to preach in the church, of which the churchwardens had the disposal, the minister being just dead. I began reading prayers at six, but was greatly disgusted at the manner of singing: (1) twelve or fourteen persons kept it to themselves, and quite shut out the congregation; (2) these repeated the same words, contrary to all sense and reason, six or eight or ten times over; (3) according to the shocking custom of modern music, different persons sung different words at one and the same moment; an intolerable insult on common sense, and utterly incompatible with any devotion. [5. 281]

With that, compare this, less amply expressed, from a few years earlier:

[5] *29 February, 1764.* I heard *Judith*, an oratorio, performed at the Lock. Some parts of it were exceeding fine; but there are two things in all modern pieces of music which I could never reconcile to common sense. One is singing the same words ten times over; the other, singing different words by different persons, at the same time. And this in the most solemn addresses to God, whether by way of prayer or of thanksgiving. This can never be defended by all the musicians in Europe, till reason is quite out of date. [5. 47]

In this case, the music was that of Thomas Arne (1710–78), one of these pestilent modern fellows of whom Dr Pepusch disapproved. "The Lock" is the Lock Hospital Chapel, presided over by Martin Madan, a charity-school which became during these years a major church music centre. It was referred to in quotation [2] above, and was the best known of the many charitable foundations inspired by early Methodism. It had its own hymn-tune book, the *Lock Hospital Collection* (1769), which is the source of several evangelical hymn tunes that are still well known (for example, *Carlisle*, EH 190). Wesley was fond of the place and took every opportunity of visiting it.

Dr Arne, then, was disapproved of. But not Handel.

> [6] *17 August, 1758.* I went to the cathedral [at Bristol] to hear Mr Handel's *Messiah*. I doubt if that congregation was ever so serious at a sermon as they were during this performance. In many parts, especially some of the choruses, it exceeded my expectation. [4. 282]

John Wesley appreciated organ music when it did not conflict with his principles or his convenience. His first approving reference is something of a backhanded compliment:

> [7] *7 April, 1751* (being Easter Day). After preaching, I went to the new church, and found an uncommon blessing, at a time when I least expected it, namely, while the organist was playing a voluntary! [3. 520]

This was in Manchester. We would give much to know what the organist was playing, but probably we never shall know. However, the next reference is less guarded:

> [8] *29 August, 1762.* At the cathedral [of Exeter] we had a useful sermon, and the whole service was performed with great seriousness and decency. Such an organ I never saw or heard before, so large, so beautiful, and so finely toned; and the music of "Glory to God in the highest", I think, exceeded the *Messiah* itself. [4. 526]

Nehemiah Curnock, who edited the classic edition of the *Journal*, tells us that this organ was built by John Loosemore in 1665, enlarged in 1713, and rebuilt by Jordan in 1741. The original instrument is described by W. L. Sumner as "Loosemore's masterpiece".[1] The rebuild by Abraham Jordan very probably contained an example of that historic invention of Jordan's, the swell box.[2] So this may have been the first time John Wesley heard a "Swell" effect; if it was, it was his introduction to what has come to be regarded as one of the great impediments to good organ playing. But Wesley was captivated by it. When we come to Samuel Sebastian, we shall have occasion to refer to the scarcity of good organs in parish churches and even cathedrals a mere hundred years later than this. So to John Wesley, whose itineraries took him into considerable churches only during the later years of his crusade, hearing a fine instrument will probably have been a new and unfamiliar experience in 1762.

There are two friendly references to the parish church of Macclesfield, Cheshire, the first of which carries this same thought a little further.

> [9] *29 March, 1782* (being Good Friday). I came to Macclesfield just time enough to assist Mr Simpson in the laborious service of the day. I preached for him morning and afternoon; and we administered the sacrament to about thirteen hundred persons. While we were administering I heard a low, soft, solemn sound, just like that of an Aeolian harp. It continued five or six minutes, and so affected many that they could not refrain from tears. It then gradually died away. Strange that no other organist (that I know) should think of this.    [6. 346]

That is a tantalizing comment if ever there was one. How did the organist of Macclesfield church (one Aeneas Maclardie, unknown otherwise to history except as the father-in-law of a worthy Methodist scholar and hymn writer, Dr Bunting)

[1] *The Organ*, by W. L. Sumner (Macdonald, 1952); p. 117.
[2] *The Organ*, by W. L. Sumner; pp. 161, 182.

contrive this effect? A modern ear would suspect a Voix
Celestes stop, or a Dulciana with both octave couplers, but
either Celestes or octave couplers would be an anachronistic
conjecture. We must here, once again, conjecture a Swell effect.
(An Echo organ is a tempting notion, but less so when one
notes the specification of the "Echo" organ at St Martin-in-the-
Fields, London, c. 1727, which mentiones four stops, all
diapasons, clearly designed as a secondary diapason chorus.)[1]
The secret has died with the good Aeneas Maclardie. But four
years later John is back at Macclesfield enjoying the music—
probably not of the same instrument:

[10] *2 April, 1786.* We had a large and serious congregation [*sc.*
at Macclesfield] at the new church, both morning and afternoon. The organ is one of the finest-toned I have ever heard;
and the congregation singing with it make a sweet harmony.
[7. 152]

In Lincolnshire, however, it was otherwise:

[11] The last time Wesley visited the place [Louth] crowds came
to hear him. Many stood round the door; he gave out the
hymn with emphasis, "I thirst, thou wounded Lamb of
God". The organ annoyed him. After the first verse he said,
"Let that organ stop, and let the women take their parts."
"They cannot sing without, sir," replied Mr Robinson.
"Then," he retorted, "how did they do before they got
one?" [7. 411 n.]

That is, of course, not from the *Journal*, but from an article in
the *Primitive Methodist Magazine* for March 1850, by the Rev.
Henry Kendall. An entertaining entry in a much earlier page of
the *Journal* shows how on one occasion an organ was used as an
instrument of offence against Wesley's preaching.

[12] *13 August, 1746.* At three in the afternoon I preached at
Builth, designing to go from thence to Carmarthen; but

---

[1] *The Organ*, by W. L. Sumner; p. 370.

notice having been given by mistake, of my preaching at Leominster in Herefordshire, I altered my design, and, going to Llansaintffrydd that night, the next day rode to Leominster.

At six in the evening I began preaching on a tombstone, close to the north side of the church. The multitude roared on every side, but my voice soon prevailed, and more and more the people were melted down, till they began ringing the bells; but neither thus did they gain their point, for my voice prevailed still. Then the organs began to play amain. Mr C., the curate, went into the church and endeavoured to stop it; but in vain. So I thought it best to remove to the cornmarket. [3. 251]

Once again the story tells us too little. What kind of an instrument must they have had at Leominster which could compete with Wesley preaching outside the church more effectively than the bells? It looks as if John felt that the indications that he was unwelcome were after all compelling, once the organist began to play. The organist's name, we are told, was Paul Francillon.

The other musical reminiscences are of literary rather than musical interest. There was the time when John was agreeably surprised by a new hymn tune which turned out to be an old favourite:

[13] *29 March, 1774.* Abundance of people were soon gathered together [at Newcastle-under-Lyme], who surprised me not a little by mistaking the tune, and striking up the march in *Judas Maccabaeus.* Many of them had admirable voices, and tolerable skill. I know not when I have heard so agreeable a sound; it was indeed the voice of melody. But we had one jarring string: a drunken gentleman was a little noisy, till he was carried away. [6. 13]

The "March" is no doubt "See the conquering hero comes", which occasionally turns up in hymn books of the early nineteenth century, and which has in recent years become well known internationally through being set to a French hymn,

"*À toi la gloire*", and to its English translation, "Thine be the glory" (M 213). One other note about Exeter Cathedral gives high praise to a setting of the Communion service (6. 365):

> [14] . . . the solemn music at the post-communion, one of the finest compositions I have ever heard.   (18 August, 1782)

The composition, whatever it was, being played by William Jackson (1730–1803), composer of a once famous *Te Deum in F* and of one or two hymn tunes still in use (e.g. *Exeter*, EH 528: M 982). And there is the endearing little note on his meeting with J. F. Lampe (1703–51), the bassoon-player in the Covent Garden orchestra who became editor of one of the best of the early Wesleyan tune-books, and composer of some of the best of its tunes:

> [15] *29 November, 1745.* I spent an hour with Mr Lampe, who had been a Deist for many years, till it pleased God, by the *Earnest Appeal*, to bring him to a better mind.   [3. 226]

### ON THE POWER OF MUSIC

These scraps of information and introspection indicate only that Wesley's interest in music was no more than that which a naturally observant man would have. It hardly occurred to him to pursue the subject any further, except on one occasion. Whether the slightly impatient remark in a letter to his brother Charles, which he preserved in his *Journal* [5. 295], "I have no time for Handel or Avison now" (December 1768), represented more than a passing mood we can hardly tell. Most of his jottings on music are from about that date or later, but it is as if he knew that if he gave himself to the study of music he would be distracted from his chief work. And yet he did once go into the matter systematically, and set down what amounted to his musical creed. The provenance of his tract *On the Power*

*of Music* (1779) is a choice example of the Wesleyan way of life.
Begin from this entry in the *Journal*:

[16] *9 June, 1779.* We had another rainy day, so that I was again
driven into the house; and again I delivered my own soul,
to a larger congregation than before. In the morning, we had
an affectionate parting, perhaps to meet no more. I am glad,
however, that I have made three journeys to Inverness. It has
not been lost labour. Between ten and eleven I began preaching at Nairn. . . . About two we reached Sir Ludovick
Grant's . . .

Inverness! Whether John felt about the Scottish scenery and
climate as did his eminent contemporary, Dr Johnson, was his
own business; he shared no opinions with his readers. But in
June 1764 and April 1770, he had included that town in his
apostolic journeys—his sixty-first and sixty-seventh years—and
now here he is again, at seventy-five, as strenuous as ever. It
seems that on 9 June, 1779 he visited Inverness, then Nairn, and
then the home of Sir Ludovic Grant, which was in the place
that since 1694 had been called by the family name, Grantown
(now Grantown-on-Spey). The tract on music is dated from
Inverness in 1779, a year also famous in hymnology as the
date of John Wesley's classic preface to the definitive congregational edition of his brother's hymns. "London, October 20,
1779" is its date, and it is reprinted in the current (1933) edition
of the *Methodist Hymn Book*. Perhaps the imminent publication
of *Hymns for the People Called Methodists* had brought the subject
of music at last to the front of John's mind. However that may
have been, this is what the now aged evangelist wrote.

### THE POWER OF MUSIC

*Note: numbers above the text refer to the notes immediately following the tract*
*(pp. 20-22).*

I. By the power of music,[1] I mean its power to affect the hearers;
to raise various passions in the human mind. Of this we have very
surprising accounts in ancient history. We are told the ancient

Greek musicians in particular were able to excite whatever passions they pleased; to inspire love or hate, joy or sorrow, hope or fear, courage, fury, or despair; yet, to raise these one after another, and to vary the passions just according to the variation of the music.

II. But how is this to be accounted for? No such effects attend the modern music, although it is confessed, on all hands, that our instruments excel theirs, beyond all degrees of comparison. What was their lyre, their instrument of ten strings, compared to our violin?[2] What were any of their pipes to our hautboy or German flute? What were all of them put together, all that were in use two or three thousand years ago, to our organ? How is it, then, that with this inconceivable advantage the modern music has less power than the ancient?

III. Some have given a very short answer to this, cutting the knot which they could not untie. They have doubted, or affected to doubt, the fact; perhaps they have even denied it. But no sensible man will do this, unless he be utterly blinded by prejudice; for it would be denying the faith of all history, seeing no fact is better authenticated. None is delivered down to us by more unquestionable testimony, such as fully satisfies in all other cases. We have, therefore, no more reason to doubt of the power of Timotheus' music than of Alexander's arms[3] and we may deny his taking Persepolis, as well as his burning it through the sudden rage which was excited in him by that musician. And the various effects which were successively wrought in his mind (so beautifully described by Dryden, in his Ode on [St] Cecilia's Day) are astonishing instances of the power of a single harp to transport, as it were, the mind out of itself.

IV. Nay, we read of an instance, even in more modern history, of the power of music, not inferior to this. A musician being brought to the King of Denmark and asked whether he could excite any passion, answered in the affirmative, and was commanded to make the trial upon the king himself. Presently the monarch was all in tears; and upon the musician's changing his mood, he was quickly roused to such frenzy, that snatching a sword from one of his assistants' hands (for they had purposely removed his own) he immediately killed him, and would have killed all the room had he not been forcibly withheld.

V. This alone removes all the incredibility of what is related concerning the ancient music. But why is it that modern music in general has no such effect on the hearers? The grand reason seems to be no other than this—the whole nature and design of music is altered. The ancient composers studied melody alone, the due arrangement of single notes; and it was by melody alone that they wrought such wonderful effects; and as this music was directly calculated to move the passions, so they designed it for this very end. But the modern composers study harmony, which in the present sense of the word is quite another thing—namely, a contrast of various notes, opposite to, and yet blended with each other, wherein they

"now high, now low, pursue the resonant fugue".

Dr Gregory[4] says, "This harmony has been known in the world little more than two hundred years." Be that as it may, ever since it was first introduced—ever since counterpoint has been invented, as it has altered the grand design of music, so it has well nigh destroyed its effects.

VI. Some indeed have imagined, and attempted to prove, that the ancients were acquainted with this. It seems there needs but one single argument to demonstrate the contrary. We have many capital pieces of ancient music that are now in the hands of the curious. Dr Pepusch, who was well versed in the music of antiquity (perhaps the best of any man in Europe) showed me several large Greek folios, which contained many of their musical compositions. Now, is there, or is there not, any counterpoint in these? The learned know there is no such thing. There is not the least trace of it to be found: it is all melody, and no harmony.

VII. And as the nature of music is thus changed, so is likewise the design of it. Our composers do not aim at moving the passions, but at quite another thing—at varying and contrasting the notes a thousand different ways. What had counterpoint to do with the passions? It is applied to a quite different faculty of the mind; not to our joy, our hope, or fear; but merely to the ear, to the imagination, or internal sense. And the pleasure it gives is not upon this principle—not by raising any passion whatever. It no more affects the passions than the judgment: both the one and the other lie quite out of its province.

VIII. Need we any other, and can we have any stronger, proof of this, than those modern overtures, voluntaries, or concertos, which consist altogether of artificial sounds without any words at all? What have any of the passions to do with these? What has judgment, reason, common sense? Just nothing at all. All these are utterly excluded by delicate, unmeaning sound!

IX. In this respect the modern music has no connexion with common sense, any more than with the passions. In another, it is glaringly, undeniably, contrary to common sense: namely, in allowing, yea, appointing different words to be sung by different persons at the same time! What can be more shocking to a man of understanding than this? Pray which of those sentences am I to attend to? I can attend only to one sentence at once and I hear three or four at one and the same instant! And, to complete the matter, this astonishing jargon has found a place even in the worship of God! It runs through (O pity! O shame!) the greatest part even of our Church music! It is found even in the finest of our anthems, and in the most solemn parts of our public worship! Let any impartial and unprejudiced person say whether there can be a more direct mockery of God.

X. But to return: is it strange that modern music does not answer the end it is designed for, and which it is in no wise calculated for? It is not possible that it should. Had Timotheus pursued "the resonant fugue", his music would have been quite harmless. It would have affected Alexander no more than Bucephalus; the finest city in the world had not been destroyed; but

*Persepolis stares, Cyrique arx alta maneres.*[5]

XI. It is true the modern music had been sometimes observed to have as powerful an effect as the ancient, so that frequently single persons, and sometimes numerous assemblies, have been seen in a flood of tears. But when was this? Generally, if not always, when a fine solo was sung; when "the sound has been an echo to the sense"; when the music has been extremely simple and inartificial, the composer having attended to melody, not harmony. Then, and then only, the natural power of music to move the passion has appeared. This music was calculated for that end, and effectually answered it.

XII. Upon this ground it is that so many persons are so much affected by Scotch or Irish airs. They are composed not according to art but nature; they are simple in the highest degree. There is no harmony, according to the present sense of the word, therein; but there is much melody. And this is not only heard, but felt, by all those who retain their native taste, whose taste is not biassed (I might say corrupted) by attending to counterpoint and complicated music. It is this in its counterpoint, it is harmony (so-called) which destroys the power of music. And if ever this should be banished from our composition, if ever we should return to the simplicity and melody of the ancients, then the effects of our music will be as surprising as any that were wrought by theirs; yea, perhaps they will be as much greater as modern instruments are more excellent than those of the ancients.

## Notes on the tract, *On the Power of Music*

[1] The notion that music has direct power over human minds and emotions is found wherever music is made. Broadly, there are three modes in which it appears: (1) the strictly "demonic" or superstitious mode, which gives rise to such stories as the famous one of David charming the madness out of Saul by playing on an instrument. This appears in I Samuel 16.23, a passage very often quoted in early Christian literature on the subject; (2) the philosophical and analytical mode, which attempts to explain what was formerly attributed to supernatural influence, and which is found in Plato; and (3) the moralizing mode, derived from Plato (especially from the earlier pages of *The Republic*), which appealed especially to early Christian writers. On all this, see the first two chapters of my book, *The Church and Music* (2nd edition, 1967), together with quotations in the Appendix of that book. The only serious attempt to detach music altogether from affective impulses has been made in the twentieth century by the composers of serial, aleatoric and electronic music (for whom see my *Twentieth Century Church Music*, Chapters 9 and 10 together with the references there).

Mode (2)—the philosophic mode—was always capable of leading in a scientific direction; the Greek philosopher Aristoxenus codified a musical system in quasi-mathematical terms, and the history of musical instruments shows how an intuitive understanding of the basic association between music and physics gradually emerged into a physical understanding, and then a technical understanding, so that in the end the organ, the most technological of instruments, became the first instrument to be used as a "precision instrument"—in the hands of Olivier Messiaen (see *Twentieth Century Church Music, ad loc.*).

[2]. *Violin.* In Wesley's day (and although he was writing in 1779, he was drawing on a lively musical experience that probably dates from as much as fifty years earlier), the violin as we know it was still a comparatively recent invention. No precise date can be found for its emergence: but Antonio Stradivari died in 1737, the year before John Wesley's conversion, and his pupil, Giuseppe Antonio Guarneri, in 1745. It was the Amati family who first developed the violin as we know it, an instrument which added so much boldness and richness of tone to the traditional sound of the viols, and whose development was a process covering at least three long generations: the first, Andrea Amati, *c.* 1520–1611 and

20

his younger brother Nicola (exact dates unknown); the next, Antonio (1550–1638) and his brother Geronimo (1551–1635); and the third, Nicolo (1596–1684), in whose workshop Stradivari served his apprenticeship.

*Flute.* In the same way, the "German flute" was becoming familiar during the days of John Wesley's youth. The "English flute" was what we now call a recorder, held vertically and blown from the end: the "German flute" was the Continental instrument held transversely and blown from the side.

[3] *Alexander.* Wesley refers explicitly to Dryden's *Ode on St Cecilia's Day*, one of the great classic evocations of the diverse power of musical instruments, and the reference to Alexander and Timotheus is derived also from Dryden—from his *Alexander's Feast*. There is plenty of doubt about the historical existence of the musician Timotheus here referred to.

> Now strike the golden lyre again:
> A louder yet, and yet a louder strain!
> Break his bands of sleep asunder
> And rouse him like a rattling peal of thunder.
> Hark, hark! the horrid sound
> Has raised up his head:
> As awaked from the dead
> And amazed he stares around.
> Revenge, revenge, Timotheus cries,
> See the Furies arise!
>
> (lines 98–107)

The only Timotheus known to history as a musician died at the age of about ninety in 357 B.C., the year before Alexander was born. Curiously enough, his entry in Smith's *Classical Dictionary* contains these words:

> He was at first unfortunate in his professional efforts. Even the Athenians, fond as they were of novelty, were offended at the bold innovations of Timotheus, and hissed off his performance . . . He delighted in the most artificial and intricate forms of musical expression, and he used instrumental music, without a vocal accompaniment, to a greater extent than any previous composer.

So that this Timotheus would have been a peculiarly unfortunate example to cite in support of Wesley's conservatism. The Timotheus in Dryden's poem is a purely mythical figure.

[4] "Dr Gregory" is no doubt Dr John Gregory, F.R.S., Professor of Medicine at Edinburgh University. He lived from 1724 to 1773, and in 1774, while himself at Edinburgh, Wesley records that "in the way to Perth I read that ingenious tract, Dr Gregory's *Advice to his Daughters*". (18 May, 1774: *Journal*, 6. 20). Gregory moved in the highest literary circles and was a person of wide culture. His works were collected and published together in 1788.

[5] The quotation is an adaptation of *Aeneid*, II 56:
    *Troiaque nunc staret, Priamique arx alta maneres,*
in which, with a typically eighteenth-century conceit, Wesley has adapted "Troy" to the capital of Persia, and with a high hand, such as he deplored when others applied it to his own and his brother's works, altered Virgil's subtle change of person to suit the ruder needs of his own argument.

The chief general point in this tract is that melodic music with words was always more potent in arousing the emotions than instrumental music. Wesley has no use for music of the intellect. He is a Platonist, and a follower of the early Christian fathers, in his approach to music.

He writes therefore of the post-Restoration instrumental music just as a modern cleric might write of twelve-tone music, or the experiments of Cornelius Cardew. The commonest ground for disparagement of what we now call "modern music" is its emotional aridity; the less experienced the critic, the narrower the band of music which he regards as emotionally evocative. Indeed, there are plenty of people, clergy among them, who regard only music written between about 1840 and 1920 as emotionally satisfying. Tudor polyphony is, to them, hardly less "cold" than Schoenberg or Lutyens. The judgment is, of course, subjective and musically meaningless. But its social implications happen to be important, and we shall return to them when we are considering the genuinely musical Wesleys.

John's judgment has a strongly Puritan colour, in that he seems to be uninterested in music which does not carry words: he further insists that the words shall be clearly heard—neither too often repeated nor obscured by counterpoint. Obviously there must be some parts of the *Messiah* that he could not strictly approve. The *Hallelujah Chorus*, for example, would get low marks in both parts of the examination. Why then does he speak so highly of the *Messiah*? The answer is because there is in him a conflict—which in other spheres became marvellously creative—between the residue of Puritanism and a proleptic Romanticism. All accounts of him leave the impression that he was the quietest and least demonstrative of Methodist preachers, and yet that none ever achieved such profound emotional effects as he did on his hearers. That is the pattern exactly. Puritan preachers of Richard Baxter's generation were not histrionic; they were ruthlessly logical and lengthy and (on the surface of the argument) rational. But their doctrine of conversion was a doctrine, not an experience like John Wesley's. Those emotions they permitted were strictly private; their emotional literature is always introspective, never persuasive. Wesley's emotional equipment was directed to public purposes, and all through his life he had to justify this to himself. No seventeenth-century Puritan would have dreamt of saying that it was music's purpose, in or out of church, to arouse emotions; if it did, they did not approve it. But to John, music's primary purpose was just this. So he conflates the Puritan love of the word with his new insight into the importance of emotional excitement as an agent of conversion, and the result is what we read in this tract.

What gives us a better notion of the practical consequences of this approach to music is to be seen in the early Methodist hymns, to which we are about to turn. In these there is a collision—again, sometimes wholly creative—between the newly liberated religious emotions and the Puritan disciplines.

John's natural instincts led him, as they lead any musical innocent, to enjoy "a good tune". Of course he enjoyed psalm-singing in Scotland (§ XII); it was unaccompanied—any accompanying instrument would have been illegal—and it was confined to a very restricted repertory of magnificent melodies. Millar Patrick[1] tells us that, at the beginning of the eighteenth century, there were twelve tunes which were "canonized as embodying the inexpansible musical tradition of the Church of Scotland"; these appeared in a Psalter published in Aberdeen in 1666. Very probably, since progress and innovation were as slow in the north-east of Scotland as they would have been anywhere in that century, these, or a small selection of them, would be the Inverness repertory in 1779. The tunes were *Common Tune, King's Tune, Duke's Tune, English Tune, French, London, Stilt, Dunfermline, Dundee, Abbey, Martyrs* and *Elgin*, with the addition (because of its Aberdeen origin) of *Bon Accord*. Many of them still survive, and a glance at them shows how most of them keep that timeless quality which makes them acceptable to every possible kind of musical taste.[2]

You have to hear a highland precentor "lining out" such tunes as these to get their full flavour. This is still possible in the remoter regions; perhaps John was fortunate enough to hear something of the kind, there and in Ireland.

Since Methodism was so intimately associated with music, it

[1] *Four Centuries of Scottish Psalmody*, p. 111.

[2]

|  | English Hymnal 1933 | Church Hymnary 1927 | Scottish Psalter 1929 |
|---|---|---|---|
| Duke's Tune |  |  | 50 |
| French (= Dundee) | 428 | 227 | 61 |
| London | 394 | 520 | 82 |
| Stilt (= York) | 472 |  | 146 |
| Dunfermline | 64 | 295 | 52 |
| Dundee (= Windsor) | 332 | 276 | 51 |
| Abbey |  | 455 | 24 |
| Martyrs | 449 | 520 | 86 |
| Elgin |  | 246 | 57 |
| Bon Accord |  |  | 192 |

is necessary to know its founder's mind on music; and what we find is that his judgments are technically naïve, and temperamentally characteristic of the culture from which he came. He was never in favour of the florid tunes which his people soon learned to sing; he cannot have been pleased with tunes that demanded many repetitions of the words; and the "fuguing" style must have irritated him greatly. On the tunes in one of the early tune books of his society, Thomas Butts's *Harmonia Sacra* (1753), he commented that the more florid tunes were irreverent, and the old psalm tunes were dull. But he was not easy to please. He confessed once in his *Journal*:

> [17] *3 July, 1764.* I was reflecting on an odd circumstance, which I cannot account for. I never relish a tune at first hearing, not till I have almost learned to sing it; and, as I learn it more perfectly, I gradually lose my relish for it. I observe something similar in poetry. I seldom relish verses at first hearing; till I have heard them over and over, they give me no pleasure; and they give me next to none when I have heard them a few times more, so as to be quite familiar . . . Oh how imperfectly do we understand even the machine which we carry about with us!

Few people mention it, but this is actually the condition in which most, if not all, non-technically minded people approach the arts; they suspect, they enjoy, they cool off. It may have been hard for people to work with so strenuous a person as John Wesley when their own specialities were concerned; this was simply because, being himself no specialist in any ordinary discipline, Wesley remained to the end of his days a strictly normal human figure writ large. He carried all the mediocrities and prejudices and half-formed opinions and impatiences of the "layman" into everything he turned his hand to, as well as all the flexibility that marks off the layman from the pedant. Therefore he would advise, in music as in other matters, not what he imagined the ordinary man would need, but what he himself needed, backing his opinion that he was himself an ordinary man in all things except in the work he had been

2*

divinely appointed to do. The whole point of his preaching was that what had happened to him in his conversion could happen to anybody who would allow it to happen. "Universal salvation" was the spiritual charter of the common man; the denial of calvanist spiritual aristocracy.

## A NOTE ON THE "CONVERSION"

It is almost time to look briefly at early Methodist hymns, but there is one more matter concerning John Wesley to be cleared up. His conversion on 24 May, 1738, followed hard upon the hearing of a piece of church music, as he records in the most famous pages of his *Journal* [1. 472 ff.]. This was the anthem, "Out of the deep", words from Psalm 130, which he heard that afternoon at St Paul's Cathedral. Sanctified hindsight on his part associated this with the experience which overtook him at "a quarter before nine" that same evening. At the time, it must have been a purely musical experience. Susceptible as he always was to "atmosphere", and especially to that generated by the august appointments of an English cathedral, he was brought up all standing by this performance in St Paul's. But whose was the music? Conjectures have favoured several settings. Sir Frederick Bridge's guess that it was Purcell's is underwritten by Curnock in the standard edition of the *Journal* (*loc. cit.*).

The determining factor, however, is the contents of the choir-books in use in St Paul's at that time. These manuscript part-books, dated about 1690, are still preserved at St Paul's, and they contain two settings of the Psalm; one by Henry Aldrich (1647–1710), Dean of Christ Church and sometime Vice-Chancellor of Oxford University, and one by William Croft (1678–1727), organist of St Anne's, Soho, London. Taking all other probabilities into account, the opinion at St Paul's (for which I thank Dr Dykes Bower, the organist and

Mr Maurice Bevan, Vicar-Choral) favours the setting by Croft. It does not appear in full in any modern edition, but an abridged edition was published in 1963 by Abingdon Press (U.S.A.), arranged by Dr Austin Lovelace.

The impressive thing about this setting is that it opens with a solo, highly expressive, and exactly what John later confessed appealed to him most. The settings by Purcell, Morley and Batten, though in existence in 1738, do not seem, from these manuscript books, to have been in the cathedral repertory at that time. Morley and Batten were organists of St Paul's; Purcell, like his protagonist, Bridge, was organist of Westminster Abbey. But it may be judged safe to say that it was Croft's setting that John Wesley heard on that fateful day.

Example 1
By William Croft

# 3

# Charles Wesley and
# Methodist Music

"I am a poor creature on such occasions, being soon cast down." So Charles Wesley wrote of himself when confronted with the grim pastoral problems that faced him in the early days of his ministry. Four years younger than his dynamic brother, his was the gentler and in some ways the weaker spirit. Historically, he was absolutely indispensable to the Methodist movement, and his contribution to it has ensured that his name is by no means less illustrious among English-speaking Christians than that of John. They were in some ways complementary; yet, in fact, they saw less of one another than brothers engaged in such work as theirs might be expected to do, and their approach to religion and life differed in matters so fundamental that open disagreement between them was not only possible, but was probably as infrequent as it was only because they spent so little of their time in company.

Pictures of John always show us a memorable face, a Wellingtonian nose, a piercing eye, and a spare figure. Those of Charles show a man of more comfortable habit. History insists that John was an inspired administrator, Charles basically an artist. Both regarded themselves as faithful priests of the Church of England; yet this opinion found different formulations in the two men's lives. Obedience to the church meant something to Charles; to John it meant nothing. You cannot obey what you are in process of reforming. This was why Charles was so distressed by John's decisive action in the "ordinations" (if that is what they were; it is a controversial matter into which I shall not here enter) of 1784. John loved his church through rebuke; Charles loved it directly.

Certain things they have in common. Both lived to over eighty. Both went to Oxford. Both were instrumental in founding and keeping alive the Holy Club. Both went to America. Both returned from there disillusioned. Both were converted in the same week of May 1738, Charles three days before John. Both married late, but John unsatisfactorily, Charles happily (to Sarah Gwynne, 8 April, 1749).

But where John was indefatigably itinerant, Charles was essentially stationary. His ministry (irregular at first) at Bristol began in late 1739, and he last visited the city in 1787, the year before he died. Like his brother, he suffered a good deal of persecution in the early days, but lived to see a large acceptance of his preaching and principles. He made two visits to Ireland with his brother in 1747 and 1748, and his last visit to the North of England was as early as 1756. Thereafter, he divided his time between Bristol and London, and (as we shall see) strove to keep up a household which should blend (at times uneasily) strict piety with high culture.

There is no sign that he was personally any more of a musician than his brother was; but he enjoyed music, and had more time both to hear it and to cultivate the society of musicians. He was "musical" enough to be profoundly influenced in his hymn-writing by the chorales of Germany. And of course it is by his hymns that he is now known to a world-wide Christian company.

People always ask how many hymns Charles Wesley wrote, and the answer to that question depends on what you call a hymn. It is of some importance at this stage of our journey to find out just what Wesleyans thought, or were taught to think, constituted a hymn, and therefore we must attend briefly to this.

The best answer to the short question how many hymns Charles Wesley wrote is that given by Frank Baker (*Representative Verse of Charles Wesley*), who says that 8,989 of his religious poems have survived for his personal examination, and implies that it is a matter more or less of private judgment how many of these can be called hymns. This astonishing total could be expressed as three hymns a week for something over fifty-seven years. In fact, hymn books edited and partly written by Charles Wesley appeared over a period of forty-seven years. The first was a joint effort with his brother entitled *Hymns and Sacred Poems*, which appeared in three successive editions in 1739 (John had edited a book by himself the previous year, called *Collection of Psalms and Hymns*, which was strictly the first hymnal of the Evangelical Revival); the last was *A Pocket Hymn Book* (1786). New hymns were appearing even in *Hymns for the Nation* (1782), and the tradition is that "In age and feebleness extreme" (*Methodist Hymn Book*, Additional Verses No. 47) was written at the very end of his life.

It was in this way that Charles expressed himself; his hymns did his travelling for him. And his purpose in writing them was threefold; to provide a body of Christian teaching, to provide material for public praise, and to objectify his rich personal faith.

The didactic purpose is, in his own time, as great as the poetic or devotional purpose. This is where he differs subtly from Isaac Watts, his only serious competitor for the affections of eighteenth-century hymn singers. Isaac Watts, standing in the Calvinist tradition, sought to expound the Bible first and last. His hymns were a lyrical extension of Calvinist preaching. What was not direct quotation or powerful reminiscence of Scripture in his hymns was direct gloss on Scripture. Their language never departs from the vocabulary of the Authorized Version. They were written for a settled congregation (at Mark Lane, London), which knew its Bible and would pick up allusions, and delighted primarily in preaching. The services at which they were used were exclusively minister-centred, and the attentive, but (apart from the hymns and metrical psalms) entirely un-vocal, congregation asked only to be edified in terms of the Bible. Watts's one departure from tradition was to provide for singing not only paraphrase of Scripture but comment on it. "When I survey the wondrous cross", for example, was a quite new invention, because it introduced the first personal pronoun, and celebrated not only Christian doctrine but also Christian experience. Metrical psalms celebrated Christian doctrine in that they implied the unique value of Scriptural words for singing. All that was permissible in the metrical-psalm tradition was the rearrangement of the scriptural words in such fashion as to make them singable to easy tunes. Beyond the bare necessities of this, no alteration was tolerated. Compare "The Lord's my Shepherd" in the familiar Scottish version of 1650 with George Herbert's version of the same psalm, "The God of love my shepherd is" [EH 93: M 50], and at once you can see that George Herbert's line, "while he is mine and I am his", would be inadmissible to the metrical psalmists; it is neither quotation nor close paraphrase, but gloss. But although Watts rebelled against the tyranny of this kind of literalism, his hymns were always gathered round Scripture. "When I survey the wondrous cross" is really a lyric sermon on Galatians 6. 14, and the one thing Watts would never have contemplated is the common, present, English habit of omitting the fourth verse, "His dying crimson, like a robe . . ."

Charles Wesley had a wider loyalty. While he equals Watts in his handling of Scripture, and excels him in his faculty for juxtaposing Scriptural references and allusions ("Love divine" quotes from II Corinthians 3, Psalm 106 and Malachi 3 among other sources), it is not only Scripture that is his guide ("Love divine" finishes with a quotation from Joseph Addison, and was written with a tune by Purcell in mind). Classical and contemporary literature provide some of his sources—as in the quotation made famous by Bernard Manning, "Those amarynthine bowers, inalienably ours"—but so does contemporary religious literature (a few of his hymns are direct versifications of passages in Matthew Henry's Commentary; the most celebrated is "A charge to keep I have"), and so above all does The Book of Common Prayer. Indeed, Charles Wesley is as Anglican as Watts is Dissenting. Charles Wesley has a seasonal hymn for each of the great Christian seasons—many of these have survived into contemporary use, such as "Lo, he comes" for Advent (much altered as we sing it), "Hark the herald" for Christmas (again somewhat altered), "Christ the Lord is risen to-day" for Easter and "Hail the day that sees Him rise" for Ascension. A quick look at the last of these shows how liturgical teaching weighs with Wesley. "Grant . . . that we may in heart and mind thither ascend . . .", from the Collect for Ascension Day, has its place in the hymn; for Watts, that would not have been possible. For Christmas, Charles Wesley, making a mosaic of Scripture, relies on the doctrine of the Incarnation, and ranges from Genesis 3 to St. John 1 in the course of the original of "Hark, the herald". Watts has no "Christmas" hymn, because Christmas was not celebrated in his church; the only hymn of his in any way associated with the season is "Joy to the world", which is really a paraphrase of the first part of Psalm 98.

Charles Wesley filtered high culture through to ordinary people by way of Scripture. His mind was stored with all the best in the literature of the English, Latin and Greek languages. By associating this culture with Scripture and using it to illuminate Scripture, he produced the amazing spate of lyrics by which his people were taught. But the small fraction of his work that most Christians now sing (even English Methodists, with 240 of his hymns in the current hymnal, are singing hardly two and a half per cent of his output) largely hides from them the fact that their author was primarily a teacher, and that his hymns were a body of divinity designed to illuminate not only Scripture but also the Prayer Book.

When writing, he must have often been hardly conscious of

any need to decide whether he was writing for a singing congregation or not. We must recall (it has, as a matter of fact, been a great surprise to me that many people are now unaware of this) that hymn books, from the time of Watts onwards, were designed as much for reading as for congregational singing. It is still true that people, seniors at least, in the Dissenting traditions use their hymn books as those of the Catholic tradition use their spiritual literature and their breviaries. Most certainly they were expected to do so in the eighteenth-century evangelical tradition. Hence the number of "pocket hymn books" that appeared in those days. The assumption must have been that any instructed Christian would possess a hymnal, would be personally familiar with it, would bring it to church, and would be prepared to sing whatever the minister called for. The distinction we make nowadays between what is "congregational" and what is "devotional", which excises from modern hymnals even such matchless works as Charles Wesley's "Come, O thou traveller", was unknown then. The personal acquaintance of the singer with the contents of his book removed any sense of incongruity when he was called on to sing some of the devotional profundities which embarrass modern singers. Looking at the full text of "Come, O thou traveller", a modern critic is tempted to wonder whether Wesley ever meant it to be sung, but we know for a fact that John called for it in a public service on the Sunday after Charles's death (and we can be tolerably sure that they sang it to one of John's and Charles's favourite tunes, *Vater Unser*). The close knowledge of Genesis 32, and of the words of the hymn, which could be presupposed in the congregation, made this not in the least an incongruous choice.

Now all this is not really straying far from our central subject, because it prepares us for what we find in the music to which hymns were sung in Charles Wesley's own day. Just as we must be aware of the social assumptions that underlie the style of Charles's verse, so we must be aware of those that lie behind the music that became generally accepted. And just as there is a touch of what we now would call individualism in nearly all Charles's hymns, so there is the same touch in early Methodist music. Put it this way: Charles's "individualism" is, or is meant to be, the authentic touch of the good teacher; he hooks his teaching on to something already present in the consciousness and affection of his pupil. He does not speak all the time *de haut en bas*. Watts prepares the way for the teaching of Galatians 6. 14 to do its work by getting his pupil to say, "When *I* survey". A teacher may even do as Paul did: prepare the way for dogmatic penitence by saying, "Wretched man that *I* am"; by magnetism, or by the more primitive method of appearing to lead, but really thrusting from behind and within (the principle of the couplings in railway trains or motor trailers), the teacher makes his direct contact. And it was so with the extraordinarily popular and persuasive music of Methodism.

John Wesley, we recall, was worried about this music, and he rationalized his suspicion by claiming to detest polyphony and the liberties it took with the diction of words. But John, for whom this was a marginal matter, had no leisure to analyse his objections. Had he done so, he would have been faced with an issue which no leader can face without misgiving; the persistent claims of individualism even in the best organized community. We really cannot say that it just happened coincidentally that the Handelian style (a translation of the Italian style) in music was available for assimilation into Christian worship. We can only say that the individualism of Charles Wesley's religious approach and that of Handel's music flow from a common cultural source. The country was ready for the Wesleys, just when and for the same reasons for which it was ready for Handel.

Not only Handel; perhaps, in our field, not chiefly Handel, but rather Gay and Pepusch and other minor but popular practitioners of the graces of the modern music. The central point is that the music which came naturally to the composers who furnished the tunes for the early evangelical hymn books was the music of the opera house and the concert room, the music of solo and chorus, melody and bass, aria and continuo.

Now this was to a large extent outside the control of the two leaders of the revival. We know what John thought about some of it. We may guess what strains were put on Charles's tolerance when we remember that Charles got that astonishing variety of metres, in which he broke clean away from the Watts tradition, very largely from Germany. It was the contacts with the Herrnhut Moravians and with the lyric chorale school of Freylinghausen that inspired the writing of so many hymns in metres before then unknown in England. The genesis of the very characteristic six-eights stanza-form in both the translations of John and the original hymns of Charles was the tune *Vater Unser*.[1] Many other curious Wesley metres are of German origin. If then Charles had the original German tunes in mind when he wrote in these metres, he soon had to come to terms with the incapacity of English singers for appreciating them, and their eagerness to write their own.

To illustrate this point, take two examples, tunes written in the same metre and published within the same quarter-century. The tune *Eltham* (Example 56a), which will engage our attention again when we come to S. S. Wesley, first appeared as one of the relatively few new tunes in *Harmonia Perfecta* (1730), a book of psalm-tunes compiled for the (then Presbyterian) congregation at the King's Weigh House Chapel, London, and designed to be used with the metrical psalter and with the hymns of Isaac Watts—for one of which this particular tune is marked. The tune *Invitation* (later called *Kent* or *Devonshire*) (Example 2) was published in *Hymns for the Greater Festivals* (1746), an early evangelical tune book edited by J. F. Lampe. It happens that both tunes are remarkable for their musical architecture. As I ventured to point out in the *Companion to Congregational Praise* (1953), *Invitation* has a quite unusual

---

[1] To this day it is a matter of conjecture whether this venerable tune was really conceived by its composer in three groups of two phrases or in two of three. There is just an outside possibility that Luther in his translation of the Lord's Prayer distorted the musical metre by converting 888.888 to 88.88.88, but that we will leave to others to deal with.

melodic symmetry in that the distance separating the two
highest notes of the first two lines is exactly equal to that separating the highest notes in the third and fourth, with the result
that the constant rising of the melody is in strong tension with
the natural "gravitation" of a tune to its final tonic.[1] *Eltham* is,

Example 2
*Invitation* from *Hymns for the Greater Festivals* (1746)
Cf. EH 347: AM 71: M 496

in a different way, an equally good architectural model, in
which we notice the various uses to which the composer puts
his opening four-note phrase, not forgetting the appearance
of it in the bass of the third line.

But now observe the manner in which *Invitation* was set out
by Lampe when it first appeared. It becomes an excellent
example of the "subjective" manner, adorned with grace-
notes and trills, set out as a solo melody with continuo accompaniment, where *Eltham* was set out on four vocal staves
with the melody in the tenor. Looking at the original score of
*Invitation*, you can hear it being sung by a solo voice with a
violin accompaniment putting in the trills, and a keyboard
continuo filling out the figured bass.

This manner of writing out is the one used throughout
Lampe's very fine little collection. (Another very good example

[1] See *Companion to Congregational Praise* at no. 395 for the details.

can be seen in *The Music of Christian Hymnody*, Example 109.) The true genesis of this style is in German pietism, which used a highly decorative style in its devotional lyrics (see Examples 83 to 98 in M.C.H.); this decorative style reached its highest pitch of grace and discipline in the sacred lyrics of J. S. Bach published in the Schemelli *Chorale Book* of 1736, and it was a departure from the more restrained and severe style of Crüger and his school. It developed over the period 1670–1740, and it was this section of German piety which especially influenced the Wesleys. In itself, the *music* was probably hardly known to John and Charles Wesley personally, but this was the style of music associated with evangelical religion in Germany, and it found its way at once into Methodism through the agency of the German-born Lampe. That was its religious origin, but we repeat that in any case this musical texture was common to sacred and secular music, and this musical material was that which, in their own different ways, Handel, Bach and Haydn applied to their special purposes.

This was the "sacred solo" style. The parallel style in the other texture is the choral style of the opera and the oratorio reduced to the part-song scale. Opera and oratorio specialized in the alternation of solo and chorus, with the emphasis very much on the solo. But the chorus, when it came, would quite normally be a fairly extended treatment of a very brief text, with many repetitions of the words and plenty of musical flourish. The end-product of this choral tradition is seen in the "repeating" tune of which the early evangelicals were so fond. Occasionally there is a touch of fugato about it, but more commonly the fashion is for antiphonal treatment of repeated phrases. As good an example as any is the last verse of *Amesbury* (Example 3).

Example 3

*Amesbury* (last verse), from the *Lock Hospital Collection* (1769)

This raises another point. The fashion of developing hymns into miniature oratorios, setting different verses to quite different tunes in different textures. Example 4 shows a fairly simple example of this style associated partly with a choral texture and partly with a solo (or unison) texture. The third and final verse of this tune is in fact a choral piece.

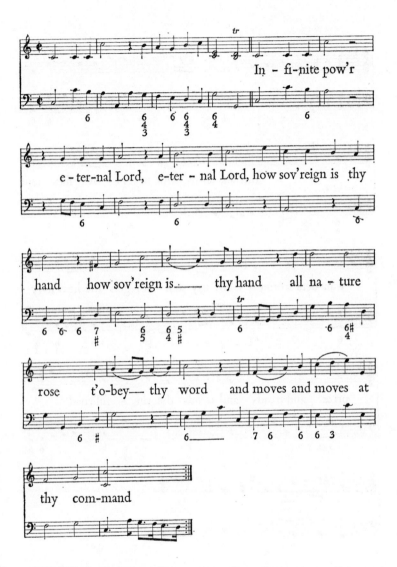

Example 4
"Mr Evance", from the *Lock Hospital Collection* (1769)
Verses 1 and 2

But ah, how wide my spi - rit___ flies and wan-ders from my God: my soul for-gets the heav'n-ly prize and treads and treads the sin - ful road

Verse 3

The question will at once be asked; who sang these sophisticated pieces? Were congregations then much more biddable
than ours are now, or than they had been before? The answer
is that the evangelicals had their choral foundations, and that
this was, as it were, their cathedral music. At any rate, the
multiform hymn tunes were. Their choral foundations were
mainly the charity orphanages and homes for the destitute and
fallen, the metropolitan "cathedral" among these was the Lock
Hospital Chapel under the direction of Martin Madan (for
whom, see below, pp. 72–3). It is from the *Lock Hospital Collection* (1769 and onwards) that we get many of the classics of
extended evangelical hymn music. The "solo" style in simple
hymn-tune form like *Invitation* would, of course, be appropriate to any Methodist service or "class meeting", in a meeting house or in the open air. But we may suppose that when
a congregation sang all together, they did not necessarily sing
the more florid of the evangelical tunes. Later, in more settled
circumstances, they did learn to sing some of them, and therefore tunes in this style continued to be composed and included
in hymn books up to the middle years of the nineteenth century.
*Diadem*, a still well-known evangelical tune in the "repeating"
style (*Methodist Hymn Book*, Additional Tunes, 6), is dated
1840. But the simpler occasions of Methodist preaching (those
on which John was most in his element) will have more probably been diversified by the singing of simple hymns, not
necessarily by Charles Wesley, to well-known psalm tunes.
There is no reason to believe that then, any more than now,
every tune in a collection was well known. Almost certainly,
those most sung were the pre-Wesley tunes, and the words
used most often will have been those which fitted the psalm-
tune style of music. The repertory will have widened as time
went on, but basically, hymns remained hymns, and congregations did not transform themselves abruptly into choral
societies.

We might mention one other matter; Charles Wesley never
seems to have been interested in writing hymns with refrains

in the style of the late nineteenth-century evangelicals. There is no better way of making the illiterate sing than by writing narrative hymns with simple choruses—which is what so many of the old carols are, and what the "Sankeys" are at their best. Why then, in his crusade to reclaim the dispossessed and barbarous people of Cornwall and the Black Country, few of whom could read at all, did Charles Wesley not employ this technique? Because the Wesleys distinguished sharply between the educated, whom they sought to interest in singing their complex and profound hymns (and this includes the children who were being educated under the influence of their movement) and the utterly illiterate, who could be reached only by direct teaching and appeal. Hence the mannered language and the mannered music. These have nothing to do with the reclamation of the illiterate and the poor. They are for the building up of the literate and substantial, John Wesley's "rich sinners". Therefore, no choruses of the Sankey kind, and no folk-tunes of the carol kind or even of the Luther kind. It really was not at all like a Billy Graham campaign in an age of literacy. It was more as if a new revival turned its back on the music of the hymn books and carol books and of the whole of past history, and fed its congregations on Hindemith, Poulenc and Britten, leaving all those who could not achieve appreciation of it to the techniques of direct Bible-teaching and the singing of hymns they had known from their childhood.

That needs modifying, of course. In our chapter on Charles and Samuel, the sons of the hymn-writer, we shall supply the needed modification. But broadly speaking, that is the background of the Wesley hymnody and the first-generation evangelical music. (For further details about its development the reader may refer to *The Music of Christian Hymnody*.)

What we must now proceed to is the account written by Charles of the remarkable musical gifts of his sons. We shall reproduce this as it stands in Charles Wesley's journal, adding such notes and glosses as will make the story historically clearer.

# 4

# *The Rev. Charles Wesley's Account of his Two Sons*

Charles was born on December 11th, 1757. He was two years and three quarters old, when I first observed his strong inclination in music. He then surprised me by playing a tune readily, and in just time. Soon after, he played several, whatever his mother sang, or whatever he heard in the streets.

From his birth she used to quiet and amuse him with the harpsichord; but he would never suffer her to play with one hand only, taking the other and putting it on the keys, before he could speak. When he played himself, she used to tie him up by his back-string to the chair, for fear of his falling. Whatever tune it was, he always put a true bass to it. From the beginning he played without study, or hesitation; and, as the learned declared, perfectly well.

Mr Broadrip[1] heard him in petticoats, and foretold he would one day make a great player. Whenever he was called to play to a stranger, he would ask, in a word of his own, "Is he a musicker?" and if answered "Yes", he played with all readiness.

He always played *con spirito*.[2] There was something in his

---

[1] This is probably J. Broderip (1710–85), organist of Wells Cathedral from 1741. The note in the *Journal* favours his son, Robert Broderip (d. 1808, date of birth uncertain) because he is said to have been "of Bristol". But in 1761 he would hardly have been old enough to carry great authority. J. Broderip is composer of the hymn tune *Calvary*, no. 211 in the 1904 (Historical) edition of *Hymns A & M*.

[2] "Intelligently", not "spiritedly".

43

manner above a child, which struck the hearers, whether learned or unlearned.

At four years old I carried him with me to London. Mr Beard[1] was the first that confirmed Mr Broadrip's judgment of him, and offered to get him admitted among the King's singing-boys; but I had then no thoughts of bringing him up a musician.

A gentleman next carried him to Mr Stanley,[2] who expressed his pleasure and surprise at hearing him, and declared he had never met one of his age with so great a propensity to music. The gentleman told us he had never before believed what Handel used to tell him of himself, and his own love of music, in his childhood.

Mr Madan[3] presented my son to Mr Worgan[4] who was extremely kind to him, and, as I then thought, partial. He told us he would prove an eminent master, if he was not taken off by other studies. He frequently entertained him on the harpsichord. Charles was greatly taken with his bold, full manner of playing, and seemed even then to catch a spark of his fire.

At our return to Bristol, we left him to ramble on till he was near six. Then we gave him Mr Rooke for a master: a man of no name, but very good-natured; who let him run on *ad libitum*, while he sat by, more to observe than control him.

Mr Rogers,[5] the oldest organist in Bristol, was his first and very great friend. He often set him upon his knee, and made him play

---

[1] John Beard (*c.* 1716–91), actor and vocalist, who took Macheath in the *Beggar's Opera* in London in 1743 and became manager of Covent Garden in 1761.

[2] John Stanley (1714–86), the blind musician and composer was a pupil of Maurice Greene and a well-known London organist (fifty years organist of the Temple Church). He was manager, with J. C. Smith and later T. Linley, of the Handel Oratorio Concerts from 1760 and Master of the King's Musick from 1779. He wrote an opera, some cantatas, a good deal of incidental music for the stage and much organ music, some of which is celebrated today.

[3] Martin Madan (1726–90), barrister 1748, converted to methodism by John Wesley's preaching, and became chaplain of the Lock Hospital, 1750–80; see below in Chapter 5.

[4] John Worgan (1724–90), organist at Vauxhall Gardens, London, 1751–74. Composer of church music, including chant in E flat (*New Cathedral Psalter*, ed. Martin, 1909, no. 149).

[5] Rogers is untraceable. He is certainly not the composer of *Rogers in E flat* (*New Cathedral Psalter*, ed. Martin, 1909, no. 243), who was born too late.

to him, declaring he was more delighted to hear him than any of his scholars, or himself.

I always saw the importance (if he was to be a musician) of placing him under the best master that could be got, and also one who was an admirer of Handel, as my own son preferred him to all the world. But I saw no likelihood of my ever being able to procure him the first masters, or of purchasing the most excellent music, and other necessary means of acquiring so costly an art.

I think it was at our next journey to London, that Lady Gertrude Hotham[1] heard him with much satisfaction, and made him a present of all her music. Mrs Rich[2] had before him Handel's songs: and Mr Beard, Scarlatti's lessons, and Purcell. Sir Charles Hotham was particularly fond of him; promised him an organ, and that he should never want any means or encouragement in the pursuit of his art. But he went abroad soon after, and was thence translated to the heavenly country.

With him Charles lost all hope and prospect of a benefactor. Nevertheless, he went on with the assistance of nature, and his two favourite authors, Handel and Corelli, till he was ten years old. Then Mr Rogers told me it was high time to put him in trammels; and soon after, Mr Granville,[3] of Bath, an old friend of Handel's, sent for him. After hearing him, he charged him to have nothing to do with any great master; "who will utterly spoil you", he added, "and destroy anything that is original in you. Study Handel's Lessons, till perfect in them. The only man in London who *can* teach you them is Kelway,[4] but he *will* not, neither for love or money."

---

[1] Lady Gertrude Hotham was mother of Sir Charles Hotham, Groom of the Bedchamber to King George III. She was a sister of Lord Chesterfield. She opened her house for Methodist preaching. See the *Journal* of John Wesley, 4. 358 and 5. 175, and Madan's tune *Hotham*, named after this family. Charles Wesley wrote an ode on the death of Lady Hotham in 1756 (*Journal* of C.W., 2. 327 ff.), but this was the wife of Lady Gertrude's son, who died soon after her marriage.

[2] Mrs Rich: no doubt the widow of John Rich (*c*. 1682–1761), who opened Covent Garden Opera House in 1732.

[3] Granville: of the Granville family formerly of Buckland, Oxfordshire. See John Wesley's *Journal* (Introduction), 1. 25 f. and Martin Schmidt, *John Wesley*, 95 f.

[4] Kelway: not Thomas Kelway, famous for a single chant in D (*New Cathedral Psalter*, as above, 62), who died in 1749, but Joseph Kelway (d. 1782), organist of St Martin-in-the-Fields, and harpsichordist, among whose pupils was Queen Charlotte, consort of George III.

Soon after we went to town, Charles notwithstanding Mr Granville's caution, had a strong curiosity to hear the principal masters there. I wanted their judgment and advice for him. Through Mr Bromfield's[1] recommendation, he first heard Mr Keeble[2] (a great lover of Handel), and his favourite pupil, Mr Burton. Then he played to them. Mr Burton said "he had a very brilliant finger"; Mr Keeble, that "he ought to be encouraged by all the lovers of music; yet he must not expect it, because he was not born in Italy". He advised him to pursue his studies of Latin, etc., till he was fourteen, and then to apply himself in earnest to harmony.

Mr Arnold[3] treated him with the utmost affection; said, he would soon surpass the masters; and advised him not to confine himself to any one author, but study what was excellent in all.

Dr Arne's[4] counsel was, like Mr Keeble's, to stay till he was fourteen, and then deliver himself up to the strictest master then could be got.

Vento[5] confessed "he wanted nothing but an *Italian* teacher."

Giardini,[6] urged by Mr Madan, at last owned "the boy played well"; and was for sending him to Bologna or—Paris!

---

[1] William Bromfield (1712–92), first surgeon at the Lock Hospital; he collaborated with Madan (q.v.) in planning it.

[2] John Keeble (1711–86), organist of St George's, Hanover Square.

[3] Samuel Arnold (1740–1802), still a young man at this time, but already composer to Covent Garden. He published a collection of cathedral music in 1790, and became organist of Westminster Abbey in 1793.

[4] Thomas Augustine Arne (1710–78), composer to Drury Lane 1744–60, and after 1760, to Covent Garden. He was one of the leading eighteenth-century English composers.

[5] Matthias Vento (*c.* 1735–76), born in Naples, came to London about 1763. He is credited with three operas as well as a good deal of study-music.

[6] Felice de Giardini (1716–96), Italian by birth, cosmopolitan by nature, was a noted violinist and a composer of slight merit, whose public conversation with Haydn is reminiscent of that between Wesley and Toplady. Two of the hymn-tunes he composed for the Wesleys are in currency today; one is the very well known *Moscow* (EH 553, named after the place where he died—it was originally called *Trinity*); the other, a much more characteristic tune, is *Pelham* (M 191). Perhaps "at last" in Wesley's report indicates a dour temperament. At any rate, Charles senior recorded this in his *Journal* under Tuesday, 28 May, 1770: "Charles was happy in making his master so; but Mr Kelway was very angry at G......i, for his cool approbation of the scholar. 'G......i does not so much as know what is in this boy; neither does any master in London'."

They all agreed in this, that he was marked by nature for a musician, and ought to cultivate his talent. Yet still I mistrusted them, as well as myself, till Mr Bromfield carried us to Mr Kelway. His judgment was decisive, and expressed in more than words: for he invited Charles to come to him whenever he was in London, and generously promised to *give* him all the assistance in his power.

He began by teaching him Handel's Lessons; then his own, and Scarlatti's, and Geminiani's. For nearly two years he instructed him gratis, and with such commendations as are not for me to repeat. Meantime Charles attended the oratorios and rehearsals, through the favour of Mr Stanley, and invitation of Mr Arnold.

As soon as he was engaged with Mr Kelway, his old friend Mr Worgan kindly offered to take him without money, under his auspices (as he expressed himself), and to train him up in his art. Such a master for my son was the height of my ambition; but Mr Kelway had been beforehand with him.

Mr Worgan continued his kindness. He often played, and sung over to him, whole oratorios. So did Mr Battishill.[1] Mr Kelway at one time played over to him the *Messiah*, on purpose to teach him the time and manner of Handel. For three seasons Charles heard all the oratorios, comparing the performers with each other, and both with Mr Worgan and Mr Kelway.

He received great encouragement from Mr Savage.[2] Mr Arnold was another father to him. Mr Worgan gave him many lessons in thorough-bass and composition. Mr Smith's[3] curiosity drew him to Mr Kelway's to hear his scholar, whom he bade go on and prosper, under the best of masters. Dr Boyce[4] came several times

---

[1] Jonathan Battishill (1738–1801), distinguished composer of church music, organist of three churches in London, and from 1762, harpsichordist at Covent Garden, where he produced an opera, *Almena*, in collaboration with Arne.

[2] Possibly the Rev. Samuel Morton Savage (1721–91), pastor (1757–87) to the Independent congregation at Duke's Place, St Mary Axe, London.

[3] No doubt, John Christopher Smith (1712–95), mentioned above in the note on John Stanley. Organist of the Foundling Hospital, 1754, having been a pupil of Handel and, later, of Pepusch and Roseingrave. Amanuensis to Handel when the composer went blind.

[4] What happened to the "hymns" of Boyce? The tunes at present in common use (*Chapel Royal*, AMR 316; *Halton Holgate*, AMR 186; and *Portsea*, AMR 124) were all published in 1765 as settings for Christopher Smart's metrical paraphrases of the Psalms. *Kingsland* (SP 452; MHB 795) was published in 1791, and Lightwood suggests that it was by William

to my house to hear him; gave him some of his own music, and set some hymns for us; asked if the King has heard him; and expressed much surprise when we told him, No. His uncle enriched him with an inestimable present of Dr Boyce's Cathedral Music.

It now evidently appeared that his particular bent was to church music. Other music he could take pleasure in (especially what was truly excellent in the Italian), and played it without any trouble; but his chief delight was in the oratorios. These he played over and over from the score, till he had them by heart, as well as the rest of Handel's music, and Corelli, and Scarlatti, and Geminiani.

These last two years he has spent in his four classical authors, and in composition. Mr Kelway has made him a player, that is certain; but he knows the difference betwixt that and a musician; and can never think himself the latter, till he is quite master of thorough-bass.

Several have offered to teach it him. One eminent master (besides Mr Worgan), equally skilled in Handel's and in the Italian music, told me, he would engage to make him perfect master of harmony in half a year. But as I waited, and deferred his instruction in the practical part, till I could find the very best instructor for him, so I keep him back from the theory. The only man to teach him that, and sacred music, he believes to be Dr Boyce.

Thus wrote Charles Wesley, finding himself, well past fifty, the father of a musical prodigy. Well might he be dismayed; well might he flounder in unaccustomed emotions. For Charles Wesley senior was no pale imitation of his brother. He was, in his own way, just as powerful a character, but it was his own way.

The Wesleys publicly repudiated classic Puritanism, but nobody was a more consistent temperamental Puritan than John Wesley, except his brother Charles. Puritanism was a theology and a way of life up to the end of the seventeenth

---

Boyce junior. The three best known were then in print by the time Charles Wesley is speaking of (1767-9). The tunes that Boyce composed for the Wesleys seem to have disappeared altogether.

century. In the eighteenth century it was transformed—one might well say corrupted into a temperament. In the matter of music, this is easily illustrated, as, indeed, it has been in that classic work, *The Puritans and Music* (1936), by the late Percy Scholes. He shows there how the seventeenth-century Puritans had no hatred of music; indeed they were lovers of music in its own right, suspicious only of the associations of certain kinds of public music-making. The irrational and emotional philistinism which later associated itself with the word "Puritan" was an eighteenth-century manifestation, which continued into the nineteenth century.

Compare the attitudes to music of Milton on the one hand and the senior Wesleys on the other, and little more needs to be said. Milton, like his father, was devoted to music. Music is never far from his mind when he is writing poetry and music was built into his theology. His special predilection (this John Wesley did share) was for music sung rather than played.

> Blest pair of Sirens, pledges of heaven's joy,
> Sphere-born harmonious sisters, Voice and Verse . . .

It was song that he loved best; Henry Lawes was his contemporary hero. In John Wesley, however, we found an eclectic pleasure in music when he had time for it—the kind of judgment that one would expect from a busy industrial executive or cabinet minister to-day; what he likes best is what he heard in his young manhood. He is saved from superstitions about music by that special quality of strenuous and objective observation which was, among that odd family, uniquely his. Charles was in all things more central, more "normal". And therefore he was vulnerable to that superstition of the neopuritan, that music was a somewhat second-rate subject. The culture which was to insist that the army, the law and the church were occupations for gentlemen, that "trade" was worthy but vulgar, and that music was well below either in the social scale was already in the making. Wesley's cousin,

Lord Mornington, was (we observed before) thought a strange fellow for allowing himself to be seen carrying his fiddle-case about in the street.

Therefore, Charles senior not only "had no thought" of his son's becoming a musician. Had it not been for Kelway and Worgan and the rest of them, he would probably have resisted it. Observe how in his own reminiscences he never once observes that he himself took the least pleasure in his son's music-making. He shows a proper deference to the musical authorities —and in this he did a good deal better than a Victorian father might have done—but it is all incomprehensible to him. If Kelway says it, it's probably true, but he has to make an effort to believe it. He must have had rueful thoughts on reflecting that of the eight children born to himself and his wife only three survived, and two of those became professional musicians. (The third, Sally, would obviously have made a handsome living as a cartoonist had she lived two hundred years later. The drawing attached to a letter to her brother Charles junior, reproduced in F. C. Gill's *Charles Wesley, the First Methodist* [1964, p. 193], is sufficient evidence for that.)

All this has a curious, but typically eighteenth-century, flavour about it. That century in England was a field of strange social contradiction. It was the age in which distinction in all walks of life received quick honour, in which those who reached the top found themselves separated by immense distances from those who did not. It was the age of the building of colossal mansions for the newly rich, of the concentration of wealth in a few hands, of the expansion of trade, of the beginning of the building of the Empire. It was also the age in which a John Wesley found work to do. In intellectual achievement, the eighteenth-century Englishmen cannot come near those of the seventeenth century, nor yet those of the later nineteenth. But in the patronage of the arts, England took its cue from the Continent and often did handsomely by the sculptors, the portrait painters, the architects and the landscape gardeners. It was the "useful arts" that prospered, together with those modes of the "fine arts" which the wealthy could find useful.

The one protest against the studied and serene urbanity of the eighteenth century had to be a social protest; and where this was associated with religion, it had to be an evangelical protest. John Wesley really did take religious truth and comfort to forgotten people. People really could be forgotten. In France, the forgotten people staged their show-down in a social and anti-clerical revolution. In England, they found their champions in the evangelical Wesleys, under whose inspiration not only did these people hear the Gospel, but they were provided with pioneer projects in orphanages, homes for fallen women, hospitals, prison reform and the abolition of slavery. There was no social reform of the late eighteenth century that did not owe its inspiration to the evangelical eruptions of the early eighteenth century. The only anti-clericals, in the heyday of the Wesleys, were the philosophers—pre-eminently, David Hume, a Scotsman. It was several generations before the spirit of the French Revolution invaded England.

Religious social protest naturally went with an attitude of opposition to those things especially associated with the affluent peak of society. And most unfortunately for the musicians, music had gathered to itself that association. The cause of this was in the cultural revolution of the Restoration, which swung the whole course of music-making away from the home and the village to the city and the court. During the ensuing generations, music became in a quite new way *expensive*; the characteristic music of the eighteenth century is not the carol, the village dance-tune or the chamber music of house or church; it is opera, orchestral music, and oratorio. The central musical instrument is becoming, not the pipe or the viol, but the harpsichord, and by the end of the century, the piano. The human voice is characteristically used not for the song with lute accompaniment, but for the formal and often exacting aria. The vocal chorus is not the quartet or quintet of the madrigal, but the choir of the *Messiah*. And even if that choir was not, in

Handel's day, the size of the Huddersfield Choral Society, it was an instrument from which modern large choruses were directly and naturally derived.

The evangelical, obsessed with compassion for the poor, suspects all this except where it is specifically associated with religion. He is obliged to. That was Charles Wesley's attitude exactly. He was a loyal priest of the Church of England. In 1784, at the end of their lives, Charles and John came very near to an open breach because of John's "emergency ordinations" of ministers to serve in a quasi-episcopal capacity in America. Charles insisted on being buried in a parish churchyard, not on Methodist premises. The older he grew, the more he insisted that he was a loyal priest, seeking only reform from within, and the more of his earlier indiscretions in writing of episcopacy he retracted. This made him all the more ecclesiastical-plus-evangelical in his attitudes to specific decisions. If his sons were going to be eminent musicians, they were virtually bound to abandon the way of life and the ideals for which their father had stood, and he knew this. But he could not step out of his age, and he could not possibly turn a deaf ear to Kelway and Worgan. For his age supported the doctrine that the words of the great and the distinguished were to be taken seriously. They were, in the eighteenth century, strangers to the more recent doctrine that a musician is the last person to consult about music, because he will give the partisan judgment of an expert. The pattern of life we associate with Berlioz could only have formed itself in the nineteenth century, in the context of a quite different set of values. Mozart, the true progenitor of the race of musicians who live and die for music, was hardly a year older than Charles's son.

That is by way of being a prologue to the main contention of this book, which will be worked out in a later chapter. For the moment, we must consider what we know of the early childhood of the younger brother, Samuel Wesley.

We owe the preservation of the document we quoted on Charles junior, and of the evidences we are about to quote, to the industry of a certain Daines Barrington (1727–1800). Barrington was an eminent lawyer, Bencher of the Inner Temple, and (what is especially relevant here) Recorder of Bristol from 1764 to 1778. (He was also a well-known naturalist, and is said to have persuaded Gilbert White to write *The Natural History of Selborne*.) He contributed to the *Philosophical Transactions* of 1781 a document which contained Charles Wesley's own account of his two sons, and also some personal reminiscences. From these we shall now give an abridged quotation.

### THE CHILDHOOD OF SAMUEL WESLEY

Samuel was born on St Matthias's day, February 24th, 1766, the same day which gave birth to Handel eighty-two years before.[1] The seeds of harmony did not spring up in him quite so early as in his brother; for he was three years old before he aimed at a tune.[2] His first were "God save great George our King",[3] *Fischer's Minuet*, and such like, mostly picked up from the street-organs . . .

Mr Arnold was the first who, hearing him at the harpsichord, said, "I set down Sam for one of my family." But we did not much regard him, coming after Charles. The first thing which drew our attention was, the great delight he took in hearing his brother play. Whenever Mr Kelway came to teach him, Sam constantly attended, and accompanied Charles *on the chair*. Undaunted by Mr Kelway's frown, he went on; and when he did not *see* the harpsichord, he crossed his hands on the chair, as the other on the instrument, without ever missing a time . . .

He was between four and five years old when he got hold of the Oratorio of *Samson*, and by that alone taught himself to read

---

[1] Not 82, of course, but 81. Handel was born in 1685.

[2] Barrington adds a footnote that Mrs Welsey assured him that Samuel played a tune when he was two years, eleven months old, and that she had an elder son, who died in infancy (this will have been John, or "Jack", born 1752), who sung a tune and beat time when he was twelve months old.

[3] The "National Anthem" was by this time popular, but it was a new tune. It was first printed in something approaching the form we know, in 1744. See P. Scholes, *God Save the Queen* (1954).

words. Soon after he taught himself to write. From this time he sprung up like a mushroom . . .

He was full eight years old when Dr Boyce came to see us, and accosted me with, "Sir, I hear you have got an English Mozart in your house: young Linley[1] tells me wonderful things of him." I called Sam to answer for himself. He had by this time scrawled down his Oratorio of *Ruth*. The Doctor looked over it very carefully, and seemed highly pleased with the performance. Some of his words were, "These airs are some of the prettiest I have seen. This boy writes by nature as true a bass as I can do by rule and study. There is no man in England has two such sons." He bade us let him run on *ad libitum*, without any check of rules or masters.

After this, whenever the Doctor visited us, Sam ran to him with his song, sonata, or anthem, and the Doctor examined them with astonishing patience and delight.

As soon as Sam had quite finished his Oratorio, he sent it as a present to the Doctor, who immediately honoured him with the following note:

TO MR SAMUEL WESLEY
Dr Boyce's compliments and thanks to his very ingenious brother-composer, Mr Samuel Wesley, and is very much pleased and obliged by the possession of the Oratorio of *Ruth*; which he shall preserve, with the utmost care, as the most curious[2] product of his musical library.

Mr Madan now began carrying him about to his musical friends. He played many times at Mr Wilmot's,[3] to many of the nobility, and some eminent masters and judges of music . . .

---

[1] Thomas Linley (1732–95), usually called "the elder", but "young" to Boyce, a member of a large musical family, now mostly forgotten. At this time, he was concert manager in the Bath Assembly Rooms, his son Thomas the younger (1756–78) being leader of the orchestra. Possibly Boyce is indeed referring to Thomas II.

[2] "Curious" means here, of course, not "odd" but "precious".

[3] This sounds like a member of the family of Eardley-Wilmot, one of the great legal families of the time. The head at this time was Sir John Eardley-Wilmot (1709–92), Chief Justice of common pleas, but he was knighted in 1755, and it is unlikely that Charles Wesley would have omitted the title. His son, of the same name, but without the title, being born in 1750, is a little young to fit the context.

Lord Barrington,[1] Lord Aylsbury, Lord Dudley, Sir Watkin W. Wynne, and other lovers of Handel, were highly delighted with him, and encouraged him to hold fast his veneration for Handel and the old music. But old or new was all one to Sam, so it was but good . . .

Mr Cramer[2] took a great liking to him, offered to teach him the violin, and played some trios with Charles and him. He sent a man to take measure of him for a fiddle . . .

To those extracts from Charles Wesley's own records, preserved by Barrington, we may add these from Barrington's own comments:

To speak of him first as a performer on the harpsichord, he was then [1775] able to execute the most difficult lessons for the instrument at first sight; for his fingers never wanted the guidance of the eye, in the most rapid and desultory passages . . . He not only executed crabbed compositions thus at sight, but he was equally ready to transpose into any keys, even a fourth . . .

If left to himself, when he played upon the organ, there were oftener traces of Handel's style than any other master; and if on the harpsichord, of Scarlatti. At other times, however, his voluntaries were original and singular. After he had seen or heard a few pieces of any composer, he was fully possessed of his peculiarities, which, if at all striking, he could instantly imitate at the word of command, as well as the general flow and turn of the composition. This I have heard him frequently play extemporary lessons, which, without prejudice to their musical names, might have been supposed those of Abel,[3] Vento, Schobert[4] and Bach . . .

I once happened to see some music wet upon his desk, which, he told me, was a solo for the trumpet. I then asked him if he had

---

[1] William Wildman Barrington, second Viscount Barrington (1717–93), statesman. The other names sufficiently indicate the circles in which both Handel and Samuel Wesley were approved.

[2] Wilhelm Cramer (d. 1799), one of the most celebrated violinists of his day.

[3] Karl Friedrich Abel (1723–87), close friend of J. C. Bach (son of J. S. Bach), and a prolific composer.

[4] Johann Schobert (c. 1720–67), composer and harpsichordist, whose style influenced Haydn and Mozart.

heard Fischer[1] upon the hautboy, and would compose an extempore solo, proper for him to execute. To this Sam readily
assented, but found his little legs too short for reaching the swell
of the organ, without which the imitation could not have its
effect. I then proposed to touch the swell myself, on his giving me
the proper signals; but to this he answered, that I could neither
do this instantaneously as was requisite, nor should I give the
greater or less force of the swell (if a note was dwelt upon) which
would correspond with his feelings. Having stated this difficulty,
however, he soon suggested the remedy, which was the following:

He stood upon the ground with his left foot, while his right rested
upon the swell; and thus literally played an extemporary solo,
*stans pede in uno*; the three movements of which must have lasted
not less than ten minutes, and every bar of which Fischer might
have acknowledged for his own. Every one who hath heard that
capital musician, must have observed a great angularity in his
cadences, in the imitation of which Sam succeeded as perfectly as
in the other parts of the composition . . .

I can refer only to one printed proof of his abilities as a composer, which is a set of *Eight Lessons for the Harpsichord*, and which
appeared in 1777, about the same time that he became known to
the musical world . . . Numbers of his other compositions, and
almost of all kinds, may be likewise examined; particularly an
anthem on the following words, which I selected for him, and
which has been performed at the Chapel-Royal, and St Paul's:

"O Lord God of hosts, how long wilt thou be angry at the
prayer of thy people?" . . .

Mozart in Austria, the Wesleys in England and, to complete
the picture, William Crotch, who as another child-genius becomes entangled in this strange story for a moment. Crotch
(1775–1847), nine years junior to Sam, was the son of a car-
penter. His father had a great interest in organs and built himself one, upon which, at the age of twenty-seven months,
William was heard to play the tune of "God save the King";
at four, he was playing the organ in public. Barrington records

[1] Johann Christian Fischer (1733–1800), German oboist and composer,
who first visited London in 1768 and, in 1780, married Mary Gainsborough,
daughter of the painter. A minuet of his is the subject of Mozart's variations,
K 179.

the first meeting between him and young Sam, which we may suppose to have been hardly before 1779 and certainly not later than 1781 when the record was printed; Sam is therefore about fourteen and Crotch about five.

I had desired him to compose an easy melody in the minor third, for an experiment on little Crotch; and that he would go with me to hear what that very extraordinary child was capable of. Crotch was not in good humour, and Master Wesley submitted, among other things, to play on a cracked violin, to please him; the company, however, having found out who he was pressed him very much to play upon the organ, which Sam constantly declined. As this was contrary to his usual readiness in obliging any person who had curiosity to hear him, I asked him afterwards what might be the occasion of his refusal; when he told me, that he thought it would look like wishing to shine at little Crotch's expense.

# 5

# The Progress of the Two Sons

The further progress of Charles and Samuel Wesley fell short of brilliance in both cases, and even of distinction in that of Charles. Of Charles, it is remembered that he grew up to be a very good player, but a composer of scanty output and merit. Samuel's story is more romantic, but still not a story of great personal eminence in any way comparable to that achieved by European musicians of the time, either as composers or as performers.

There were certain outward impediments to Charles's progress as a professional organist. It is said that when he applied for St Paul's Cathedral, Westminster Abbey, the Charterhouse and Gresham's College, he found that the Wesley name was against him. The Chapter at St Paul's said to him, "We want no Wesleys here", and although there was a royal apology for this unmannerly rebuff, he seems to have found the highest appointments closed to him. He did hold appointments at St George's, Hanover Square, the Lock Hospital, and later, Marylebone Parish Church, all after 1794.

Most of his compositions, such as they are, came from his early years. By 1784 (when he was 27) he had published six concertos, five string quartets, eight songs, and a little church music. He wrote a few hymn tunes, of which two are at present in currency: *Epworth* (M 925) and *Berkshire* (M 48). The first of these is a cheerful and conventional composition, the second a very pedestrian effort that uses the same three opening notes for three of its four lines and a rising fourth as the first interval in every line. Neither seems to have been printed before Vincent Novello included them in *The Psalmist* (1835–43), and probably their inclusion in that collection was something of an act of piety, consequent upon Novello's friendship for the Wesley family (see below, p. 75). The first volume of *The Psalmist* appeared the year after Charles's death.

It may seem odd that there was anti-Wesley prejudice as late as the 1780s, at which time John was full of honours in the country at large. But the explanation is quite clear. The Wesley name would carry honour among those whose opinions were in line with the evangelical movement which was pervading all the churches; but not with the high Establishment: the musical genius of the boys might find them favour with the secular nobility and with the court, but music in the great churches of England was not up to the intellectual standard which would rate musicianship higher than orthodoxy.

This, however, is all secondary to the main point, which is that Charles junior was almost certainly quite incapable of finding a market for what he had to offer; and the reasons for this were psychological and temperamental.

The pattern of early musical genius always seems to be that it leads to later frustration. There are not very many musicians who have achieved the highest consistency of eminence and who have gone on uninterrupted from a prodigious youth. Some executants have, by outward appearances, had an uninterrupted run, but even then there are almost certainly inner pressures in early maturity of which the casual observer knows nothing. Heifetz is a well-known example of a violinist of international standard who never lost hold of the genius he began to show in very early youth. Elman and to some extent Kreisler were the same. There is a very well-known academic musician on the English scene at present whose name frequently appeared in the newspapers as a prodigious organist at a very early age (twelve or thereabouts).

But even these pictures, as we say, can be misleading. Certainly the career of Mozart or of Menuhin give us a truer picture—and we get it because we are allowed to know the intimacies. Mozart was a remarkable organist at the age of eight, and was able to compose in tiny, but perfect forms, at six. But some strange providence ordained that Mozart should become the great dissenter against the musical values of his time, refusing patronage, composing for a meagre living, dedicated to music in a single-minded way which never occurred to Haydn (and the lack of which did Haydn's music no harm whatever; this is not a moral issue). Mozart packed 626 musical works into a composing life of thirty years, and Schubert, nearly a thousand into rather less time; but nobody could call the careers of Mozart or of Schubert a fulfilment of the prophecies of people who stood around the infant musicians and predicted brilliance, public approbation and affluence for them.

In the other sense, the now well-known story of Yehudi Menuhin's musical reconstruction shows the rough country through which a young genius usually has to pass. Menuhin has told us that there was a time, after he had made an international reputation and played the Elgar Concerto under the composer's baton at sixteen, when he wondered whether he would ever play again, and when only a rigid and sacrificial re-forming of his technique saved him. In the result, as everybody knows, he has become one of the richest and most cultivated (not to say compassionate) musicians of our time; a great violinist, but so much else as well.

Similarly, Mozart became a great harpsichordist, but so much else as well. This is what did not really happen to the Wesleys, although Samuel came out of it better than Charles. Charles possibly fared worse because he was the elder.

We say this because it was his misfortune to be caught between two violent and unresolved forces; his parents' astonished admiration of his talents and their evangelical suspicion of music-making. We must not lay all the responsibility at the parental door, and in any case we must insist that this is not a moral affair anyway. But here is a young child, taken round to every well-known musician of his day, and approved by every one of them (except the morose Giardini, and we must resist the temptation to speculate whether Giardini was saying that the emperor had no clothes). Parents and friends and musical culture generally are all saying that he is a prodigy. This is going to make it difficult, almost impossible, for him to develop that power of self-criticism and self-sacrifice which a true artist cannot do without. And when you add to this the pressure that comes from the other Establishment—the evangelical—you have all the materials for setting up a textbook pattern of anxiety. Certainly the facts are that Crotch, that other and slightly later prodigy, though never achieving much creative talent as a composer, had a much smoother journey and found himself much better appreciated than either of the Wesleys. On which point, it is interesting that Samuel should write in his later years (with a generosity which he never lost):

> The Hon. Daines Barrington . . . makes an observation that Crotch in his childhood had but few advantages from the example of others; whereas, on the contrary, myself and brother were nursed and cherished in good music from our infancy. Therefore the rapidity of our progress was less extraordinary than his.

Yes, Crotch's background was simpler and homelier, less encumbered with social and theological complexities. But Samuel goes on in the same passage to express regret that he himself did not take advantage, as his brother had done, of the tuition of Boyce. He calls this "silly obstinacy" in himself. However, a little later we shall look at evidence for saying that this may have been one of his pieces of good fortune. Another may have been his being nine years younger than Charles, and being, at any rate at first, very much "second fiddle" to his brilliant brother.

The evidence of a slightly perplexed parental pride has already been set out, and general musical experience confirms that the "discovery" of a young genius at six or sixteen by parents, school or musical culture is not a passport to musical distinction. Evidence for the evangelical suspicion of music as a worldly plaything of the rich and godless is no less abundant. One piece of it comes from the seclusion of the village of Olney, where that strange and sometimes bitter lyricist, Cowper, was setting down his thoughts.

> Ye clergy, while your orbit is your place,
> Lights of the world, and stars of human race;
> But if eccentric you forsake your sphere,
> Prodigies ominous, and viewed with fear;
> The comet's baneful influence is a dream,
> Yours real, and pernicious in the extreme . . .
> Oh laugh or mourn with me, the rueful jest,
> A cassocked huntsman, and a fiddling priest!
> He from Italian songsters takes his cue;
> Set Paul to music, he shall quote him too.
> He takes the field, the master of the pack
> Cries—"Well done, Saint!" and claps him on the back.
> Is this the path of sanctity? Is this
> To stand a way-mark on the road to bliss? . . .
>     Occiduus is a pastor of renown;
> When he has prayed and preached the Sabbath down,
> With wire and catgut he concludes the day,
> Quavering and semiquavering care away.
> The full concerto swells upon your ear;
> All elbows shake. Look in, and you would swear
> The Babylonian tyrant with a nod
> Had summoned them to serve his golden god;
> So well that thought the employment seems to suit,
> Psaltery and sackbut, dulcimer and flute . . .
>
> *The Progress of Error* (lines 96–101; 110–17; 124–33)

Those lines were published in 1782. Occiduus, by the way, is Martin Madan, whose concerts at the Lock Hospital Chapel had already attracted a good deal of attention, not to say notoriety. It was in 1779 that the Wesleys held their first family concert, Charles being twenty-two and Samuel thirteen. It was really a series of concerts, and several more such series followed.[1] Charles senior felt he had to defend these concerts

[1] See F. C. Gill, *Charles Wesley, The First Methodist* (1964), p. 190.

to his brother, and he wrote to him expressing four grounds on which he felt that the concerts were to be justified: (a) because the boys would be kept from mischievous associations; (b) because the revenue from the concerts would help to pay the expenses of the boys' musical training; (c) that it would help to make the boys independent and to give them a faculty of private judgment rather than "swimming with the stream"; and (d) that it would encourage them to improve their skill in playing and composing.

All of which indicates that Charles senior had to wrestle with his conscience, and with the censure of the evangelicals. A musical parson was as bad as a hunting parson in the eyes of such laymen as Cowper and of such clergy as John William Fletcher (originally de la Flêchère, 1729–85), Rector of Madeley, who wrote severely to Charles senior in 1775 that his enemies complained "of your love for music, company, fine people, great folks, and of the want of your former zeal and frugality".

What we know of Charles junior—which is scanty enough—was that from the days of his early maturity he developed into a withdrawn and mildly unsociable character. "It is doubtful", says one commentator, "whether through the entire course of his life he was able to dress himself without assistance; if left to himself he was apt to appear with his wig on one side, his waistcoat buttoned awry or the knot of his cravat opposite one of his shoulders". He appeared to be in love when he was about twenty-five. Mild family resistance extinguished what was probably never a very powerful flame. His mother appears to have thought him unwise to form an attachment with a girl who had neither family nor fortune. Possibly this was prudence rather than snobbery, for by this time Charles must have been clearly a person who would rely on his wife to provide most of the temporalities. Charles's veneration for his parents prevented his applying for the organistship of the Chapel Royal; a post he might well have achieved, for he was much in the Royal favour. But it was a Court appointment, and Charles senior did not care for it, so Charles junior did not apply. This was in 1788, when his father was near his death. He remembered that when he had been invited to play at Windsor, his father had written to him that this was "stirring up a nest of hornets" and that he hoped he would not play there again. George III had on that occasion said privately to Charles, "Your uncle and your father, George Whitefield and Lady Huntingdon, have done more to promote true religion in the country than all the dignified clergy put together." But even if Charles senior knew this, it did not abate his sourness towards the court.

But all this was, musically, to ignore the facts of life, which were that music was being made in the circles of the court and the nobility. Cut off from these, forced to accept a scale of values in which the most honorific appointment for a musician was to be organist of the Lock Chapel, young Charles found neither a market for his talents nor a challenge to his habitual indolence. This is true, yet the facts of history are that what music was being made in English court circles was at a low level of quality and significance. So long as he remained in England, there was no hope of Charles junior's becoming a first-rate musician, by the standards which were about to be set up in Vienna and Bonn. The whole of the life of Beethoven fell within that of Charles junior, but Charles was obliged to live as though Beethoven had never been born, even though Beethoven's "posthumous" string quartets were written some ten years before Charles died. It was the same with Samuel; the differences between the brothers lie in other directions than this. Today it is hardly credible that so much could happen in Europe of which England was wholly ignorant, but in those days it was so. England had been invaded at the Restoration by the styles of France, and in Handel's time by those of Italy: but the influence of the intellectual and emotional mainstream was to wait a generation or two before it was felt at all. The irony of this story is that the chief agent in making that influence felt for the first time was none other than Samuel Wesley.

Samuel's life was somewhat more complex and colourful than Charles's, yet hardly less loaded with frustrations. His temperament was unlike that of his brother in that where Charles was, on the surface, withdrawn and placid, Samuel tended to the alternating elation and gloom that are the familiar signs of depression. In many things he was superficially Charles's opposite. Towards religion his attitude was ambivalent; Charles's was uniformly indifferent. Charles held down uninteresting musical jobs; Samuel lurched from one honour to the next despair. Charles was too little interested in marriage to get married; Samuel was, if anything, a rather uxorious marriage-partner. But clearly the brothers were the two halves of a single, slightly unbalanced psychological cell. (As happens not infrequently in such families, their sister seems to have been an unusually balanced and integrated person.) Where Charles withdrew from the world, Samuel was always vulnerable to it, but neither really made friends with it. Charles's music was a good deal less memorable than Samuel's, but what a disorganized heap of paper Samuel's eventually turned out to be is surprising only until one realizes what both brothers were contending with in their background and surroundings.

In his mature years Samuel wrote, "I hate public life: I always did." In the same letter he described the profession of music as a "trivial and degrading business" and regrets that his father forced him into it. That was his consistent attitude. Music, he was born to, and it was his first love; but its profession, its social overtones, repelled him. What was a rational and deliberate attitude in his father's evangelical friends was an inborn resentment in himself. The family and the evangelical culture, while encouraging him in music, had discouraged him in fitting himself for the social life that was, in that age, music's public context. So of course he loved music and hated musicians.

He spent some time as a converted Roman Catholic, and this was surely one of the oddest conversions to that church of which record has been preserved. It was a somewhat clandestine affair, but there is nothing at all surprising about that, even though Lightwood makes a good deal of it. It must have taken place about 1783 or 1784, but no direct evidence is available.

In the year 1783, we are still in the pre-Revolutionary era, and what is more important, the pre-Tractarian era, of English religion. Roman Catholicism is still a form of inhibited non-conformity. Such disabilities as were still suffered by protestant Dissenters were suffered also by Roman Catholics. There was to be no general emancipation of Catholics until 1833, no Roman hierarchy in England until 1850. It was to be 1791 before their political disabilities were first repealed. The reason for the 1791 Act was the invasion of this country by the first Catholic refugees from the continent of Europe (and it is credibly said that it was a desire to befriend these refugees who would, in Britain, appear to be members of an illegal priest-hood that caused certain Anglican parsons to adopt the round "Roman" collar in place of the traditional Protestant white cravat). Roman Catholicism was hardly a controversial faith in 1783; it was, in England, an eccentricity to which a few noble families adhered, but of which normal people took no account whatever. True, the conversion of Samuel was kept for a time from his father, and when the news was given to the aged Charles senior, he was profoundly distressed; but the climate was different from that in which the Tractarian landslide took place. Defection to Rome was a serious accident, but not a serious risk.

And it is quite clear why Samuel defected. Not only was he inoculated against evangelicalism (here again, the immuniza-tion that affected the two brothers had no effect on their sister), but the one place where really good church music could be heard in London was the Portuguese Embassy.

Even if that has to be qualified, it is a reasonably accurate account of what would have been in Samuel's mind. The London embassies of Catholic countries alone, apart from the private chapels of such families as the Howards, were the places where Catholic worship was kept alive; they were the only public places where this could happen. By standards of later years, their music was probably ill organized, but at least you could hear some form of plainsong there, and healthy eighteenth-century Catholic music in motets and sequences. There was a much closer contact there between church music and the music of the secular culture than there was elsewhere. Methodist music was becoming superficial and irresponsible; Anglican music was content to regard Boyce's *Cathedral Music* as the Bible of praise; beyond this, the Anglican musicians were doing little beyond composing Anglican chants. Samuel Wesley, born and bred in the school of Handel, was easy prey to the attractions of the music at the Portuguese Embassy. Almost certainly he will have been among the first Englishmen, for example, to hear the tune now sung to "O come, all ye faithful", which soon found its way into Protestant tune-books in association with evangelical hymns, but which had been in use at the Portuguese Embassy since about 1750. He will have heard the results of the choirmastership of the two Samuel Webbes, and of the musicology of La Feillée. For this sensitive teenager, this was probably the one kind of worship that had held any meaning.

He celebrated his new devotion to the Roman Church by composing a good deal of music, including a Mass *De Spiritu Sancto*, of which he sent a copy to the Pope, and for which he received a grave and gracious reply of thanks. Another work now performed widely which came from this period is the motet *In Exitu Israel*, of which more later. It was one of a set of Latin motets written, if not for Catholic use, at least in a Catholic context; its opening phrase derived from the eighth plainsong psalm tone is as good as a Vatican stamp.

But there is no evidence at all that he became in any sense a "devout Catholic"; this was no tractarian decision. If he ever understood Catholic doctrine, he had little use for it. He wrote later, in 1808, "If the Roman doctrines were like the Roman *music* we should have heaven on earth." That exposes the secret of it.

The next incident in Samuel's life calling for comment is his famous accident in a London street. It is thus recorded by Lightwood:

> As he was returning home one evening from a visit to an intimate friend, a member of the Madrigal Society, his way lay along Snow Hill, and here he fell into a deep excavation which had been prepared for the erection of a new building. He lay there insensible until daylight, when he was discovered and taken home. It was found that his head had been seriously injured, and the doctor who attended him suggested the operation of trepanning, which consisted in removing portions of the bone of the skull to relieve the pressure on the brain. Wesley obstinately refused his consent, and the wound was allowed to heal. He had good reason to regret this decision in after years, for it was undoubtedly the cause of the fits of irritability and nervous depression which were to be his lot, and which undoubtedly checked and darkened a career which might otherwise have been so brilliantly successful.
>
> (*Samuel Wesley:* p. 73)

It is normally assumed that this accident had a permanent effect on Samuel's life, changing his personality, making him subject to depression, and all but extinguishing his creative talent. The truth of the matter will probably never be known, but there is little more reason to be dogmatic in favour of that assumption than against it. For one thing, we have scanty medical evidence to go on, against the undoubted fact that Samuel lived fifty years after his injury. For another, in the only autobiographical work he left (part of which is copied out by Winters), there is no mention of the incident. For a third, it is hazardous to claim that he would have been a major composer had this not happened.

Snow Hill, in London, is a short rise now partly obscured by the Holborn Viaduct. How the accident happened we are never told; there might be an explanation which Samuel preferred to forget. His depressive temperament may have been aggravated by recurrent pain consequent on the unattended wound, but there is no record of any brain injury or paralysis.

Dr Percy Scholes says that the accident induced seven years' "incapacity", and that he was ever afterwards subject to fits of mental aberration. The "incapacity" cannot, even on the records we have, have been anything like complete. The reasons for this opinion will shortly become clear. He was anything but inactive during the years 1787–94, and indeed it was during that period that he married. As for the mental aberration, we have no indication that it was the result of the accident, and plenty of ground for attributing to him an unstable temperament from the first. Lightwood does mention on good authority a period of eight years, 1817–25, during which Samuel suffered from acute depression, but he adds, "the mental depression that he suffered at this time was not due entirely to brain trouble, for there were other evil influences at work." None the less, his naming of the accident as the primary cause of the breakdown thirty years later is almost certainly the origin of the assertions in reference books later than 1937 (his publication date) that Samuel was intermittently under the effects of brain damage for the last fifty years of his life.

In fact, there is nothing particularly improbable in suggesting that Samuel Wesley, through absentmindedness or some more palpable cause, fell into this hole one night in 1787, that the fall caused concussion, that there was a great to-do when he was found insensible in the morning, that the patient indignantly and perhaps with embarrassment repudiated the doctor's diagnosis of brain-damage, that he waved aside the hazards of brain-surgery (which must have been gruesomely high at that date), and that any irregularity in his subsequent life is attributable to causes far more deep-seated than an accident which, though it proved a convenient scapegoat, left him with his faculties quite unimpaired.

It is also necessary, if we are to accept the view that the accident was responsible for so much, to judge that the music of his later years was well below the standard of that which he composed before 1787. This is a view which it is quite impossible to maintain. Very little of his music was ever published, and a tiny fraction is now known, otherwise than to specialists. There are just two works which are indisputably major contributions to church music; the rest are still more or less curiosities, or pleasant but strictly minor offerings. These two works are the motets *In Exitu Israel* and *Exultate Deo*, and they happen to be works which can be reasonably accurately dated. *In Exitu Israel* is from his brief period of Roman Catholic enthusiasm—somewhere about 1784. *Exultate Deo* is dated about 1799 by Lightwood (pp. 104–8). Nobody has ever claimed that *Exultate Deo* is the inferior work; both are at the highest level of craftsmanship and of inspiration.

Not by any means all Samuel's music is dated; dates are usually ascertainable only from cross-references in his or other people's writings. The explosion of his musical output in the middle eighties is sufficiently explained by the inspiration of the Portuguese Embassy; the paucity of good music from the period after that, by sheer lack of inspiration and encouragement; the production of a good deal of organ music, by his discovery of Bach.

About this time, Samuel was engaged in a good deal of correspondence concerning the doctrines and disciplines of the Roman Church. There can, I think, be no doubt that he was, in some sort, received into that Church, although Winters takes a characteristic disparagement of Catholic doctrine in one of his letters to be evidence that he never was so received. (But Winters was writing [1874] at a time when a good Anglican would go to any length to conceal the defection to Rome of anybody in whom he was interested.) It is quite impossible that Charles Wesley should have been told of his son's conversion, resulting in such distress to himself, by people who were merely making mischief. In what manner, and after what sort of instruction, he was received we do not know; and it is quite possible that when "the Roman Catholic Church" meant the Portuguese Embassy in South Street (now South Audley Street), he was received in a manner which would, any time after 1850, have been regarded as infamously casual. None the less, this involved him in a certain amount of controversy, and he was always at pains (unlike, again, any convert of the post-1850 era) to disclaim any agreement with or responsibility for Roman teaching. Certainly, he ceased within a few years to maintain any pretence of Catholic discipline, and in 1793 he was married in the Church of England to Charlotte Louisa Martin.

The Wesleys were not notable for matrimonial success. John did not shine as a husband, and Charles junior did not attempt marriage. Charles senior was abundantly fortunate in his wife (who survived him by 34 years, dying in 1822 at the age of 96), but Samuel's first marriage was a spectacular failure. It was a mysterious business in some ways, and Lightwood tells us either too much or too little about it. Mrs Wesley was, it seems, an assistant teacher in a private school in Marylebone. After meeting her and being aroused to thoughts of marriage, Samuel, in his middle twenties, appears to have hesitated to go further, partly because he was so impecunious, but partly, as he revealingly said, because "to tie my person would be to lose my heart".

That, from what we know of these Wesleys, was a typical Wesley statement. All the Wesleys with whom we are dealing had a touch of obsessiveness about them; we shall find that even Samuel Sebastian had it. They tended to regard marriage as a distraction from higher things—the two seniors, from religion; the two juniors, from music. This was a rationalization of an almost irrational fear of losing personal integrity, at any rate in the musicians—natural enough in men who, as children, had been exposed to so many invasions of their personalities too early.

It would need a better acquaintance with eighteenth-century psychology than I myself possess to judge how remarkable it was that four months after his marriage, Samuel should write to his mother that his wife was in indifferent health because "the heat and her own weight are almost too much for her". Let us say that it evinces an objectivity unusual at that stage in married life. But he wrote in 1795 to his sister Sally of an open breach between himself and Charlotte, warning her that she was about to receive a letter from Mrs Wesley that would traduce his own character, and adding, "The worst that this woman can say of me, or of those whom I love, I am well prepared for, and her open violence will have very little other effect than that of driving me more speedily to comfort than I expected".

That is odd enough, but what makes it a good deal odder is that before his marriage Samuel had come under the influence of the later, and rather surprising, teaching of Martin Madan on marriage. This Madan has appeared once or twice already in our story, and we shall have to turn aside to attend to him for a moment. He was a younger contemporary of the senior Wesleys, being born in 1726, educated at Oxford, and called to the bar in 1748. Almost at once he sought Holy Orders, but he had already come under the Wesleyan influence, and he had a little difficulty in achieving them. Once ordained, he became at 24 years of age, chaplain of the Lock Hospital, which stood near Hyde Park Corner and became the most celebrated orphanage in London. The "Lock" was a place frequently visited by Wesley, and indeed founded under evangelical influence, but the association between Madan and the Wesleys was never personally close. Historically, it was chiefly hymnological, for Madan's collection of hymns and songs made in 1769 for the Hospital included a number of the Wesleys' hymns and a good deal of music which subsequently became thought of (not always to John Wesley's satisfaction) as typically Methodist. Madan survives in modern hymnals as part author of "Lo, he comes with clouds descending", and it was he who wrote the lines in "Hark the herald angels sing":

> with the angelic host proclaim
> "Christ is born in Bethlehem",

substituting them for a more characteristic couplet in Wesley's original.

That is what we remember now; but in 1780, at the age of forty-four, Madan was chiefly known to his contemporaries as a sexual eccentric, for in that year he published a tract entitled *Thelyphthora* (fancifully formed from the Greek for "female" and "destruction", probably meaning, "the destruction of woman"), in which he put the case for polygamy. This abruptly ended his ministry at the "Lock", and he took no other. He died in 1790 in obscurity.

It was this work that had fallen into the hands of the young Samuel Wesley. He engaged in a good deal of correspondence about it with his relatives and friends. How far he took it seriously, we dare not judge. He wrote to his sister before his marriage begging her to read Madan and do him justice. "His most sacred intention", he said, "was to save your sex from ruin, and to make those honourable whom the world delights to crush and destroy"; which I take to mean, "to make women honourable" rather than "to make adulterers honourable." What we can say reasonably reliably is that when, in his letter of 1795, he wrote of "seeking comfort", he was giving warning that he did not propose to live monogamously with Charlotte; and indeed that he had never proposed to do so ("Sooner than I expected" can hardly be interpreted otherwise).

Commentators have not been slow to attribute this aberration from convention to the Snow Hill episode, but it is quite clear that Samuel went into his marriage with a somewhat tentative acceptance of thee injunction to "keep thee only unto her as long as ye both shall live". More than this we cannot say. There were three children of this marriage, so it appears that 1795 did not see the end of it (though on this point Lightwood is elusive). They were named Charles, John William and Emma Frances. The third Charles entered the Church of England in orders, and was appointed Chaplain to the King's Household at St James's in 1833, and subsequently subdean of the Chapel Royal.

The marriage seems finally to have broken down about the turn of the century. Once again, the ambiguity of Lightwood reveals the unreliability of the evidence; but it seems that Samuel had turned for "comfort" to a housekeeper who had been in the house when Samuel and his wife were still living together. This is what we must gather from a sentence in a later letter of Samuel's. After he had finally broken with his wife, and set up house with the housekeeper, Sarah Suter, he wrote to a relative who had remonstrated with him, that he was "shamefully neglected and might have perished just at the time I was setting out to Tamworth (a journey of 114 miles) had it not been for the humane and tender attention of the very person falsely represented to you as a worthless and abandoned strumpet." This Tamworth visit appears to be the "Tamworth music meeting" of late September 1809. In writing of it, he clearly speaks as one who is visiting the place for the first time, both in the letter above quoted and in another, dated 25 September from Birmingham, on the way home. Therefore, it seems that in 1809 Samuel was still living in a house in which, at one and the same time, his wife could neglect him and his housekeeper could serve him. Exactly when his wife left him for good is not recorded. But what is beyond doubt is that on 9 September, 1810, Sarah Suter gave birth to her first child, who was named Samuel Sebastian. It is in the highest degree unlikely that Mrs Wesley was there when this baby was born, or when its arrival was given notice of; so probably she disappeared about the end of 1809 or beginning of 1810. She lived until 1845, and her gravestone in Highgate Cemetery records that she was in her eighty-fourth year (which makes her about five years older than Samuel), and that she was the "relict of Samuel Wesley, the celebrated composer".

The new union gave Samuel much happiness. There was never a divorce, so all their children were illegitimate. Among these was Eliza Wesley, who died in 1895 and who makes a further contribution to our story, and Robert Glenn Wesley, who was for some years organist at Wesley's Chapel, City

Road, London. Samuel was to know some bitter years before his life was done, but the birth of Samuel Sebastian came at the moment when he was at the height of the achievement most satisfying to himself, and most significant in history; his championship of J. S. Bach.

To this we are about to turn, but the point to be emphasized before we go further is this. During these years, Samuel never seems to have ceased composing. Historians have been unwilling to distinguish between Samuel's capacity for writing first-class music and his capacity for writing at all. In Grove's *Dictionary of Music and Musicians* there are, in a full bibliography, copious references to compositions in the 1790s and early 1800s. They have mostly disappeared into oblivion, but what with all this activity, and the stimulating friendship of Vincent Novello, which meant so much to Samuel from the turn of the century onwards, quite apart from the Bach episode, Samuel seems to have been leading anything but an aimless life.

His real difficulty was in finding a demand that drew the best from him. What seemed to be demanded, he wrote. A good deal of it was never published, which indicates that he mistook the demand or could not rise to it. There was undoubtedly a reaction after the high activity that followed his reception at the Portuguese Embassy, but it is in the general quality of the music rather than in its quantity that the falling-off is seen; and even that is not consistent. He was a busy and celebrated organist, and lived only the precarious life that is the lot of all unpatronized musicians. This, from the facts we have, seems to be the background.

# 6

# *The Music of the Two Sons*

At this point, and before we deal with the second and third of the great musical crises in the life of Samuel, we must go back a little to pick up the thread of Charles's music. Charles's compositions are too slight in content to require a chapter to themselves, but if we glance at them at this point, we shall be able to reconstruct in imagination the musical scene into which Samuel introduced the formidable figure of Bach. The meeting with Mendelssohn will naturally follow.

Charles was an able enough organist, but an almost negligible composer. We cannot but agree with Samuel Sebastian, who when he was compiling his *European Psalmist* found space for several anthems by his father at the end, but for nothing but a hymn tune by his uncle. Indeed, Charles's contribution to the choral repertory is now hardly existent at all. Nearly all his work was written for instruments, or for the organ.

There were five string quartets which he wrote about 1778, when he was twenty-one. By any standards they are juvenile works; impeccable in taste, but musically "for amusement only". Three have recently been reprinted by Hinrichsen through the piety of the late Gerald Finzi, who also has made an edition of one of his six keyboard concertos from about the same period. Of the three quartets, two take just over nine minutes to play, with all repeats; the third (no. 2 in D) takes half that time. The most interesting movement to play is the first movement of no. 1 in F, which contains some pleasant imitative strong writing and is indeed the longest movement (seventy-nine bars) in the three. No. 5 in B flat has a very charming Andante for its second of three movements. The opening movement of no. 1 is the most finished composition in the whole set, being in elementary, but plausible, sonata form. By contrast, the opening movement of no. 5 sounds like a sonata movement ending with the development, the tonic key having been reached by an oversight. The central movement of no. 2 is a good fugue. For the rest of the time, in all three of the Hinrichsen quartets, the composer relies on minuets.

As juvenilia, they hardly compare with early Mozart or Haydn, and are the kind of music which, had he lived to write more substantial music, the composer would probably have suppressed. There is a fatal tendency towards melodic writing, leaving the lower instruments with little to do beyond providing an Alberti bass. The C major concerto contains a good deal more promising music.

As an organist, Charles seems to have been moved rather late towards composition. His Voluntaries are pieces in four movements of very unequal merit. Preludes and Fugues in A minor and G minor have been extracted from two of these, worked by modern editors (Gordon Phillips and Peter Williams respectively), and in the Hinrichsen edition they do their best for the composer in their comments. The set from which they are taken is dated 1812 (1815 by Williams); being dedicated to the Regent, they must be later than 1811. Thus, they were composed when Charles was in his late fifties, but, as Phillips points out, by this time the Voluntary for organ had expanded from the one or two movement piece of the days of John Stanley to more pretentious dimensions, and Charles was not equal to the demands of what amounted to a four-movement sonata—indeed, the A minor Voluntary ends with a transcription from Handel for its fourth movement.

Charles was, in all his ways, a conservative to the point of eccentricity. It came natural to him, therefore, to write the first movement of the G minor Voluntary in the style of the "French Overture" which was in vogue anything up to a hundred years earlier. This was really his undoing. He tacked a "French Overture" onto a musical form, the four-movement Voluntary, that was brand-new. In other words, he had not the contemporary touch to bring alive a contemporary form. And generally, he lacked the faculty of thrust and confidence without which no composer can write either new music or music in new forms. His was a fugitive and world-denying temperament, sufficient for the day-to-day work of an organist in an environment insulated from rapid change, but insufficient for creative music. This is the conclusion to which you come, however carefully and exhaustively you study his music.

It is typical of Charles that when his brother Samuel "discovered" J. S. Bach, he apparently took no interest whatever in the news. Samuel despairingly refers to him as an obstinate Handelian—which was the obvious thing to be if one did not share Samuel's new enthusiasm. Everybody was to some extent a Handelian, even though there was but one Handel. Handel's genius was not in thinking of magnificent musical commonplaces (which anybody could do to some extent at that time), but in the limitless resource with which he constructed musical architecture on the most enormous scale; a scale which showed the real virtue of the simplicity of the units that made up the total structure. In building on the really large scale in the eighteenth century, nobody wanted subtlety in the units of the building. What everybody responded to in Handel was the bold, clear lines of the drawing, extended in the music in such a way as to give an impression of immense vistas of space. Once you examine a great house or a fine street of eighteenth-century architecture closely, or move about inside it, you appreciate the subtlety and originality that is expressed in proportions and in the marrying of style to use. It is very much the same with Handel's music. With him, music became really public. It lost its last vestiges of domesticity; but it was the combining of this with a complete lack of bombast and oppressiveness that made a work like the *Messiah* popular. Inevitably, anybody who wanted to "speak in public" musically, at least in church circles, wanted to use Handel's style. Everybody felt that he was the greatest of musicians, and that nobody else had anything to add. But lacking the architectonic vision of Handel, lesser composers tended to write imitations that were merely parodies. Handel is the easiest of all composers to parody. (Anybody can write a plausible Handel recitative or aria, but let him who can do that try his hand at a pastiche of a Bach recitative or aria, and he will soon see the difference between the two men's approach to music.)

The secret of Charles, despite what Samuel said, was not really that he was a Handelian, it was that he was essentially a chamber-musician, a composer who would have found himself only in music on the intimate scale. Of such composers there were dozens in any country in eighteenth-century western Europe; people whose music was of local and domestic interest; people who were not Mozarts or Haydns, with the power to make domestic conversation into something that, repeated and amplified, could command public attention, but whose music was, in the phrase we used before, "for amusement only"—blameless, graceful, urbane. This is no disparagement. It is only when such music tries to ape a public manner, as Charles's did in his Voluntaries, that it becomes aesthetically disproportioned.

The real question for composers in 1800 was, if you wished to make "public music", where was your "public"? Music was just emerging from the age of aristocratic patronage which found its best servant in Haydn, and which provided a "public" capable of drawing from Haydn 104 full-length symphonies. In any case, that kind of patronage did not flourish in England. English patronage provided a "public" only in the concert-rooms of the great houses—and it was in such a concert-room in a modest house that the two Wesley sons were brought up. But, as we have said, the special climate of *that* concert-room was emotionally uneasy. It left the sons to choose whether they would be church musicians or secular musicians. Charles became an unsuccessful secular musician while Samuel was moved to be a church musician. However, frustrated by the Puritan echoes which discouraged any composer of imagination from becoming productive in church, he had to wait for his first two musical "crises" before his inspiration found an outlet. The first of these was his contact with the Roman Catholic Church in the Portuguese Embassy, and this produced that small but precious pair of great choral works, *In Exitu Israel*, and *Omnia Vanitas*.

He was, we suppose, about twenty when he wrote these. *Omnia Vanitas* was written, we are told, "about the time of his father's death". If it was written just before or just after that event, it was written just after his accident of 1787. For if it were written before it, "about the time of his father's death" would hardly be appropriate. The matter is hardly important, except that it may contribute to the devaluing of the "accident" as an influence in Samuel's life which we have already suggested.

However, these two works show a complete mastery of musical language, and a sure touch in choral writing. All are capable of being sung unaccompanied, and *Omnia Vanitas* was originally scored only for voices. *In Exitu Israel* is for double choir, eight parts, a marvellously energetic and lyrical exposition of the opening of Psalm 114. It has a dignified opening based on a plainsong intonation, and then things gradually gather momentum. After the working out of a long contrapuntal statement, a new subject, in the home key, appears at *Jordanis conversus est retrorsum*, skilfully balanced with the first subject, not in key, but in its jagged melodic line. After this, new ideas crowd in on each other until the peroration (on page 18 of the Novello score, eight bars before letter G).

It is the music that matters. There is no attempt whatever at "word-painting" here. Imagine what a romantic would

have made of the drama of Psalm 114, and compare that
probably perilous fantasy with what Samuel does. Here are
twenty pages of B flat major, with hardly any modulation, only
the briefest of episodes in closely related keys. Everything
depends on the melodic and contrapuntal balancing of musical
values, the raising and relaxing of tensions. In other words,
this is exceedingly conventional music as Handel's was conventional, but not in Handel's style at all. A look at Example 5
will show that the various subjects are chosen not because they
reflect the imagery of the words, but because once the music
has got going, these are the subjects that the music requires to
keep the balance of values right.

As a dignified and commanding opening is conventionally
required for any weighty piece of music—the symphonists
largely agreed in taking this over from the composers of the
earlier suites—so a dignified and relaxed close is also required
(in this, neither the suite-writers nor the symphonists con-
curred; it is strictly an ecclesiastical convention). All through
the work of all three Wesleys, when they are in a church
context, we find codas, usually with plagal cadences and very
often with the highest voice sounding the fifth of the common
chord, designed to bring the music from a spanking gallop
gradually down to a walking pace and a smooth close. The
organ fugues are always designed to end, as it were, on Great
diapasons, the colourful stops having all been shut off.

That is the explanation of the extraordinary new statement
in *In Exitu Israel* on its penultimate page. There are no new
words (it is still *mare vidit*), but the composer simply cannot
bring everything to an abrupt stop after the climax of the final
*Jordanis conversus est.* What happens after this curious little
intrusion of platitude is a repetition of the opening plainsong
phrase, ending however (again using a well-tried convention)
with a touch of minor tonality, and a *pianissimo* final cadence.

This is a small point, yet it suggests much larger ones. It is
a clear sign of the urbane conventions which serious composers
always observed. Only the highest dramatic necessity would

4

Example 5
The subjects of *In Exitu Israel*

persuade a composer to finish a motet for church use without
slowing down the movement and reducing the volume.

But this actually is what Samuel does in *Exultate Deo*. This,
a rather later work, is a five-part setting of the first two verses
of Psalm 81, with organ accompaniment provided. Nowadays
it is usually sung unaccompanied, although a confident choirmaster will bring in the organ on the very last phrase, and its
effect is certainly distorted if the organ postlude is omitted.
It is a very simple musical construction, founded on two
commanding phrases (Example 6), one dancing up the common

Example 6
The subjects of *Exultate Deo*

chord, the other stumbling down it. The tonality is D major,
moving to F major just over half way through, and the part-
writing is severely contrapuntal, diversified with occasional
trumpet-like episodes of homophony (as with *sumite psalmum*
on page 18). Here, there is no slowing down at the end, only
the organ fanfare in strict time.

It is not Handel, but undoubtedly Haydn, whose music
chimes with that of these two great motets. But what is to be
said of *Omnia vanitas*? Why, this piece, in the still strange key
of C sharp minor, seems to indicate that the composer knew
his Tudor church musicians well. Here, the solemn homophonic

opening, setting the tonality and the prevailing style before the parts begin their conversation, is exactly what we have in the more reflective work of Byrd and Gibbons; for example Byrd's *Justorum Animae*. But it is a combination of that tradition with other later elements. The ruthless dotted rhythm which pervades the whole piece and is the inevitable demand of the Latin words *omnia vanitas* is strictly original, and its obsessive effect as it interrupts the contrapuntal conversation is something which Samuel borrowed from nobody. At its end, the piece quietly dies away in the conventional form of cadence, and well it may, because the tension it builds up is something of which Purcell at his best would have been proud.

This work is one of the two quoted in full by Samuel Sebastian at the end of his book, *A Few Words on Cathedral Music*, with the comment that if a composer could have written as well as this when cathedral music was in such a poor condition as it was in his day, there is yet hope for church music. The other work quoted in the same place is a short motet, *Tu es Sacerdos*, dated about forty years later (1827), but showing exactly the same blend of archaic serenity with "modern" evocative devices. Example 7, giving its opening and closing bars, shows its beautifully regulated style.

Another series of vocal works seems to come from a period separated from his "Roman Catholic" years by a good many years. These anthems are distinguished from the early motets by being set to English words and by using a much less sophisticated choral style. Indeed, they seem to have been written very much "to order", being performable by choirs of very restricted resources, and depending much more on solo-writing, or on tune-and-bass technique, than the earlier music. Indeed, it is difficult to recognize them as the work of the same composer who wrote the Latin motets. A few of these pieces are preserved by S. S. Wesley in his *European Psalmist*, and one or two are dated. But the dates are probably unreliable, which is a pity.

a

b

Example 7
From *Tu es Sacerdos*, by Samuel Wesley
a  Opening
b  Ending

One of these pieces which has recently been reprinted is "Might I in thy sight appear", a solo setting of three verses of a Charles Wesley hymn. The words appear as verses 4 and 5 of no. 346 in the *Methodist Hymn Book*, and the whole composition is no. 726 in the *European Psalmist*. It is there dated 1827; but it must be a good deal earlier, because in one of his "Bach Letters" (with which we are about to deal), Samuel ends with the salutation, "Pray remember me most kindly to Mrs ——" and follows this with the opening phrase of this song, instead of her name—the letter is dated 22 November, 1808.

However, whatever the dates of these short pieces, they show a quite different style, much more like that of Charles Wesley in places, and appropriate to the needs of the only people who were likely to buy copies. It is quite possible, for example, that

Samuel's "Might I in thy sight appear" would be sung by the choir of Surrey Chapel, where the recipient of the "Bach Letters" was organist, and which was the Dissenting "cathedral foundation" of church music in its time. Some of his other short anthems may have had the same destination, or they may have been performed under his brother; and Mr Novello was, after founding his publishing house in 1811, always ready to take anything from his old friend. The following short section of one of these pieces shows it to be agreeable, but without the ambition of the earlier works.

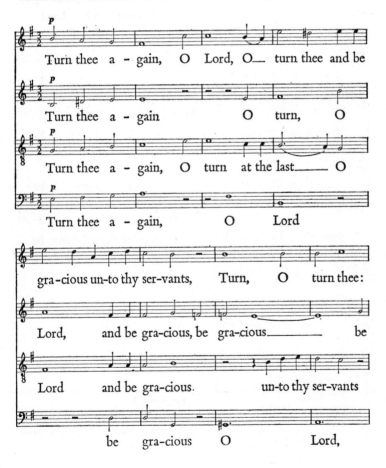

Example 8
A later anthem by Samuel
Wesley, from *The European
Psalmist*, 723

No, Samuel needed external pressure and demand to bring good music out of him. The early Latin motets were his response to the stimulus of the Portuguese Embassy; the corresponding stimulus to the discovery of Bach was in certain of his keyboard works which are sometimes used as organ pieces.

## SAMUEL WESLEY AND J. S. BACH

In England in 1800, only the learned had heard of J. S. Bach, and only the travelled had encountered his music. This need surprise nobody, for what demand would there be in England at that time for his work? His organ music was unplayable on any but a very few English organs, his church music was written in a liturgical tradition entirely foreign to that of England, his secular music supplied a demand which was, to the musical ear of the time, more attractively met by Telemann and his contemporaries, or by the minor English composers. The dissemination of the knowledge of Bach required a considerable raising of standards.

It seems that Samuel owed his introduction to the work of Bach to two contemporary musicians. He himself says in his autobiography that the first contact he had was through George Frederick Pinto, "one of the greatest musical geniuses that Europe ever produced". He also says that his reading of August Kollmann's *Essay on Practical Method and Composition* confirmed his enthusiasm for this newly discovered composer —this in a letter.

There is a touch of romance here, for G. F. Pinto was born in 1786 (and died of pneumonia at twenty in 1806), while Kollmann's *Essay* appeared in 1799, and it is only a few years after that that Samuel is announcing his "Bach crusade". Pinto was a young pianist-prodigy who had been appearing in Salomon's concerts since 1796. Kollmann (1756–1828), born in Germany, had come to England in 1784 to be organist,

4*

schoolmaster and chapel-keeper to the German Chapel in St. James's—the place of religious resort of the German entourage of the House of Hanover, and in his *Essay* he referred to Bach, printing the first Prelude and Fugue of Book I of the "48" as an example, thus becoming the first publisher in this country of a work by Bach.

Clearly, what happened was that Samuel heard Pinto play something of Bach's at a Salomon Concert, and his sensibilities were no doubt heightened by this encounter with a young player whose childhood was proving so much more productive than his own. (What might have become of Charles and Samuel had there been Salomon concerts in the seventies? But the concerts were only begun in the eighties. When they did begin, they were a most powerful source of the raising of standards of public taste by bringing the finest Continental music into the English scene.) Kollmann's book, coming out when it did, would have converged with this impression, and between them the two *habitués* of the cosmopolitan world, one mature, the other hardly yet a teenager, aroused Samuel to a new enthusiasm, and inspired him to a new phase of composition. Indeed, they gave him something to live for at a very lean time of his life.

Samuel's *Bach Letters*, conveniently made available by his daughter Eliza Wesley's edition of them in 1875, tell some of the story of his romantic quest for this new music. The story can be filled out from his autobiography and the other manuscript letters which have been preserved (and to which Lightwood makes copious and valuable reference). The *Bach Letters* number twenty-four, and were written between 1808 and 1816. All but one in this collection were written to his friend, Benjamin Jacob, who was organist at the Surrey Chapel. We know from a reference in one of the letters (VI, p. 20) that Samuel attended Surrey Chapel, and was much satisfied by the preaching of the minister, the celebrated Rowland Hill (1744–1833). "I assure you that I have not felt so much affected by any Harangue from the Pulpit for many years past as I was by the honest unstudied natural discourse Mr Hill gave us." It was also the scene of his first Bach concerts.

Samuel was much concerned to enlist Jacob's support in getting the works of Bach published in this country. By this time, Samuel's reputation was by no means high among those who did not appreciate him as a musician, and it appears that Mrs Benjamin Jacob violently disapproved of him. Probably he was not himself admitted to the Jacob household (and this may be why he was obliged to write this series of letters, for he was not by nature a ready writer). In Letter IV (p. 14) he says:

> I am glad that you brought forward the Hymn Tune for two Reasons, the former (and the better), because I know it is just in the style which particularly pleases C.W. (for his best compositions are pathetic), [this of course is his brother] and secondly, if he should venture to report the fact to our worthy Sister she will be extraordinarily chagrined in finding that a man whom she has represented (these are her own Words) as "destitute of every Sentiment of Justice, Honour, or Integrity," should have sufficient Respect to any religious Words to think of setting them to Music: I dare say she will add that they are thoroughly profaned by the experiment.

Since the following letter is that to which we have already referred as ending with a scrap of "Might I in thy sight appear" instead of the lady's name in a final salutation, it looks as if this is the tune he was there referring to, and as if the lady was Mrs Jacob.

The chief points made in the whole series of letters, where they concern Bach, are the need to get the music published, and the need to get it appreciated. Letter I contains an account (17 September, 1808) of how the previous year Samuel sought out Charles Burney (who, born in 1726, was then over eighty), and sought to remonstrate with him over a published judgment of Bach. Burney showed him a copy of *24 Preludes and Fugues* which C. P. E. Bach had given him, and Samuel found it a woefully corrupt text, full of "*scriptural* faults" (p. 3), and "a most vile and damnable copy" (p. 22). Samuel is able to tell the doctor this, and also that there is a second book of *24 Preludes and Fugues*. Samuel was so persuasive that the elderly sage began to share his enthusiasm, and to repent of his earlier judgment (pp. 4, 32, 44).

He also mentions in his first letter that he has been informed by one Canon Picart of Hereford that Bach has "written pieces for *three* organs"; probably Picart or his informant meant the concertos for three harpsichords, but Samuel was prepared to believe any miracle possible at the hands of "our Sacred Musician". He concludes that the great mass of Bach's music is "not sent to England purely from the contempt which the Germans entertain of the general state of Music in this country, and which unfavourable sentiment I am sorry to say has but too much foundation on the Truth."

The indications are, then, that Samuel had been studying Bach for some years, and that he had not been the only person to do so. The second letter (17 October, 1808) introduces another enthusiast, Karl Friedrich Horn (1762–1830). Horn, like Kollmann, was German-born, and had come to England in 1782. He had been noticed by the Saxon ambassador, and had become music-teacher to the Princess Charlotte. With his co-operation, Samuel announces that Forkel's *Life of Bach* is to be translated into English. (It was, but the work was not finished until 1820.) In this book is, he says, a complete list of Bach's musical works. Also, the "Fugues" are to be edited and published—by which he means the "48". (They appeared in 1813.) Horn has a great deal of Bach's music that is new to Samuel, especially:

Stupendous Trios for the Organ, which he used to play: his right hand played the 1st part on the Top Row of the Clavier; his left the 2nd Part on the 2nd Row, and he played the Bass *wholly* upon the Pedals. There are Allegro Movements among them, and occasionally very brisk notes in the Bass Part, whence it appears that he was alike dexterous both with hands and feet.

In the end it is hoped to publish all the music Bach ever wrote.

The works that have specially captivated Samuel at this point are evidently the organ sonatas, and he commends them to Jacob.

Letter III (19 October) adds little except some cheerful examples of the invective which Samuel is prepared to expend on those who do not share his enthusiasm, and the written source for Samuel's nicknaming "Saints in Glory" the Fugue in E from Book I of the "48". But Letter IV (17 November) expands on his sorrow that he cannot share his love of Bach with his brother. This is a subject to which he often returns. Charles is an irrevocable Handelian.

> Your playing Bach on Monday set my Brother upon his *Battle-Horse*. [He regards Charles as the victim of a conspiracy.] I think of him with some pleasure as to the *native* and *original* Goodness of his disposition, but with more melancholy when I consider such a Cruel Sacrifice to the whims and Artifices of designing Persons, who have made him the mere Puppet of their base and interested Designs.

These "designing Persons" were no doubt the court authorities at Windsor, for whom at the time Charles was conducting an almost continuous programme of Handel. In Letter V, he indicates that without the prejudice induced by these social pressures, Charles might possibly have come round, but that "amongst mere Handelians he will but too readily relapse into blasphemy."

By March 1809, he is preparing lectures on Bach which, later in the year, he delivered. The "campaign" is his sole preoccupation, and he sees an enemy in every musical rustle in the hedge. "We must for the present confine and repress our Inclination to publish *too hastily* our Creed in the transcendant Merits of this Marvellous Man" (Letter VIII, 8 March, 1809, p. 24). Thus he writes of the required strategy. In the same letter, he says that the first *Trio* (organ-sonata) has gone to the engraver. But by 18 August (Letter XI), he is writing:

> In order to ascertain who are verily and indeed "The Israelites in whom is no guile", I can think of nothing more expedient

than the Formation of a junto among ourselves, composed of Characters who sincerely and conscientiously admit and adhere to the superior excellence of the great Musical High Priest.

So it goes on. Specific references become fewer, and the letters shorter, after this half-way mark. The *Trios* appear to have been ready for publication by December 1809 (XV, p. 37, if the inadequate date does indeed mean December). In the same month (9 December), he replies to a letter from one Knight Spenser, of the "Surrey Institution", where he has been giving his lectures, apologizing in some sort for unguarded remarks in the course of one of them about people whose opinions were unfavourable to his subject, but declining to "make Amends" beyond that. The Lecture, on the subject of "Musical Deception", was one of which we may well wish the manuscript had been preserved.

Letter XVII, which most unfortunately is one of those without a date, gives the good news that "Chappell at Birchall's tells me that the People teaze his soul out for the Fugues; the eternal question is, 'When does Mr Wesley intend to bring forward the Fugues in all the twenty-four Keys?'" He also mentions that Chappell wants to publish some voluntaries of his own together with some other already published work; all of which makes him so busy that he pleads with Jacob to help in editing a section of the "48" (p. 42). He writes jubilantly,

> The Organ is King, be the Blockheads ever so unquiet. I cannot sufficiently express my Thanks . . . for making me an humble Engine of bringing into due Notice that noble Instrument by which so many Minds are brought to attend to Truths upon which the present and future Happiness depend.

Letter XVIII says that Burney, "almost 90 years old", is clamouring for copies of Bach's sonatas (Burney died in 1814 aged 88: the letter can be of any date between 1809 and that year). In Letter XXI, a very brief one, he refers to a comment in a journal he calls *The Cerberus* which concedes Bach's skill as an organ composer but says, "what strange stuff his Attempt at Vocal Music would have been". This reminds us that in the letters there is no reference anywhere to Bach's vocal works, apart from one to his chorale-harmonizations in Letter VIII. It is clear that Samuel's preoccupation was with the keyboard works, and that he had nothing directly to do with the introduction of the major vocal works into England. The first performance of the *St Matthew Passion* was in fact in London under Mendelssohn in 1829.

The upshot of this is that Samuel's Bach crusade has little to do with his contribution to church music. The exception to this is in certain of his works for organ. Most of his organ music was clearly inspired by the Bach crusade. It must have been. The best source to go to for evidence of this is the two collections of organ pieces, the *Voluntaries*, op. 6, and the *Twelve Short Pieces*.

It was clearly difficult to assimilate the organ technique of Bach to the conditions of English organ playing, in which organ music is still being written on two staves as a sub-species of piano or harpsichord music. The convention was to use the pedals simply as assistance to the manuals, perhaps, in a fugue, keeping them until the "pedal-point" preceding the final cadence, or in lyric and homophonic pieces discreetly adding a lower octave by using the 16-foot register which the pedals controlled. So at first glance, the Wesley fugues in the *Voluntaries* do not look very much like those of Bach. But it was the "48" that got into Samuel's system, rather than the great organ works to which he refers only once in the Letters (Letter IX where he quotes the first 5 bars of the Chorale-Prelude "*Wir Glauben All*" [S. 680] as something with which he proposes to astound his brother). And it is as much in the fugue subjects as anywhere that the influence of Bach is visible. Fugue-subjects in those days of English music tended to be pianistic, or to look like transcriptions from works for strings. Certainly, they were never written with any thought that they must be playable independently on the pedals. The two subjects quoted from Charles in Example 9 and the one from Samuel Sebastian's *Choral Song* that follows them show the prevailing convention. Those are essentially fugue-subjects for *manualiter*

Example 9
Fugue subjects
a    Double fugue, by Charles Wesley
b    Fugue, by Charles Wesley

compositions. Samuel is moved to experiment with the less demonstrative subjects in the later Bach style. For example, that of the *Fugue in C Minor* from the *Voluntaries* and the short *Fugue in D major* which forms the *Full Voluntary* tacked on to the end of the *Twelve Short Pieces* (Example 10). In these, the subjects suggest Bach's organ writing, the texture, his writing in the "48". The chromaticism of the *Fugue in C minor* is especially interesting, showing Samuel's attempt to rival his master in exploring the possibilities of a chromatic subject. The *Fugue in C minor* explores nearly every key in the spectrum during its long course.

Similarly, the *Twelve Short Pieces* suggest very strongly the Bach *Inventions*. The two best known today are the *Air and Gavotte* in F. In these, the Bach influence is far less noticeable than in, for example, *Fugue no. 7 in A minor* and *no. 10 in F*. The point must not be pressed too strongly. Samuel knows his limitations, and writes his own music; but there need be no doubt that he was inspired to write organ music by his contact with Bach's work, and that many points of experiment, notably his repudiation of the rather pretentious developments in

Example 10
a  Note the influence of Bach in the rhythm of this fugue subject
   by Samuel Wesley
b  Double-fugue subject, by Samuel Wesley
c  A "pianistic" fugue subject, by Samuel Sebastian Wesley: cf.
   Examples 33 and 34

the *Voluntaries* which had ensnared his brother, are derived
direct from that source.

There is much uncertainty about the dates of these works.
Peter Williams dates the *Voluntaries* between 1820 and 1830,
adding that it is "possible" that they had been composed before
1820. But Letter XVII, undated, but presumably between
1809 and 1814 (and if Eliza Wesley has put them in chrono-
logical order, nearer 1809 than 1814), tells us that Samuel is
looking out for Chappell the *Voluntaries* which Hodsall has
already published. The inevitable conclusion from this is a
date before 1810. Since Kollmann's book, which first attracted
Samuel to Bach, was published in 1799, giving him ten years
of preparation before he told Jacob of his plans, we should
probably be justified in putting the *Voluntaries* in the first
decade of the century. No attempt has been made to date the
*Twelve Short Pieces*, although Gordon Phillips gives (in his
edition of the set) a specification of the kind of organ for which

they were composed. Samuel does not refer to these in his letters; the probability is that they came a little later than the *Voluntaries*; sometime after 1816, or perhaps after about 1812, when the letters begin to become scrappy.

One thing is very clear. The influence of Bach delivered Samuel from two sins which otherwise tended to beset him; sentimentality and prolixity. Compared with other composers of his time and later, Bach's outstanding external quality is that of economy. Samuel once in his letters refers to the practical possibility of writing out every fugue in the "48" on one double sheet of manuscript paper: true, special paper had to be manufactured for the purpose, but the project was not an impossible one. Sometimes, Samuel tended to run on and on: he does so in that amusing piece, the *Voluntary in C* for four hands on one organ, which would be a great deal more entertaining if the fugue were cut down by a third. When W. T. Best got hold of his vast 187-bar *Fugue in G major*, he sought to render it more palatable by rearranging it as a virtuoso piece in much the same style that Liszt and Busoni had used on Bach's organ works in their piano transcriptions. In that work, there is nothing of Bach discernible. Nor is there in such small offerings as the *Introductory Movement in E*, which Williams plausibly puts at about 1825. This is a miserably sentimental and uninteresting piece from the hands of the Bach-inspired Samuel, and clearly shows the same kind of lapse from inspiration that we find in much of his late vocal work.

In sum, Samuel was a musician of very unequal temper. He needed outside influence to draw good work from him. He was fortunate in being as susceptible to it as his brother was impervious. One wonders, of course, what would have happened had the final "musical crisis" of his life come earlier than it did. This was the meeting with Mendelssohn. This event is well documented in a Hinrichsen volume called *Samuel Wesley and Dr Mendelssohn*, where the facts are set out by Max Hinrichsen, who uses *The Musical World* for the later months of 1837 as his source.

These last years of Samuel's life make pathetic reading. Failing in his powers as an organist, finding very little demand for his music, he seems to have been virtually dependent on the charity of publishers to keep him from destitution. His son Sebastian was still young, and although there were still the occasional recitals to be given (see below, p. 191), there was little hope yet of his son's being able to help support him. As his eminent son was to do, he turned very late in life to the composition of hymn tunes. In 1828, he compiled a volume of *Original Hymn Tunes*, and after its completion he continued to compose them for the new collection which Vincent Novello was preparing. Novello's book, *The Psalmist*, came out in four parts, each containing a hundred hymn tunes, from 1835 to 1843. Towards the end of this, there are a large number of tunes by Samuel, virtually none of which show anything more than a journeyman's talent. One thing one does notice; an occasional ascription of one of his tunes to a "Gregorian" original. In the three cases where this happens the identification of the original, or the composer's intention in so describing it, is quite impossible now. A few of these tunes are given in Examples 61–66 to show how Samuel preferred the more restrained style of the eighteenth century to the florid style, and how he strove to achieve some kind of lyric success in a form which never came naturally to him. In all he contributed fifty-seven tunes to *The Psalmist*. Very few found a home in Sebastian's *European Psalmist*, but that work did include a few of Samuel's Anglican chants, three of which, as curiosities of early nineteenth-century church music, are given at Example 11. They make it very clear that Samuel lived before the age when the congregational use of Anglican chants was contemplated. (See below, pp. 240–5 and 257–262.)

It was in the very last days of his life that Samuel met Mendelssohn; the German maestro was twenty-eight, the English veteran, seventy-one. It was not Mendelssohn's first visit, and when it was known that he was to play at St Paul's on Sunday, 10 September, 1837, the congregation refused to

Example 11
Chants by Samuel Wesley (see also Example 58a)
a From *The European Psalmist*, 703: original key
b From *The European Psalmist*, 705: original key
c From *The European Psalmist*, 672

leave the cathedral after the outgoing voluntary until, as the story goes, the organ blower abandoned his post in the middle of a piece. It was learned that Mendelssohn was to play at Christ Church, Newgate on the 12th, and it was there that Samuel joined the packed audience to hear the young German player on the new organ (built, 1835). He was entranced by Mendelssohn's playing, and hardly dared present himself after the recital; but being persuaded to play, he played a piece which he had composed three days before—a *Fugue in B minor*, which has the date 9 September, 1837 on the manuscript. Mendelssohn, says the contemporary account, was enthusiastic in his praise of it and of Samuel's playing, but the old man wistfully replied, "You should have heard me forty years ago." The

Fugue, "composed expressly for Dr Mendelssohn" (as the manuscript states), was Samuel's last work; and for that reason, but that alone, is worth a passing glance. It is little more than a two-part extemporization on its opening phrase. But there it is, and when we look at the bare score and compare it with the sophisticated elegance of Mendelssohn's organ fugues, we can only salute the occasion of the young man's kindness to the senior, and pass on. Samuel never left his house after returning to it on 12 September; he died on 11 October, and handed on the torch to the young and promising organist of Worcester Cathedral. He left an unfinished and uninformative auto-biography, laboriously copied out in capital letters, which is in the British Museum. It was Samuel Sebastian who drank deep of Mendelssohn, and to whom it was given to fight a last battle for the grand-style choral tradition in the English Church.

# 7

# Samuel Sebastian,
# His Life and Adventures

Samuel Sebastian Wesley made his appearance in the strange family of his father Samuel on 14 August, 1810, the first of several children born to Samuel Wesley and Sarah Suter in their irregular union. At that time Samuel Wesley was 44, and, at his own birth, his father, Charles senior, had been 59, so that Samuel Sebastian was 103 years younger than his grandfather. There are no indications that the precocity of the senior generation repeated itself in young Sebastian, but at nine years old he had a good enough voice and ear to become a chorister at the Chapel Royal. There, he received a very good musical training under Hawes, the choirmaster. Kendrick Pyne recorded this of the young chorister:

> Mr Attwood and a small contingent from the Chapel Royal, St James's, were commanded to do duty at the Chapel Royal, Brighton . . . Master Wesley from His Majesty's Choir at St James's took the soprano and leading parts in the anthem with sweet and divine effect.

The document there quoted (in Kendrick Pyne's reminiscences of his teacher, Samuel Sebastian, in *English Church Music* for January 1935) is dated 1823, and the building was the chapel originally attached to the Royal Pavilion, the summer residence built by King George IV when he was Prince Regent. The King showed personal interest in the boy to the extent of once presenting him with a gold watch, and of allowing him to ride part of the way to Brighton in the royal carriage. Hawes used to describe him as the best chorister who ever came under his care.

He gained his first organist's post at the age of fifteen, and during the next seven years, 1825–32, he was organist of four London churches. It is not quite clear which of these posts, if any, he held concurrently, but they were St James's, Hampstead Road, St Giles, Camberwell, St. John's, Waterloo Road, and Hampton Parish Church (with Hampton Court). The first of his five cathedral (or quasi-cathedral) appointments came in 1832, when he was twenty-two, and it was to Hereford. He had already achieved the distinction of conducting a performance of *Cosi fan Tutte* at the age of nineteen, in the (then) Theatre Royal, London.

The rest of his life, except for an interlude of seven years, was to be spent in that English West Country which had been the ancestral region of the Wesleys. His first appointment lasted three years only, on a salary of £52 a year with a bonus of £8 "to be paid by the custos and vicars", and the prospect of a further £40 when his superannuated predecessor, Dr J. Clarke Whitfeld, should die. Wesley did not stay long enough to claim the full salary; Whitfeld outlived his appointment by a year, dying in 1836. But the three years were spent to good purpose. They saw the composition of *The Wilderness* and "Blessed be the God and Father" (see below, pp. 141–157); in 1834 Samuel Sebastian conducted the Three Choirs' Festival at Hereford, where history was made by bringing the oratorio performances into the nave for the first time;[1] and just before he left, he married the daughter of the Dean.

In 1835, he applied for and achieved the organistship of Exeter Cathedral, where he remained until 1842. During this

[1] *The History of the Three Choirs Festival*, by Watkins Shaw; p. 31.

second period he gained the degrees of Bachelor and Doctor of Music at Oxford. His doctoral "exercise" was the extended anthem, "O Lord, thou art my God"—one of his longest pieces, but perhaps not one of his most successful. It was given its first performance in Magdalen College chapel in 1839, according to a custom which endured into the twentieth century, but was then thankfully dropped.

He applied, in 1841, for the professorship of music at Edinburgh University, but the successful applicant was Mr (from 1842, Sir) Henry Bishop, a musician of much slighter talents, but having the advantage of twenty-four years' seniority. He applied again for the same post when Bishop left it in 1843, but this time lost the competition to a younger man, Henry Hugo Pierson (1815–85), who very soon abandoned the post and went to live in Germany. Samuel Sebastian did not apply again. But in 1847, he sent in his application to the University of London for the chair of music there; once again, he was defeated—by Sir Henry Bishop.

Nothing else is on record concerning his time at Exeter. It is said (but not positively recorded) that his relations with the Chapter there were not happy, and that he resigned the post after a dispute with one of the canons following on a disparaging comment by the learned divine on a work by his father Samuel. But this may have been after he knew that he had the appointment to Leeds Parish Church in his pocket.

The seven years 1842–9 were the years of his exile from the West Country. He was appointed to Leeds Parish Church by the vicar, Walter Farquhar Hook, who was Vicar of Leeds from 1837 to 1859, and later became Dean of Chichester. In Hook, the musician found at last a kindred spirit. Hook was an energetic Tractarian who took full advantage of the opportunities offered by the industrial expansion of Leeds; he rebuilt his own parish church, and had a hand in the building of twenty-one new churches in the city during his incumbency, with thirty-two parsonages and some sixty schools. Samuel Sebastian could hardly have been less interested in Tractarian theology, but what will have appealed to him will have been Hook's establishment of a full cathedral service in the Parish Church, which continues today (1967) to be the only parish church with full cathedral-style musical appointments. The centenary biography indicates that Samuel Sebastian took this post in default of the appearance of any other cathedral appointment when he had his quarrel with the Chapter at Exeter; but he remained in it until 1849, and there is no reason to believe that he was any more discontented with it than he would have been with any other.

While he was at Leeds, he composed the *Choral Song* and the *Variations in F Sharp minor* for organ. Both are recital pieces of the kind which will have served him well in the increasing recital work which he was getting by this time. The *Service in E* also comes from this period.

He had the misfortune (1847) to injure a leg while fishing in the becks of the North Riding, but although he never recovered the proper use of the leg and went lame for the rest of his life, this did not, it seems, incapacitate him in his organ playing. What it was that provoked the publication, in 1849, of his most famous piece of writing, *A Few Words on Cathedral Music*, we shall never know; but by that time he had had sufficient experience of the ills of church music to be able to formulate one of the heartiest pieces of invective ever to come from a church organist's pen. We shall return a little later to this document. In 1849, the year when he left Leeds, he gave a famous performance as solo organist at the Birmingham Festival.

His next appointment was the longest of his career; sixteen years at Winchester Cathedral, with the organistship also of the College after a short delay. The centenary biography, written at Winchester, amplifies its account in the following terms:

> For a short time Dr Wesley lived in Kingsgate Street, and afterwards in the house in the Close, successively occupied by Dr Arnold and Dr Prendergast [later organists of the Cathedral].

Wesley's prime reason for settling in Winchester was that his sons should have the opportunity of being educated at the College, but a by no means unimportant secondary consideration (if indeed it was not the first) was the anticipation of the pleasure provided by the fishful Itchen.

The same writer goes on to remark that whereas his predecessor, Chard, was liable to sacrifice his duties to the demands of hunting, Samuel Sebastian was equally apt to cut engagements for the sake of fishing expeditions; and indeed, that his gifts as a player and a composer seemed to wane during his time at Winchester. The falling off of his playing prowess, the same writer attributes as much to his disinclination to practise as to the effects of the Yorkshire accident, and adds, on the authority of one "Mr Bumpus", author of a book called *English Cathedral Music*, "Even when he composed in his later years, it was usually some trifle that caused him no trouble".

"Ascribe unto the Lord" (whose opening words are written on the memorial tablet to Samuel Sebastian in Winchester Cathedral) was written at Winchester, and so was "All go unto one place"—composed on the death of the Prince Consort in 1861. Both are highly characteristic works, even if it would be fair to say that they contain nothing new. But if this judgment of the now forgotten Bumpus can be trusted, we probably have in Samuel Sebastian a touch of that hereditary disposition to *accidie* which quite evidently afflicted both his father and his uncle (and to which both his grandfather and his distinguished great-uncle were complete strangers). It is odd that the accident-motif should recur in the life of Samuel Sebastian, together with a falling-off of powers which could have been colourably attributed to it, but which in neither his case nor his father's was necessarily the direct consequence of it.

It was during his time at Winchester that he developed a special interest in hymnody. *Aurelia* was certainly written there (see below, p. 201) and he was collecting material for the *European Psalmist*. This interest had always been there, but the spate of hymn books that followed the publication of *Hymns*

*Ancient and Modern*, in 1861, increased his interest in this branch of church music. Indeed, he contributed to the hymnology of his time not only the *European Psalmist*, but also the music of Kemble's *Psalter and Hymn Book*, 1864, which he edited and to which he contributed a number of new tunes.

To the Winchester period belong also the anthem "Praise the Lord", composed for the opening of the organ in Holy Trinity Church in 1861, and the setting of the funeral sentences, "Man that is born of woman", written in the same year for the funeral of the Warden. During his time there, the organ in the Cathedral was replaced by an instrument erected by Henry Willis I out of part of the organ in the Crystal Palace, installed at the Exhibition of 1851. The staircase to the organ-loft was altered at his request to permit him to arrive after service had started without being visible to the congregation. The new organ was dedicated on 3 June, 1854, and one of the choristers who came from St Paul's to swell the choir for the occasion was John Stainer, then thirteen years old.

He made his last move in 1865. Being consulted by the Dean and Chapter of Gloucester about the appointment of an organist, he offered his own services, and thus began a ten-year period which was probably the happiest decade of his life. He probably did little or no composing during this time, but he finally brought out his *European Psalmist* in 1872. The best thing, however, that Gloucester did for him was to bring him back into touch with the Three Choirs' Festival, which he had had nothing to do with since his first cathedral appointment thirty years before. This raises a subject which must be dealt with in a moment, but although Samuel Sebastian found himself involved in a controversy concerning the festival, for once it was not one of his own making. He remained in office at Gloucester until his death; but actually Christmas Day, 1875 was the last service he played there. He played the "Hallelujah Chorus" as a voluntary, to everybody's surprise, and never returned to the organ loft. His health deteriorated rapidly, and he died on 19 April, 1876, aged sixty-five.

He was a distinguished teacher, and among his pupils who became eminent cathedral musicians were George Garrett of St John's, Cambridge, William Spark, of Leeds Town Hall, Kendrick Pyne of Manchester Cathedral, F. E. Gladstone of Llandaff and later of the Royal College of Music, and T. E. Aylward of Llandaff, Cardiff and Chichester. The number of anecdotes told of him suggest that he was a "character", and a person of somewhat forbidding manners; but, as we are about to show, the secret of the awe which he inspired in people (when he was not arousing positive anger) is probably in his unswerving dedication to professional standards. It was, in those days, necessary for somebody to assert these standards in church music, and this is never easy when one is dealing so largely with clergy, who can at any moment take refuge in "spirituality" to avoid meeting an argument. Nobody who stands up for the professional status of a church musician can hope to avoid being thought of as a profane meddler in sacred things by those who find it inconvenient to listen to him rationally; and he is lucky if he can avoid the habit of thinking contemptuously of the clergy as a pack of hypocritical philistines. Things in the later twentieth century are a good deal better than they were, and an organist who insisted as of right on appearing late for services would nowadays incur the displeasure not only of the chapter but also of his colleagues; but Wesley's dogmatic and uncompromising manner in such disputes is not particularly surprising when one reckons with the astounding conditions under which most church musicians worked in the mid-nineteenth century. The improvement of those conditions is owed as much to Samuel Sebastian Wesley as to any other single musician.

# 8

# The Condition of Church Music in the Early Nineteenth Century

## WHAT IS NOW OWED TO THE TRACTARIANS

In the study of church music it is now a commonplace to say that most of what we now value in it we owe to the Tractarian movement. Even so, it is hard for anybody today to imagine the conditions under which any church musician of conscience worked in the days just before that movement made its impact on English church life. If a personal statement may be permitted here to be brought in evidence, allow me to mention that in mid-April 1967, I attended morning prayer at a certain parish church in the remoter part of north-west Somerset. The church was small and kindly, the congregation numbered about thirty.

The hymn book in use was the standard edition of *Hymns Ancient and Modern* with second supplement (edition of 1922). This hymnal was a direct outcome of the Tractarian movement. The three hymns sung were "Christ, whose glory fills the skies" to *Ratisbon*, "O Jesus, I have promised", to *Day of Rest*, and "O praise ye the Lord" to the tune by Sir Hubert Parry. The words of the first were by Charles Wesley, and its tune the one popularized by the first edition of *Hymns Ancient and*

*Modern.* The words of the second were by J. E. Bode of
Charterhouse, written for a school that had come directly
under the influence of the new post-Arnold public school
movement, itself infected by the Tractarian revival; and its
tune again was an *A & M* tune. The words of the third were
by the original *A & M* editor, and the tune was the work of
the most notable composer in the Edwardian revival, which the
new spirit of purpose and seriousness in worship had made
possible.

The psalms were sung from the *Cathedral Psalter*, the chanting equivalent of *Hymns Ancient and Modern*. The priest wore a
white surplice—a Tractarian device. Holy Communion followed the morning service, and although the Tractarian
opinion would have placed it earlier in the day, it was that same
opinion which in remote parish churches aroused the con-
sciences of priests to celebrate it at all. The organ was a
venerable and beautiful little instrument at least a century old,
still hand-blown, and standing in the chancel, where the
Tractarians tended to put their organs. There was now no
choir, but in former days a surpliced choir sang from the
chancel, where the Tractarians advised them to sing.

It would have been easy to ascribe to Tractarianism the
worship-forms and customs of a downtown city church in
neo-Gothic style where everything was light, sound, scent and
movement. But in the Parish Church of Fitzhead they would
still say they were "low church". Nonetheless, there is hardly
anything visible or audible there which has not the touch
of Keble and Newman on it. Not the least of these touches was
a quite admirable dogmatic and expository sermon. There was
much that the Royal School of Church Music Commissioner
might seek to criticize; but in the days before 1833, the decency
and purposefulness of this religious exercise would have been,
in the depths of the country, a rare discovery.

## PRE-TRACTARIAN UNCERTAINTY

The trouble was that in the period 1800–33, English religion simply did not know where it was going. The rude shocks of continental anti-clericalism had hardly penetrated to its mind, and where they had done so, they had met blank incomprehension. The issue in England was a simple one; the Establishment versus evangelicalism. Evangelicalism was Wesleyan in origin, but not only Methodists embraced it. A great deal of the Church of England, especially in the new cities, embraced it. It was effective and hospitable, and to the Establishment a menace. The Establishment itself (meaning by this a body of opinion, not the whole of an established church) was hamstrung by its Puritan heritage. It was helpless before the needs of the new poor—as Puritanism always had been—it was hopelessly entangled with the values of the aristocracy. So the rising forces of anti-clericalism found it on the defensive, and it was chiefly concerned to defend itself against nonconformity and against evangelicalism. A climate of this kind could not be friendly to the development of church music.

Naturally, there were protesters among church musicians, but they were disorganized and individualistic. Samuel Wesley and his son Samuel Sebastian would have been at the centre of such a group of reformers, had it been distinguishable as a group. What in fact happened was that Samuel senior gave all his enthusiasm to the arousing of interest in Bach, while Samuel Sebastian played a lone hand in his efforts to establish some kind of professional standards, and produced, on his own, the manifesto which we are shortly to examine.

That the people interested in the reforming of church music knew one another is all that we can reasonably say. Those in whom we are interested here are, apart from the Wesleys, the La Trobe family and Vincent Novello. In what they wrote, they give us some useful insights into the state of things in church music that they observed. We can begin with John Antes La Trobe.

## THE JUDGMENT OF J. A. LA TROBE

The La Trobes were a family of Moravian religious association who flourished in England about 1800. Christian Ignatius
La Trobe, the father (1758–1836), was a musician and man of
letters who held office as "Secretary for the Unity of the
Brethren"—roughly, a senior denominational executive—in
England from 1795. He composed a small quantity of church
music, and edited *Hymn Tunes Sung in the Church of the United
Brethren*, the first Moravian official tune book, in 1790. Eight
of his tunes survive in *Moravian Liturgy and Hymns* (1914), and
one got into the 1904 *Methodist Hymn Book* (no. 115); but
otherwise, they are now forgotten.

Christian Ignatius had three sons. Peter La Trobe (1795–
1863) became a Moravian minister and secretary of the
Moravian mission. He too was a musician, and contributed
tunes to the enlarged (1826) edition of his father's tune book.
The youngest son, Charles Joseph (1801–75), after being educated for the Moravian ministry, became a traveller and
explorer, ended up as Lieutenant-Governor of Victoria,
Australia, 1851–4.

The second son was John Antes La Trobe (1799–1878), who
took Orders in the Church of England and eventually became
(1858) an honorary canon of Carlisle Cathedral. He was not a
practising musician but an interpreter and critic, and became
one of the very few priest-musicians of his generation. It is his
book, *The Music of the Church, considered in its Various Aspects,
Congregational and Choral*, published in 1831, which we are
here bringing in evidence. At that time J. A. La Trobe was
curate of St Peter's, Hereford. He may well have regretted that
he published his book the year before the new organist of the
Cathedral arrived. During the years 1832–5 they must have
known each other; but the interest in La Trobe's book is in its
criticism not of cathedral music, but of the music of ordinary
parish churches.

The book is a garrulous tract of 454 pages, unindexed and

leisurely. There is plenty of good reading in it for the patient, but its contentions can be summarized with reasonable economy.

He starts out by lamenting the evil state into which music has fallen. There is, he says, a very slight improvement in the cities, though "not proportioned to the general advance in science"; but things in the countryside (which he knows best) are appalling. The trouble is ignorance and lack of interest. The clergy are learned enough: "volumes upon volumes are continually issuing from the press upon subjects of religious obligation", but upon music there is nothing:

> some indeed so closely connected with this degraded art, that a stretch of ingenuity seems requisite to pass over it in silence; and yet in vain do we peruse the crowded pages, for one solitary remark on its preciousness.  [p. 3]

Quite soon, he declares his interest. Commenting on an essay by one the Reverend J. Jones, he quotes him as ascribing the low state of church music partly to "exuberant harmony". This turns out to be an objection very much in the terms that John Wesley used; any kind of complexity was undesirable in church music. To this he declares himself implacably opposed. It is, he says, a Puritan corruption. "Harmony!", he exclaims, "the very essence of all solemnity of sound!"

The difficulty is partly (he goes on) that the rubrics on this subject are treated as discretionary rather than as mandatory; the result is a distressing lack of uniformity or of intelligible standards.

> Few churches pursue the same plan. The chief practices, deviously and arbitrarily adopted, are the following:— A preludial voluntary upon the organ; one or more of the introductory sentences chanted [sc. "monotoned"], or a part of the hundredth Psalm sung; a short voluntary after the Psalms; the Doxology chanted, with the Te Deum and Canticles; a Psalm after the Litany; the Response after each commandment chanted; before the sermon a [sc. metrical] Psalm; another after the service; and a closing voluntary.  [pp. 8–9]

5

A little later he says: "It is one thing to avoid forcing the vegetation of a plant, and quite another thing to neglect it altogether."

After a considerable discourse on the history of church music, he comes to the parson. He characterizes the clergy as on the whole indifferent, slothful and oppressive [pp. 72–3]. The mischief is that the clergy are taken as an example: what they neglect, their people neglect [pp. 73–4]; indeed, the people feel themselves obliged to be more negligent than those pastors and masters who are held up as their superiors.

> May not the clergyman, then, congratulate himself as one cause of the decline of his psalmody?—The solemn liturgy is concluded. After a moment's silent prayer, all rise from their knees, their minds prepared for the cheering invitation, "Let us sing to the praise and glory of God." The psalm is given out. The singers elbow themselves into notice, and the tune advances. Verse follows verse—but he appointed to lead the public devotions is no longer in his place in the house of God.   [p. 74]

Here is a pre-Tractarian notion of the parson's duty to psalmody; La Trobe is referring to the disappearance of the clergyman to the vestry during the Psalm between the office and the sermon. It is a practice which he often refers to as an irritant, and he would certainly have been all at sea with the liturgical use of congregational hymns to cover the essential movements of the clergy at Mass. All the parson was doing in the vestry was, no doubt, changing into his preaching gown; but La Trobe wants him in the pulpit.

Psalmody seems to have become, says he, "a wedge to keep asunder the divisions of the service". Its servile state should be the parson's concern.

> How would [he] act if, when he entered his church upon the Sabbath, he found the cloth of the desk torn and drooping, the door of the pulpit off its hinge, the sound-board threatening him by its sloping direction, or a shingle from the roof admitting the wind to play with the leaves of his manuscript?   [p. 78]

To repair this shabbiness, La Trobe wants the incumbent to cultivate a working knowledge of music and to use this, allied with that good taste which is natural to a gentleman (but not natural to most of his flock), for the instruction of his people. He should encourage the use of "sober" psalm-tunes (such as the *Old Hundredth, St David, St Anne, Irish*) [p. 91], see that people sing tolerably in tune, extrude the bassoon which is an uncouth instrument and replace it by a 'cello, make use of the children's voices to shame the sluggish taste of their elders, appoint a good precentor, and hold congregational practices [pp. 92–5]. The parson, he says, is the best choirmaster.

The background of this statement (what Samuel Sebastian would have said about it in his Leeds years beggars imagination) is the country parish church in which it was accepted that the parson was probably the only literate person in the place (the squire's place in these plans is carefully overlooked by La Trobe). It is understood that there will be hardly anybody else who can read, let alone direct music. If the parson must, as clearly he must, do something about the prevailing irreverence of choirmen and women (especially about the terrible irreverences that can come from their proximity in the privacy of choir-lofts [p. 118]) he may as well go one step further and be musical director.

Choirs under the La Trobe scrutiny come out as an unruly and wayward company, and organists are not much better. There is a perceptive and entertaining aside on the psychology of organists which wears a good deal better than some of La Trobe's exhortations:

Of all inanimate creatures, the organ is the best adapted to portray the state of mind of the individual who performs upon it. If pride and musical foppery possess the seat of intelligence, the faithful instrument will be sure to proclaim it in the ears of the congregation. The unfortunate player, puffed up with the idea of his own importance, and dazzled with the brilliancy of his talents, is as it were transported into Madame de Genlis' enchanted palace of truth, when the tongue was the undesigned index of the real intentions of the mind. Every "fond and frivolous ornament" proclaims his conceit, however he may seek to smother it under high-sounding stops, and loaded harmonies.  [p. 122]

The organ, in other words, is a very good lie-detector, and its playing a serviceable truth-drug. Itinerant singers tend to corrupt church music by injecting into worship an undesirable notion of personal vanity [p. 129]. Bad performances of good music are pretentious and worse than bad performances of bad music [pp. 130 f.]. A moral and aesthetic congruity is needed in church music, and secular values should be suspected.

> The preservation of this distinction [sc. between sacred and secular music] depends mainly upon the organist. It is his duty to mark it by broad and intelligible lines, so that the instrument may speak a language comprehended by the devout, however dark and uninteresting to the profane.  [p. 136]

In his words on congregational singing, he asks for a more zestful, more dutiful and more orderly performance of psalmody. "In the country the psalmody is exposed to the intrusion of ill manners more coarsely, if not more openly, than in the town" [p. 172]. But it is not only boorishness that is the enemy of psalmody; some are too proud to sing, for fear of the sound they will make [p. 158], and others [p. 162] are too disgusted by the nature of the music they are asked to sing to have anything to do with it. But it is not in all respects that the parish churches are the worst off. At least in the country parish there is some sense of status and rank to induce order. (La Trobe quotes with approval an anonymous writer who says that "high breeding and religion go hand in hand", and that if you enter a country church you will always be able to distinguish the high-born from the poor by their better deportment [p. 169].) The worst irreverences of all are often to be found in the cathedral and collegiate churches.

> During the whole morning and evening service, the pacing of feet, and shutting of doors, too often occasion one continued

course of interruption—persons coming and going, not entering into the choir and taking their station reverently with the congregation, but lounging in the ante-chapel, conversing and promenading during the prayers, crowding the door of the screen for the few moments while the anthem is performed, and at its conclusion, turning their backs upon the remaining petitions, and unceremoniously taking their departure.  [p. 170]

This is enough to give the general drift of La Trobe's opinions. He goes on to consider hymn-singing in detail, offering such judgments as that the practice of "lining-out" ought to be abolished, that simple and grave metres and melodies are better than those which display levity, that "Drink to me only" (called *Prospect* in current hymn books) is an unsuitable hymn tune, that "fuguing" tunes are intolerable in decent worship, that hymns tend to be too long [p. 222] and therefore sung too fast. He also asserts that there are too many tunes in currency, and it is better for congregations to learn tunes by ear than to have them printed in their hymn books, for the presence of tunes "will encourage them to sing their discords with the greater boldness and to assume that the music in their books will amply atone for the want of music in their heads" [p. 226].

Chapters follow on the chanting of psalms and on the singing of anthems. He pleads for variety in the choice of chants, as against the prevailing custom of singing all the psalms for the day to the same tune. He advocates "the plain chant" for the singing of the *Te Deum* and the Canticles: but this almost certainly means an Anglican chant as opposed to a cathedral setting [pp. 270–6]. In the singing of anthems, he pleads for the reintroduction of instruments in defiance of the Reformers' prohibitions; indeed, he has plenty of use for the church instrumental band, provided it really is a band and not a collection of indifferent players. He mentions the unsuitability of a solo fiddle [p. 328], which he has heard in some churches, saying that it reminds him too much of the customary violin-accompaniment to country dancing. His observations on the organ are what one would by now expect. They are interesting in reminding us that an organ voluntary in the middle of morning and evening prayer, as well as at either end of the office, was the accepted custom in those days. He seems to accept the custom of having it before the First Lesson (i.e., after the Psalms for the day). He has the expected things to say about the playing of interludes between verses of hymns—a common custom which has disappeared for the most part in Britain, but which was derived from Lutheran practice and whose revival in our own time, in the right hands, has much to commend it.

The conclusion of the matter [pp. 392 ff.] is that sacred music is a high calling which simply does not come naturally to mortals, and for which proper training under authority is a necessity.

> There is nothing of natural inclination, precept or example to inspire a wish like David's after the music of the sanctuary, "O let my mouth be filled with thy praise! . . ." How can it be expected that there should enter into the giddy mind, in its cease-less whirl of intoxicating delight, the duty of the creature to the Creator, the real vanity of all earthly enjoyment, the responsibility that rests on the abuse of a talent, the awful account which is waiting the quick and the dead, the claims of the worship of God over Satan and Self! [p. 393]

We quote La Trobe at such length, because he is such a convenient example of the paternalistic and moralistic tone which music reformers have tended to use in church, not only in his time, but in the ages before and after him. He comes of an "enthusiastic" religious tradition, but he seeks now for a typically Anglican dignity and reserve. But his plea is not for the establishment of professional standards among musicians; rather for the inculcation of what he and his kind called "religion". The very close association between "religion" and the decorous behaviour of the ruling class will nowadays escape nobody, but in those days it would not have been questioned by anyone, least of all by those against whom the censures were directed. Music, undoubtedly, was in a state of disorganization, and musicians in the parish churches were a fumbling and witless lot; but the cure is not the cure that Samuel Sebastian looked for. It is "religion" pure and simple, respect for the parson, the putting away of the "vanities of the world", silence, attention, and the performance of liturgical duty.

## THE TESTIMONY OF NOVELLO

Alongside that document we may place a shorter but hardly less interesting one; the Preface to Vincent Novello's *The Psalmist*. This is, in many ways, an admirable collection, and the foundation of the more sober and dignified style of hymnody which later came to prevail under the more widespread influence of *Hymns Ancient and Modern*. It contains a few "discoveries"; among them, the tune now called *Westminster Abbey*, adapted from part of a Purcell anthem, which in recent years has come to be widely associated with the hymn "Blessed city, heavenly Salem" (see AMR 620). It also contains, as we have seen, a large number of hymn tunes by Samuel Wesley.

The preface to this work is a considerable essay of some 6,000 words, crammed into the oblong pages set in microscopic type. It contains a good deal of music history, and then some reflections on the condition of church music in the time of which La Trobe had also been writing. Here is an extract from it:

It is somewhat difficult to assign a plausible reason for the . . . decay in the public taste with regard to *Psalmody* at a period when music of the highest order is so generally cultivated. The names of Handel, Haydn, Mozart, Beethoven are familiar as household words, and there is scarcely a town of any note, where their works are not intimately known. Had there been at any time a scarcity of good Psalm Tunes, the adoption of those complained of would be easily accounted for on the ground of necessity; but not only have the publications of former eminent Composers been suffered to go out of print, from the want of demand, but those of several distinguished Musicians of the present day, comprehending selections from the Old Masters, together with originals of the same sterling character, have failed to command the circulation due to their superior merits; whilst the only compilation to which this remark will not apply, is unhesitatingly condemned by every judge of Music, as unworthy of the popularity it exclusively enjoys.[1]

In attempting to investigate the cause of a preference so singular and undeserved it will be found that some of the best compilations before the public are too expensive to be generally accessible. Others are considered deficient in the number and variety of tunes requisite for Congregational purposes. Some appear to contemplate no other Harmony but that supplied by the Organ, and are therefore useless where *Vocal Harmony only* is permitted; whilst others present a formidable barrier to popular adoption, by retaining the Tenor Clefs for the inner parts, a knowledge of which few persons will take the trouble to acquire. Such are presumed to be the principal reasons for the comparative indifference of the public to the *best compilations* extant; and will account for the general use of a Selection, which, while it is free from these objections, is destitute of any other claim to the preference it has obtained . . .

With regard to Singing as a part of the worship of God, both in Churches and Chapels, there has for some years prevailed such a disregard of the nature and design of that sacred service, as must excite astonishment and regret in the minds of those who can appreciate it aright. In the Churches there exists a lamentable indifference to its performance as a duty, that by no means characterized the earlier times of the Reformation, when many of their finest tunes were composed—an apathy, which is not only unjust to the gifted Composers of their Music, but strikingly inconsonant with the fervid and sublime character of the other parts of their public service, and the devotional feelings it is alike intended to inspire and to express. On the other hand, the *Wesleyans* and *Dissenters*, if not chargeable with *indifference* to its performance, have too generally degraded its quality, by the admission of light and trivial Music before alluded to, which has

---

[1] The publication thus complained of is almost certainly John Rippon's *Collection* (1796).

gone far to displace the beautiful Melodies which originally distinguished the worship of the former, and the sober and dignified, though somewhat monotonous strains to which the almost seraphic aspirations of Watts were written and adapted.

Although this essay is subscribed "The Compilers of The Psalmist", and contains in its closing passages eulogistic references to Novello, it is very probably in its greater part the work of Novello himself; and it expresses very well the opinion of a cultivated musician about the needs of church music in the 1840s. The only people who care about singing in church are the "Wesleyans and Dissenters", and they lack all proper taste and discretion in its use. One notable point is Novello's very aristocratic assumption that "good music" is "good for people,"—an assumption shared by La Trobe. It is, to him, terrible that a society which accepted Handel and Mozart should accept such trivial music in church. And this view persisted a very long time before it was questioned. Even those who wrote really good nineteenth-century hymn tunes, such as Parry and Stanford, based their vocabulary on that of the Continental classics. Vaughan Williams was the first to say that good hymnody is good folk music, not good "classical" music; and in his own day, that too was an "aristocratic" view (indeed, Vaughan Williams was a man of very "good family"). It has been much later that others have seriously assailed the view that Handel and Mozart, or their later equivalents, are the proper norm for hymn-writers to follow. But in their different ways, Elizabeth Poston in the *Cambridge Hymnal* (1967) and Sydney Carter in his famous ballads, have been saying just that.

## THE THREE CHOIRS' FESTIVAL

Returning to Samuel Sebastian, we can illustrate this same point by referring to the Three Choirs' Festival, in which he

5*

was involved briefly during his early years, at Hereford (when he conducted the Festival of 1834 there), and later on more closely, in his last appointment at Gloucester.

Dr Watkins Shaw, who has written the history of the Three Choirs Festival, tells us that its inception goes back to an inaugural meeting in 1717, and an inaugural Festival opening on 1 August, 1719. These seem to have been from the first festivals of both secular and sacred music, with the accent rather on the secular. As the eighteenth century advanced, the music of Handel tended to take over, and Watkins Shaw tells us that in the years 1745–1784 no fewer than forty-eight Handel performances were given, including nine of *Samson*, and seven of *Judas Maccabaeus*; the *Messiah* was first sung at the Gloucester meeting of 1757, and has been sung "in whole or in part" at every meeting since [Shaw, p. 10]. During the same period, the Festival attracted increasing numbers of "Persons of Quality and Distinction" (here Watkins Shaw quotes from the advertisements of the time), and the "Concert and Ball" became a central feature of the Festival.

In the nineteenth century, the Handel emphasis continued in works performed in the Cathedrals. The programme of the Hereford "Grand Selection of Sacred Music", in 1816, lists one work by Beethoven, one by Haydn, one by Calcott, and eleven by Handel. But Watkins Shaw tells us that in the Festival of 1829, the corresponding programme featured the work of no fewer than fourteen composers. And indeed, even more than now, the selection of music depended very largely on the enterprise of the musician at the host Cathedral.

But it happened that Samuel Sebastian's Gloucester Festival took place under the shadow of what Watkins Shaw calls "the gravest crisis ever to befall the Music Meetings" [pp. 54–5]. The nature of this crisis has nothing to do with Wesley himself, but gives a clear indication of the difficulties into which English Church Music had fallen. The crisis arose through the appearance of a body of opinion that the Festival was taking on far too secular a character. The opinion had been forming itself over the previous twenty years and more. The first sign of it was when, at Gloucester in 1853, the innovation was introduced of holding choral Matins, sung by the combined choirs, on the three days following the opening service. The custom had grown up of suspending all cathedral services during the Festival, and it was in answer to a protest by the cathedral chapter that these services were held. In 1854, the same programme was followed at Worcester, but Hereford did not follow until 1861. This was not due, apparently, to any complaisance on the part of the chapter there, who openly opposed the efforts of the then organist to support the Festival. In fact, in all three cities, the chapters were agreed in viewing the Festival with a suspicion which grew, towards the end of the sixties, into open hostility.

In the year 1865, the Earl of Dudley added his support to the chapter of Worcester by offering a gift of £10,000 towards the restoration of the cathedral, together with a pound-for-pound addition to the traditional charity collection, on condition that the Festivals were discontinued. The gift was declined, but only because Lord Hampden had, in opposition to the Earl of Dudley's views, managed to raise an equivalent subscription from other sources.

From the accounts given by the historian of the Festivals, it seems that from this point onwards the matter became political, and emotion overreached reason in most places where it was discussed. Ironically, it was a very mild sermon preached at the Gloucester Festival by Canon Barry of Worcester, but containing one reference to the possibility of changes in the Festival, which brought things to a head, and which provided the occasion for Samuel Sebastian's only contribution to the controversy—which was the playing of the "Dead March" in *Saul* as a voluntary after the sermon. However, the diocese of Worcester got no share in the charitable proceeds of the Gloucester Festival of 1874, and early in the following year, the Worcester chapter announced that they would withhold permission for the use of the cathedral for the Festival unless certain conditions were met. These were that "no orchestra or solo artists were to be engaged, no platform was to be erected in the cathedral, no tickets of admission were to be sold, no secular concerts were to be held, and no works of the oratorio class—not even *Messiah*—were to be performed."

The Festival of 1875 became known to its historians as the "Mock Festival", and Watkins Shaw mentions that it consisted of six choral services, "with music that sank as low as Smart in F, Attwood in D, and Mendelssohn in A."

It was, apparently, the townsfolk, and especially the trades-men who lost heavily on the 1875 Festival, whose opinion quickly saw to it that this was not repeated. But the point here is that this episode was the result of the complete failure of nerve in English church music by the 1870s. It is interesting to note how low the music sank in 1875, but what was it like in 1874? It was a dispiriting affair, by all accounts. Samuel Sebastian was responsible for four Festivals at Gloucester. At his first, the major works performed in the Cathedral included not only Mendelssohn's *Elijah*, *Hymn of Praise* and *St Paul* (Part 1), but also Beethoven's *Mount of Olives* and Mozart's *Requiem*. The 1871 Festival was distinguished by the first Festival performance of the *St Matthew Passion*. But at the other two, he had attempted nothing on that scale, keeping more unswervingly to the middle of the road with Mendelssohn and Spohr (whose *Last Judgment*, a marvellously light-hearted account of the mysteries of the *Book of Revelation*, was a Festival favourite through a whole generation, getting eleven performances between 1865 and 1901).

But if it is true, as it seems to be, that Samuel Sebastian's own powers of composition had deserted him by the time he got to Gloucester, and if his contemporaries were of the meagre stature at which we are bound to assess them, what was left but the dilemma of either performing fashionable Continental music, or relying on fourth-rate English music? The modern answer would be, of course, to go back into history and cele-brate England's past triumphs in singing Byrd, Gibbons and

Purcell. The answer to that is historical. It was still not the practice, either in English cathedrals or elsewhere, to celebrate the past. A somewhat conservative tradition in the Three Choirs' Festivals (no doubt supported by those tradespeople) made its promoters unwilling even to experiment with some of the music which the early Victorian antiquarians were un-earthing. Samuel Sebastian thought plainsong barbarous; but outside the circle of Havergal, Helmore and Neale, few church musicians thought it, or Tudor polyphony, anything else. One anthem by Gibbons found its way into the 1875 "Mock Festival", but that was no doubt because it was something they happened not to have forgotten at Worcester. If the fashion was—as it had been for many generations and remained until the end of the century—to perform music not more than a generation old, then there was nobody who could stand up to Mendelssohn and Spohr; nobody, except Samuel Sebastian himself, and he had lost heart.

Not that the Festival authorities were averse from good music when they could get it from a contemporary. Brahms's *Requiem* (1868; first London performance, 1873) was in the 1877 programme; Dvořák's *Stabat Mater* (1877) was performed in 1884 and his *Requiem* (1890) in 1894. By the time Elgar was fairly launched, the tradition of great choral works had revived, and resentment at their secular appointments—orchestras, soloists, platforms and the rest—had quietly vanished.

But 1875 was too soon to expect any sign of this invasion of major choral works from the Continent. It was right at the end of the really barren period. (We have to exclude Berlioz from all these considerations because, although he died in 1869, it was to be many years yet before any English concert-going audience would listen to him.) So there the choice was—a secular emphasis, appropriate not only to the secular concerts, but also to the kind of music available for the religious occa-sions, or the poor best that English composers could provide. There is no indication why Samuel Sebastian appears so little in the music lists in his lifetime: his only personal contribution was an overture specially written for the Hereford Festival of 1834. A work of his was, we gather, turned down at Worcester in 1866, an occasion from which he absented himself, and on which he had the sympathy of the *Times* music critic. What all this tells us is that neither the moralisms of such as La Trobe nor the exhortations of such as Novello had had any effect on church music. Church people were still incurably secular in their values. They behaved secularly—irreverently, said the chapters—at cathedral Festival concerts—they thought, apparently, that the final chorus of the *St Matthew Passion* could be treated as an outgoing voluntary, left their seats, and began talking to their friends. The time had not yet come when people in general regarded music as something worthy of their whole attention; and the Three Choirs' Festival was no good to the cathedrals, the tradespeople, or the designated charities if it did not get the support of plenty of "people in general" as well as specialist musicians.

It is entertaining to speculate on what might have happened had Samuel Sebastian moved to Gloucester when he in fact moved to Leeds. Had he been in his full vigour, musically creative and socially destructive, the issue might just possibly have been settled more violently and more quickly; but then the result might have been the final demise of the Festivals. As things were, they survived to become a lively centre of music making, to be a source of demand for good new music, and to keep the standards of large-scale church music healthy; which is just about the last thing you would have expected had you been in a pew at Worcester in 1875.

# 9

## *Samuel Sebastian on Cathedral Music*

Samuel Sebastian achieved a reputation for being choleric, obstinate, and difficult. Quite clearly, he inherited the slightly depressive temperament of his father, and shared it with his uncle; but what they entirely lacked, and what he recovered, was the pugnacity of the previous generation. A reading of his one contribution to letters, entitled, in the spacious style of his age, *A Few Words on Cathedral Music and the Musical System of the Church, with a Plan of Reform* (1849), one feels that had he had a readier pen he might have got a good deal more "out of his system". *A Few Words* is a seventy-eight-page tract, written with the diffuseness of incompletely organized indignation, the number and length of whose footnotes indicate a certain inexperience in writing, but whose clarity and severity of purpose are nonetheless beyond any possibility of mistaking. It is of historical interest, both for the light it throws on the state of cathedral music at the time and for the clues it gives to Samuel Sebastian's general approach to music. It was written at the end of his stay at Leeds, and published both there and in London, when the author was in his thirty-ninth year. By 1849, he had had experience of two cathedrals and one unique parish church with a cathedral-approach to music, and he reckoned that he was ready to outline his criticism and his plans for reform.

The first fifty-six pages of his tract elaborate an indictment which can be gathered under three main heads: (1) that the condition of cathedral music in England is deplorable; (2) that the indifference of the clergy to music is staggering; and (3) that the only hope for the reformation of cathedral music is the establishment of professional standards.

(1) It will be no surprise to any reader of these pages, that somebody judged the condition of cathedral music to be poor. This had to be said, and it was only a man of dissenting and cultivated mind, like Samuel Sebastian, who could say it. He opens with the statement that hardly any cathedrals in England (of which there were at the time twenty-eight) can raise the bare minimum for a resident choir, which is, he says, twelve voices. Even a choir of twelve makes the singing of verse-anthems something of a mockery, because one voice is obliged to sing a "chorus" or *tutti*. But he would make do with twelve for a start; his complaint is that even so few are not to be found. In earlier days, he says (pp. 14–22) things were better. In Edward VI's time, the staff of the Chapel Royal numbered seventy-three. Whereas now (p. 40), the choir of St. Paul's, in ancient times numbering forty, has but six voices.

(2) The trouble, he roundly (and repetitively) asserts, is with the clergy. "It would not be difficult to shew that the Clergy and men of literary pursuits are, on the whole, less susceptible of musical impressions than any other class of the community" [p. 11].

The trouble is, not that the clergy are recruited from some congenitally tone-deaf order of society, but that they have a vested interest in the suppression of music. This he traces to Puritan influence. The Genevan party in the Elizabethan Settlement, he says, quoting Peter Heylyn the seventeenth-century historian, in their opposition to all "ceremonies" in

the church caused a body of "ignorant and illiterate" opinion
to prevail in many places. This opinion was strongly supported
by the Cromwellian regime. Two long quotations support
the view that Puritanism was death to church music. (In one of
these a misprint, or possibly a misapprehension on the author's
part, produces the surprising statement that the Puritans
repealed the Act of Uniformity in 1664, "stigmatizing the
Liturgy and Service Book as burdensome". He almost certainly
means the Westminster Assembly, which was in full session in
1644. By 1664, the Clarendon Code was in operation against
Dissenters.)

Samuel Sebastian detects a lingering of Puritan opinion in
the Cathedral chapters. He gives, in one of his extended footnotes (p. 38 f.), an example from Bristol, in the very year in
which he is writing. "The Dean and Chapter elected to the
office of Minor Canon a person who could not chant the Service, and shortly afterwards abolished the Choral mode of
performing certain portions of the Service altogether." He goes
on to say, with satisfaction, that popular opinion was aroused
in the city to such good purpose that the choral services were
soon restored in obedience to a legal decision; but he further
observes that the cause of this attitude in the Dean and Chapter
was the view that "the Service would become more devotional
by being read, and Preaching was the thing of moment at
Cathedrals."

This is perfectly good history. The Genevan tradition, of
which John Knox was the most famous interpreter to Britain,
emphasized the reading and exposition of Scripture; it was
strictly cerebral, a celebration in religion of the new literacy
that the printing press had brought, and the new freedom of
interpretation that the Reformers claimed for the people. Inevitably, the pedagogic emphasis of Geneva suppressed the
imagination, which to the pedagogues was the gate by which
superstition entered the mind; and cathedral music (to say
nothing of cathedral architecture) was incompatible with such
ideals as those. He is quite wrong to attribute this to the time

of the Restoration [p. 27]: but essentially right to attribute the trouble complained of to a Puritan stream in the English character and the English church.

The consequences of this Puritan suppression are, in the first place, economic. Cathedral foundations simply will not now find money for music. Again, he shows how much better things were in other countries and in other times. But now parsimony (a Puritan virtue, of course) has strangled church music. It is almost a matter of "two cultures". Look, he says (in another long footnote), at what has happened to the Reid Chair of Music in Edinburgh. (He knew about this: he had applied twice for it without success.) The Reid bequest, he says, provided for a stipend for the Reid Professor of "not less than three nor more than eight hundred pounds a year"; but the electors to the Chair were nearly all medical men, and they kept the stipend down to the minimum so as to leave more money free for medical research. The same mind is at work in the church (for the church recruits its leaders from the same social stratum as do the universities). "The pious founders of Cathedrals never contemplated the ludicrous and profane state of things we now witness" [p. 36].

Further, he complains of the unwillingness of Cathedral authorities to buy copies of printed music. In secular life, music printing is a booming industry. Attwood at St. Paul's (he was organist there from 1796 to 1838) had to provide all copies of new anthems at his own expense. Boyce lost heavily on his *Cathedral Music*. "The late Samuel Wesley published a most beautiful and masterly 'Service' for Cathedrals. Only one Cathedral purchased copies, and the plates were eventually melted down by the publisher, Balls of Oxford Street, to be re-stamped with a set of Quadrilles." Again, "On a recent application of the kind [a subscription for a new publication] being made to the Organist of a Cathedral"—not the Chapter —he replied: "I am glad you do not ask me to get our Chapter to subscribe to your work. They never spend a pound to purchase music; and if they did, the Choir is in such a wretched state, we could not sing it." [pp. 52–4]. One wonders if this last is a reference to the author's own *Service in E*, which came out in 1847, but which can, under those conditions, have been rarely sung in his lifetime. Samuel Sebastian goes on [p. 55] to concede that chapters are not as wealthy as they had been, or as they were supposed to be, and that some thought out to be taken about clergy stipends if the required standards were to be preserved. But on the whole [ib.], the musicians "feel that the Clergy either systematically disparage music, or at best view it with a cold side-glance; and this for no better reason than that the interests of religion were far above those of music; and that the claims of a vastly increasing population have been great and pressing." So music is debased because it goes too cheap.

> Mr Landseer, it is said, has in eight days painted the picture of a horse for which he has received a thousand guineas . . . Were the musician who should produce a work of the highest merit in eight days, to ask not a thousand guineas but a thousand farthings, the reply would be, invariably, "NO!" Let him study hard in his art, from the age of eight to thirty-five, sacrificing every interest to this one sole pursuit, let him offer his work as a present at *some* Cathedrals, and they would not go to the expense of copying out the parts for the Choir! [p. 52]

Naturally this attitude has affected the composers. Nobody demands music of a high standard, so none comes. It is, he says, remarkable how the architecture of a cathedral will cover up a choir's deficiencies; so that the paltry stuff that is normally sung sounds tolerable where, sung in a room, its defects would be ruthlessly shown up [pp. 37–8].

(3) The only answer, as he sees it, is in a new attitude in the church to professional standards. In this argument, a key phrase is once again found in a footnote [p. 24]: "The sacred and the secular are here somewhat strangely intermingled, in order to show that all must conform to one standard, when viewed

professionally". He finds himself, against his instincts (certainly against Wesleyan instincts), driven to argue that the assumption of one standard for the church and another for secular music is an error. Concerts, he says [ib.] in Exeter Hall (London) are properly appointed; by contrast, church choirs are shockingly impoverished. Later, he says:

> the improved state of public taste must be remembered, and the giant strides of Secular Art . . . The present state of the art, and of public taste, is such as to warrant our claiming for Church Music the sympathetic regard arising from involuntary but well-grounded admiration. Without deferring too much to public opinion, we may hope that its criticism will be searching in all cases where the Choral Service of the Church is in process of restoration.   [pp. 50–1]

And in yet another footnote, near the end of his second section, he writes, "Would that the zeal, the talent, order, and general good conduct of persons engaged in Theatres could be transferred to Cathedrals! In Theatres, talent is sure to be rewarded and error exposed, and punished by dismissal" [p. 71].

Having thus framed his charge, he proceeds to "The Plan". His suggestions are first financial, second academic. In the first place, he wants, as an absolute minimum, twelve choirmen in every Cathedral, paid at least £85 per year, with a sufficient number of deputies to allow for absences, paid at £52 a year. But immediately, he admits that this is only part-time pay, and that a minimum salary of £150 for a choirman should be regarded as essential, if they are to give their full time to the needs of the choir, as they should. Voluntary assistant-singers could be recruited, but only against the background of a properly paid professional establishment [pp. 56–8].

Secondly, he calls for the establishment of a "Musical College" which would set and keep proper standards, and from which singers and organists could be recruited. There was, of course, nothing of this kind in his time. The Cathedral choir schools provided all the musical training that was available, and where these had suffered from the slump in musical affairs they were negligible; this applied to most of them. The answer to this prayer came with the foundation, in 1856, of St Michael's, Tenbury, through the munificence and initiative of The Reverend Sir Frederick Ouseley: this was the first of our post-Reformation Anglican music schools, and it is still flourishing more than a hundred years after its foundation.

Allied with this demand, is a parallel one for a "Musical Commission" in the church, "exercising authority in the Musical Affairs of the Church generally". The nearest thing we have to this is the institution of the Archbishop's Diploma in Church Music, associated with the foundation of the Royal School of Church Music.

Those are the two main heads under which he gathers his plan, but he amplifies them a good deal, both with subsidiary demands and with historical references. He pleads, of course, for better status for the cathedral organist. He says that the normal organist's stipend is £200 plus whatever he can raise by incidental teaching and conducting and other musical engagements. In "The Plan", Samuel Sebastian suggests that a cathedral organist should receive £500 to £800 a year, and be required to take no outside engagements. Answering the argument that curates are sometimes paid as little as £60 or £80, he says that "the artists pointed to are the *bishops* of their calling . . . set apart for duties which only the best talent of the kind can adequately fulfil".

He cannot resist some extra exhortation in the course of outlining his "Plan". The poverty of musicians is, he says, a scandal. It is no answer to him to point out that Mozart and Beethoven were scandalously poor. At least Mozart and Beethoven had somebody to appreciate and perform their work, even if their patrons were niggardly in payment for it. But the English church musician feels neither secure nor even wanted; therefore, it is fair to say that if a Palestrina appeared in 1850, he would find his talents so stunted that he could offer nothing. Palestrina's famous letter asking the Pope for a rise is quoted in full [pp. 65 ff.]; but the argument is that Palestrina had at least a Pope to appeal to and a choir to write for.

So much for Samuel Sebastian's arguments and protests. There is not much evidence that they in themselves achieved anything. The improvement in cathedral music that eventually took place is traceable to other causes more potent than the writings of one well-known but irascible cathedral organist. The opinions which he expressed here were opinions which others held in different forms; but his was, in 1849, a lonely voice. During those days, it was only Maria Hackett (1783–1874) who invaded the cathedral scene from outside, in her very successful crusade for the improvement of the lot of choirboys, principally at St Paul's Cathedral. As for the lot of organists, if the normal stipend was £200 in 1849, then they have actually fallen further behind in the economic race. There are very few cathedrals today which offer the equivalent sum (which must be well over £1,000) to their organists. Cathedral organists are able to live today in tolerable comfort only by adding far more outside work to their cathedral duties than they would have been able to gain in Samuel Sebastian's day. There are more choral societies needing conductors, there are local universities and schools, there are the BBC and the independent television companies. The affluence which these and other modern patrons can bring to the fortunate among cathedral organists conceals the fact that not infrequently an organist is obliged to overdraw his mental and physical strength to a sometimes alarming degree in order to make ends meet. There is not really much evidence that the specific terms of Samuel Sebastian's demands have been substantially met. What has happened is the raising of standards in church music through the pressures of secular standards. Amateurism cannot now be tolerated in church by a public much better indoctrinated than Wesley's was to the demands of professional standards in secular music.

Generally speaking, we can hardly call *A Few Words* an influential document; but it is an historically revealing one.

It is also interesting in the evidence it gives us of Samuel Sebastian's personal taste and of the extent and limitations of his musicianship.

We shall refer again to the fact that among church musicians he was unusually well-cultivated in music, and well-read in history. His field of musical consciousness extended far beyond that in which his colleagues worked. But it had its limits.

He is almost desperately conscious of the inferiority of English music, not only in his own day, but ever since the Reformation, to that of the Continent. In an historical sketch designed to reinforce his argument that since the Reformation, England has been incurably philistine [pp. 46 ff.], he shows first the supreme quality of "Ockenheim, Josquin des Pres, and Isaac" (the last being the Heinrich Isaak of *Innsbruck*), "whose merit was such as to set aside all probability of England's having been able to compete with the Netherlanders, at this early period". He compares the great merit of Josquin with what he calls the far inferior merit of Tallis, but a footnote makes an exception of (of all things) the Tallis *Responses*. He goes on to mention Willaert, Schütz, Gabrieli, and to say that Dowland, Byrd, Wilbye, Weelkes and Gibbons have no chance of competing with them. "Whether the inferiority of England may result from the want of genius in our musicians, or the deficiency of encouragement from the powers that *were*, is a question." A question, be it said, to which Samuel Sebastian knows the answer.

It is the small scale of English music that distresses him. True, Giovanni Gabrieli (it will be he of whom Samuel Sebastian is thinking) did have St Mark's Venice to write for, and Palestrina, the Pope's Chapel. Demand in those centres of ecclesiastical opulence brought out the grandest music in these composers. But Samuel Sebastian is relatively blind to the *chamber*-music qualities in the English composers, to the subtlety which elevates Byrd to a peak at least as lofty as that on which Palestrina sits, to the madrigal genius of Weekles, equally impressive in church music as in secular.

What is interesting is that he knew these men's music pretty well. He complains [p. 48] of other people's ignorance of Gabrieli, and this in itself shows how he yearned for the grand and magnificent style to be honoured in English church music. Well he may have done; our modern horror of the pretentious would have been out of place in those musical slum-conditions.

But although he is a good musicologist, Samuel Sebastian is no antiquarian. He would have us know our Gabrieli, but he would not have us content to sing the great music of a past age. Plainsong, he utterly abhors. He is often quoted on this [p. 49]: "Some would reject all music but the unisonous chants of a period of absolute barbarism—which they term 'Gregorian'. All is 'Gregorian' that is in the black, diamond, note! These men would look a Michael Angelo in the face and tell him Stonehenge was the perfection of architecture!" He must be thinking of Havergal, Helmore, Redhead, Neale, and all the other enthusiasts for plainsong, who will have been rejoicing in the publication in 1848 of the Mechlin *Graduale*. And before we, from our modern musical affluence, turn down too quickly the choleric comments of a Victorian on plainsong, it might be as well to glance over some of the efforts of the early plainsong-men to rationalize the ancient music in the *ore-Solesmes* era. Well-intentioned though they were, the efforts, for example, of Helmore in *The Hymnal Noted* (1852) to revive plainsong and other ancient music are hardly by any standards distinguished for their musicality. They manage to be restrained without being powerful; the result is a coldness and withdrawn-ness which is exactly what Samuel Sebastian liked least in music. "This exalting of the past upon the ruin of the present is unjustifiable", he wrote [p. 51]. Indeed it is, and always was. The secret of Samuel Sebastian's enthusiasm in his best days (and in 1849, he was at the height of those powers from which too early he declined) was a belief, against all evidence, in the possibilities of the present. If English music had so little to offer, what was surprising in his turning to Continental styles for his own music? If English musical customs were so securely bound

by convention, naturally almost anything he wrote under conviction would appear original and even adventurous in his day,
however hackneyed it sounds to modern ears. "This country
will never . . . be without talent which can impart to Church
Music the highest qualities of art." Truly, Samuel Sebastian
hoped the best things in the worst times.

# 10

# S. S. Wesley's Choral Works

The fascinating thing about English music in the nineteenth century is not so much its astonishing capacity for bathos as its wrestling with the influences of Continental music. Professor Arthur Hutchings, in *Church Music in the Nineteenth Century* (1967), has warned us not to take too insular a view of English church music. True, there was something very insular about the English churches at this period, but insularity in English music had to wait for Vaughan Williams.

We shall have to examine this phenomenon from the other end in our next chapter, when we discuss Samuel Sebastian's treatment of that very English musical form, the hymn tune. At this point, however, we must look at the English musical scene as set within that much larger historical scene in which England's cultural relations with the Continent are seen to be the subject to a recurring rhythm of approach and withdrawal. It seems a long time now since the English King was King of France also. It is a long time—half a millennium. During that time, since the victory of Henry V at Agincourt (classically and inaccurately celebrated by Shakespeare), England succeeded in drawing farther and farther away from the Continent in economics and politics. In the sixties of the twentieth century, England's great perplexities in her economic relations with the countries of northern Europe are an indication of the distance to which that withdrawal was allowed to go.

But in music, more than in any other field except architecture, the English nineteenth century was dominated by the
Continent, and especially by the cultures of Italy and of
Vienna. In secular music, England failed to keep up with the
creative genius of those musical centres, and her social and
political insularity, assisted by a political and dynastic pre-
disposition to favour the German-speaking countries and suspect
the Gauls, prevented any *rapprochement* between England and
the musicians of France. It was Beethoven, not Berlioz, whom
Englishmen regarded as music's cultural norm; and if Gounod
was popular and Fauré hardly heard, this would be because
Gounod was essentially Teutonic where Fauré was essentially
French.

Puritanism depressed the condition of English music to such
an extent that it had neither the capacity nor the nerve to compete with Vienna. The result was that England's contribution
to music in the nineteenth century was a twin spate of church
music and drawing-room music; music answering the two
major demands of English culture at the time—those of a
church slowly emerging from a psalm-based tradition and of a
bourgeoisie for whom the pianoforte was a convenient and
substantial status-symbol.

The influences in English music generally were, therefore, the
Italianate tradition of the eighteenth century—through Handel
and the eighteenth-century English composers—and the
Germanic tradition of the nineteenth century, principally by
way of Mendelssohn. The former influence is basically aristocratic, courtly and formal; the other is basically bourgeois-
romantic. Therefore, the extrovert church music of the nineteenth century in England is mostly eighteenth-century music
revived. Steggall's *Christ Church*, for example, perhaps the best
hymn tune written in the nineteenth century, is pure Croft,
and, as we shall later see, half the hymn tunes of S. S. Wesley
are good post-John Wesley congregational music, while the
other half are uneasy translations of the German chorale-idiom.

English music of the nineteenth century, then, was at its best on the smallest scale; its condition was so precarious that for several generations it was really true that the better cultivated a musician was, the less likely was he to produce anything flawless. A musician of relatively little composing power might produce a perfect miniature, as Dykes could in his hymn tunes or Stainer in his Anglican chants. But as soon as a musician essayed the larger forms, and allowed himself to be open to the influences of European music in general, he became unreliable. He had not the staying power to handle the new resources. This is the historical reason why the influence of Beethoven on English music is hardly discernible, whereas that of Brahms was enormous. Nobody here could begin to handle Beethoven's vocabulary; but Brahms spoke through Elgar, often through Parry, occasionally (somewhat muted) through Walford Davies, and certainly through Charles Wood. The musicians of the Edwardian revival threw in their lot shamelessly with the Continentals, recovered their nerve for a space, and wrote their music with confidence. No subconscious "censor" was by then disturbing their urge to make music; the church and secular society were both breaking their Puritan aesthetic silence. Abruptly, the scene changed with the rise of "national music" and the cult of the Tudors and of folk-song; but neither the boisterous confidence of the Edwardians nor the pedagogic archaism of the early Georgians was there to make things easier for the true Victorians.

Since Samuel Sebastian Wesley was easily the most cultivated musician of his day; since he not only had his contacts with Mendelssohn and Spohr, but knew well the music of J. S. Bach and therefore was almost the only historically-minded musician in business, he was vulnerable to all available influences, and liable to all the hazards that they brought. Therefore, he is best judged not so much as being the most interesting of a poorish bunch, but as the most adventurously unreliable musician of his time. He could write every cliché in the book; he could also induce a sense of spaciousness and authority which none of his contemporaries could approach.

Grove mentions twenty-six of his anthems in print; at the present time there are sixteen generally available, together with the expansive *Cathedral Service in E* and three chant-services. Of his anthems, a few are still to be found regularly in the Cathedral lists.

Probably the best-known of all, both in his time and in our own, is "Blessed be the God and Father". It seems to have been one of his earliest works, having been written at Hereford, which puts its date before 1835, while the composer was in his early twenties. It was written for an Easter Day service at Hereford, and we are told that for its first performance, there were only a row of trebles and a single bass available. It was sung both at Winchester and at Westminster Abbey on the centenary of its composer's birth, and it has appeared in the service-list of at least one royal wedding (that of the present Queen, in November, 1947). Although it is an early work, it conveniently exemplifies its composer's qualities and habits, and therefore we may begin with some account of it in detail.

"BLESSED BE THE GOD AND FATHER"

(1) *The Text.* The first thing to observe about this anthem is its text. There was a consensus of opinion among church musicians of the time that the proper source of anthem-texts was the Psalms. Few ventured beyond them. But Samuel Sebastian—no doubt it is his evangelical background showing through—shows a quite unusual sensitiveness to the possibilities of other Biblical texts for musical settings, and even of interesting collocations of texts from several sources. Here, he confines himself to I Peter 1, but selects verses 3–5, 15–17 and 22–5.

(2) *Form.* The anthem is constructed in five short movements which follow each other without breaks; it is, therefore, a short example of the "verse anthem" form which goes back to the

Restoration composers and was developed by the school of Greene, Boyce and Battishill. Its length (161 bars) and time of performance (about six minutes) are somewhat less than the composer allows himself in his other extended choral works. The scheme is this:

(a) Slow introduction (20 bars at 22 bars to the minute)
(b) A contrasting unison passage for the three lower voices, in the same tempo, followed by a soprano solo (40 bars)
(c) After 6 bars of organ interlude, a soprano aria, *moderato* (40 bars at 26)
(d) Recitative for the lower voices, one bar of free time plus 10 bars in $\frac{4}{4}$, at roughly the same speed as the overture
(e) *Tutti, allegretto* (44 bars at 50).

(3) *Key*. Movements (a), (c) and (e) are all firmly in E flat, with only the most conventional and episodic modulations. Contrast is provided by the B-flat opening of (b) and by an emphatic statement towards its end in G major—a modulation of which the composer was particularly fond; and by the dramatic introduction of E flat minor at the end of (b) and in the second half of (d). Samuel Sebastian showed a marked preference, among major keys, for those lying between E flat and G, in his choral music.

(4) *Diction*. In this, one of his earlier works, the composer already shows his sensitiveness to words, and his resources for expressiveness. The music itself is unequal, but his intentions and principles in interpreting the words are quite clear, as also are the difficulties he had to contend with. The basic principle is the accepted one that diatonic music is the rule, and chromatic episodes for points of heightened tension the departure. The chromatic points are, in this anthem, all in the second and fourth sections, the main movements being almost obsessively concerned with the key of E flat.

But here as elsewhere, it is in the small details that the composer shows himself at his best. Take the first opening paragraph. At once we notice that sections (a) and (b) together set words that form a single sentence (actually part of a very long sentence in the Authorized Version, from which the composer eventually breaks away). Similarly, sections (d) and (e) set a single sentence, but the technique in the two pairs is different. In the second pair, the sentence itself points a contrast—"all flesh is as grass . . . but the Word of the Lord . . ." In the first pair, the thought is carried through to the end of the sentence, and the composer's treatment of it is masterly.

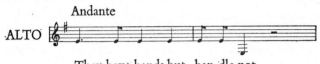

Andante

ALTO

They have hands but han-dle not

Example 12
From "Ascribe unto the Lord", by Samuel Sebastian Wesley

Note three things especially, of which the first is the placing of the notes in the opening chord. That low alto G is quite deliberate. Wesley showed a great pleasure in deep alto notes; indeed, in his other anthems, he frequently writes for the alto right down to the lowest parts of the tenor register. He always assumed that his altos would, where necessary, become tenors or even baritones in recitatives or in part-writing (Example 12), and in this work, he asks the altos to join in the male chorus in both the linking passages. But in that first chord, he is not only exploiting the richness of deep tone, he is laying the first stone in a structure which ends with exactly the same chord an octave higher (on the word "dead", bar 20). In that final chord, the tenor and bass double on E flat; that is the only difference. Its effect is made by that high bass note.

The intention is, of course, to provide a musical intimation of Easter in this first paragraph. But that is not the end of the story, for having opened thus prayerfully and serenely, he introduces an abrupt change of texture, without any change of tempo. "*L'istesso tempo*" is of the utmost importance at bar 21. The effect is even better if the composer's intention of silencing the organ after the first chord until the beginning of bar 21 is followed. As the second section continues, the tension is tightened by the swing of the harmony suddenly into G major.

In the soprano solo that follows, notice the darkening of the tone at "pass the time of your sojourning here in fear", with the B-flat minor tonality and the hanging cadence on the repeated "in fear"—the first time words have been repeated so far in the anthem.

In the dialogue between solo and full trebles that follows, all is very peaceful; musically, there is more than a hint of inertia because of the impossibility of getting out of the key of E flat. Here and there (e.g. bars 76–7, Example 13), a touch of chromaticism in the bass attempts to help ease the tonal monotony, but the interest is all in the melody. Once again there is a

Example 13
From "Blessed be", by Samuel Sebastian Wesley

momentary repetition—"that ye love, that ye love . . ."—with Mendelssohnian suspensions and a very brief excursion to the subdominant.

But the insistent E-flattery of this section throws the subsequent recitative into greater prominence. Here, we move very decisively into E flat minor, and then, quite surprisingly, into F minor with a major chord at the end.

(5) *Style*. But what of the quality of the music? These details are in themselves craftsmanlike, but what of the construction of the whole? This is where the composer runs into deep water,

and where we have to analyse influences and separate, if we can, the true originality from the derivative material. It is the extent to which the composer accepts influences from outside that determines where the "creaks" come in his music.

It is not easy to analyse influences in the work of a composer whose output is so small and whose field is so restricted as they are in Samuel Sebastian's case. *A priori*, we can say only that he was open to more influences than his contemporaries were, and that we must be careful. Beyond that we can judge only on what can be deduced from what we might call the inspirational texture of this or that passage.

In respect of the anthem here under review, we find three points at which the composition raises doubts; and in each case I think we can say that the weakness is the result of an insufficiently assimilated musical tradition or convention. They are the key-tied harmonic structure of section (c), the same quality plus the sheer banality of most of section (e), and that quite remarkable combination of naïve drama with musical bathos in the violent organ chord which ushers in section (e).

The listener is tempted to say of section (c) that it is tolerably good Mendelssohn; but if, as the historians tell us, the anthem was composed at Hereford, this is a hazardous judgment. The latest date for its composition is 1835, in which year Mendelssohn was twenty-six (he was a year older than Samuel Sebastian), and by which time to be sure, a good deal of his well-known music had been written. His four symphonies had all been composed by then (but not the *Lobgesang* which is sometimes counted as *Symphony no 2 in B flat*); the Overture to *A Midsummer Night's Dream*, op. 21, but not the incidental music op. 61; the *Hebrides*, three works for piano and orchestra, and two volumes of *Songs Without Words*, but the dates of these are 1834 and 1835. *St Paul* was not finished until 1836, and only one choral work comes before it: the rest of his sacred music is later. Mendelssohn had paid one visit to London, in 1829—when he astonished everybody by conducting with a baton "in the German manner"—and another in 1832, when he played his *Capriccio Brillante*, op. 22, for piano and orchestra. But his celebrated meeting with Samuel Wesley was not until 1837.

It is not certain, then, whether we ought to say that this very well-known passage in "Blessed be the God and Father" is directly influenced by Mendelssohn, or whether it is better to say that Samuel Sebastian and Mendelssohn were both drawing on a common store of early Romantic slow-movement style. I prefer the latter judgment as being, by a slight margin, the more psychologically probable. If we proceed on it, we are able to say that the two composers used the style in importantly different ways. Indeed, we can make the general judgment that Mendelssohn showed higher skill than Samuel Sebastian, or any other of his contemporaries, in the use of this particular style. For the Romantic "Song without words"-style depends on a balance between attractive melody and the use of a chromatic background. Mendelssohn, at his best, was a highly refined composer, who showed a degree of skill in the manipulation of this perilous musical vocabulary that Samuel Sebastian did not quite reach. The test is a simple one. Samuel Sebastian is always at his most interesting and characteristic when his music is most chromatic in the foreground; it is in his diatonic paragraphs that he is always in danger of falling into bathos. He was (as Mendelssohn was not) markedly better at expressing musical subtlety in chromatic terms than in the more exacting terms of balancing musical values in a diatonic framework. This, incidentally, is the special gift of the really good hymn-tune writer, and on the whole, Samuel Sebastian, as we shall see when we come to them, showed himself far more interesting and enterprising when he was exploiting the chromatic possibilities of the hymn tune than when he was writing straight diatonic music.

Of the quasi-fugal passage at the end, we need say little because we shall have to notice Samuel Sebastian's fugal work again when we come to his organ music. But once again, the whole paragraph is key-tied and unilluminating. This is because of a lack of craftsman's grip, which is at its most obvious in bars 149–50 (Example 14. What precisely, you must ask, is that alto G flat doing there?). This is the kind of thing that too often happens when the composer, bowing to a notion of conventional duty, introduces a fugal climax in a choral work. It is just this "sense of duty", this writing what he feels is expected of him, that is his undoing. Once again, therefore, it is a drying up of originality, a derivativeness, a touch of musical servility instead of mastery, that lets him down.

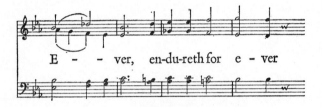

Example 14
From "Blessed be", by Samuel Sebastian Wesley

So we come to that pivotal chord. Now that passage, beginning with the chord introducing (e) and continuing through the two bold statements of "But the word of the Lord", is unusually interesting. The fugato has not yet started. This introductory passage is very good stuff indeed; it is bold, and it is certainly, in English church music, strikingly original. Where before this will you find anything to approach the effect of that *sforzando* dominant-seventh following the sinister close of the recitative? Why, it is a gesture worthy of Beethoven himself. It must have electrified the congregation that first heard it. So must the very satisfactory crunch of full organ chords that follows the choral entry. Organists still love it, and no organist should ever play it without giving its redblooded ferocity the fullest value.

Then secondly, the treble phrase on "but the word of the Lord" at this point is pure and sincere Wesley. We must diverge for a moment from the main course of our argument to point out that this phrase, the direct and uninterrupted striding over the notes of the common chord for four or even as here five degrees is just about the one distinctive "composer's signature" in Samuel Sebastian's music. We even find it in his hymn tunes (see below, pp. 226–7); but we find it remarkably often in his anthems, used with all kinds of effect from the riotously triumphant, as here, to the passionate, as in Example 15b; and the imploring, as in the cadence of "Wash me throughly", Example 15d.

a   Allegro

But the word of the Lord

b   Lento

Tru–ly my hope is   e – ven in thee

c   Lento

Thou Judge of quick and dead_____

d   Larghetto

And for–give me all____ my sin

e      Allegro moderato

ALTOS

O give thanks un–to the Lord.

f                    Allegretto con moto

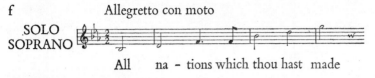

**SOLO SOPRANO**

All     na - tions which thou hast made

Example 15
Samuel Sebastian Wesley's "signature"
a    From "Blessed be"
b    From "All go unto one place"
c    From "Let us lift up"
d    From "Wash me throughly"
e    From "O give thanks"
f    From "O give thanks"

All this is first rate. He is, just here, writing what is most clearly his own music, even as he is equally certainly writing it in his opening paragraph and in the recitative. But the trouble is that viewed from another angle, it is all wrong. In his introductory chord he contrives a modulation from F minor (an F major chord actually) to E flat; and that modulation, shifting the keynote a whole tone up or down, simply cannot fail to give the impression of "hidden octaves", or, in other words, of acute discomfort. It is worse when the whole composition suffers, as this one does, from key-tiedness. That chord, in its own right an excellent sound, thrusts us once more and ruthlessly back into the home key. The elementary harmonic analysis of sections (c) and (d) in Example 16 shows what has happened: the danger-sign is the recurring bass E and the consecutive octaves at the end.

E. H. Fellowes, in *English Cathedral Music* (pp. 205 ff.) says that the best things in Samuel Sebastian's anthems are his recitatives and his arias. Certainly he was capable of writing good arias, and he has at least one superb example that stands alongside the best things of its kind in all church music—the aria "Thou, O Lord God" in the long anthem, "Let us lift up our hearts". The dialogue-aria in "Blessed be the God and Father" is not really one of the best examples. But the recitative is admirable. Of both arias and recitatives, Fellowes says

Example 16
Analysis of bars 67–117 of "Blessed be", by Samuel Sebastian
  Wesley

that they are "definitely English in style". The lack of this
quality is probably the weakness in "Love one another", but
"Being born again" exemplifies it very well. It is obviously
in the direct line from Purcell's great recitatives, not in the
least Handelian or Bach-like.

This early anthem, then, is a good summary of Wesley's
strength and weakness; it is attractive, melodious, and zestful.
It has a very good and rewarding organ part; and, in this, it
was something of a pioneering gesture. T. A. Walmisley, four
years younger than Samuel Sebastian, is always supposed to
have written the first setting of the Evening Canticles to include

a significant and independent organ part. The eighteenth-century masters, of course, provided excellent instrumental parts in their verse-anthems, but the Hereford organ inspired Wesley to explore the possibilities of the instrument for providing more than a background *continuo*.

### THE WORCESTER AND LEEDS PERIOD

"Blessed be the God and Father" was a good start. The next eighteen years find the composer taking his place as the last of the grand-style verse-anthem composers. In 1835, he published a set of twelve anthems, which includes "Blessed be", and also the following:

> "Ascribe unto the Lord"
> "Cast me not away"
> "Let us lift up our hearts"
> "Man that is born of woman"
> "O give thanks"
> "O Lord my God"
> "O Lord thou art my God"
> "The face of the Lord"
> "The Wilderness"
> "Thou wilt keep him in perfect peace"
> "Wash me throughly".

These provide a compendium of all that is best in his music, and if we look at a few of them we shall learn all that he has to tell us. After 1853, he never achieved again the expansive freedom in composition that is in the best of these. We must add to this set the *Service in E*, which is dated 1845.

### THE WILDERNESS

We can begin with *The Wilderness* because it also comes from the early Hereford period. This is a true "verse-anthem", running 341 bars and taking some twelve minutes in performance. In these crowded times, it is too long for the usual evensong, yet, being too short for a cantata, it loses its place in recital programmes. So it is, like the other long anthems of Samuel Sebastian, heard less often than it should be.

He takes verses from the 35th chapter of Isaiah, and expounds them in music as faithfully as his grandfather or great-uncle would have expounded them in words. It is written for full choir and organ, with the organ part on three staves and registration-directions inserted by the composer. Remembering that the Hereford instrument was one of the two English cathedral organs that had pedal pipes, we can see what caused him to write the celebrated second movement and mark the pedal part "Choir with 16-foot pipes".

The work is divided into three movements, running continuously, with a coda. The Muse was kind to the composer in supplying him with a really first-rate epigrammatic subject to work on. The opening tune to "The wilderness and the solitary place" (Example 17) is clearly the origin of both the trumpet-like motif on "For in the wilderness shall waters break out" (Example 18a) and of the fugue-subject "And the ransomed of the Lord" (Example 18b). The business begins at once in a grand Purcellian manner, featuring commanding dotted rhythms and this very good simple musical motif based on the major triad. The key is a firm E major—E and E flat were Wesley's favourite choices for great and dignified occasions. The whole of the opening section (46 bars) is devoted to the words of the first verse.

The second section is one of Wesley's two best male-voice solos, a strenuous piece in A minor with the Hereford organ pedal pipes sounding in a persistent staccato quaver figure while the voice declaims with rhythmical zest the words of verse 4.

Larghetto

Verse, Bass

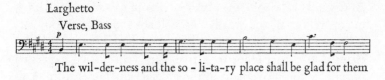

The wil-der-ness and the so - li-ta-ry place shall be glad for them

Example 17
From *The Wilderness*, by Samuel Sebastian Wesley

a      Moderato e legato

Verse, Alto

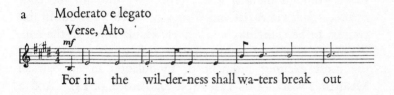

For in    the    wil-der-ness shall wa-ters break    out

b      Allegro con spirito

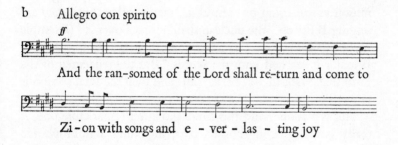

And the ran-somed of the Lord shall re-turn and come to

Zi - on with songs and  e - ver - las - ting joy

c      2nd Sop.

Bass

Example 18
From *The Wilderness*, by Samuel Sebastian Wesley

6*

At the end of the solo, the organ swells out towards a jubilant A major, reflecting the words "he will come and save you".

"Then shall the lame man leap as an hart" (verse 6) is declaimed in a brief tenor recitative, the "leap" being expressed simply by the movement in three detached chords from A to F-sharp major. After this four-bar interjection, the "verse" choir comes in with the opening notes of Example 18b. This and a counter-subject in sequential thirds occupy the next 74 bars and deal with the rest of verse 6. Once again this is all E major—though there is a key-procession through the augmented triad, via A flat and C major, which turns out in this context to be cheerfully and naïvely exhilarating. In the end, the organ takes over again and swerves into what is just about the most exciting moment of modulation in all Samuel Sebastian's work—bars 174-7 (Novello score, p. 14). "And a highway shall be there": unaccompanied male-voice unison on G sharp. Thus begins a characteristic dramatic passage, the unison voices rising one semitone, then another, until they are singing B flat on "the unclean shall not pass over it" (Example 19); the B flat becomes an enharmonic A sharp, a bright B major B major is reached with the words "But the redeemed of the Lord shall walk there" (v. 8a, 9b); and then the final section is ushered in.

This is a fugue; and this time, though a remarkable one, it really is a fugue. It runs 88 bars, including a homophonic peroration, and it has two subjects. The first is something like an inversion of the opening theme (Example 18a) and the second, a contrasting florid tune in the Handelian style (Example 18b). The entertaining thing is that the second subject turns out, at its very first appearance, to be in direct counterpoint with the first. They are knit together not, as one might expect in the classical form, near the end, but near the beginning (Example 18c). The fugue begins as a five-voice composition, but while every voice is allowed at least one turn with the counter-subject, the altos never sing the main subject. The main subject is introduced by the basses accompanied by the tenors, altos

Example 19
From *The Wilderness*, by Samuel Sebastian Wesley

and second sopranos—a choirmaster's puzzle when all are marked *ff*. After 37 bars, the two sopranos join in a single line, and the music becomes more and more concerned with the coloratura of the counter-subject. Then, just when we feel that the composer has run out of energy and is settling down to a homophonic series of clichés, there is a splendid excursion into C major, with a new colour for the word "return" (bars 263–5, letter N). Immediately after this, there is a prolonged cadence in the dominant demanding full sustained tone in the middle of the voice sung *fortissimo*—another choirmaster's crux.

What happens after this is, in the context of that culture, inevitable; it is a quiet ending, at half speed, *piano*. It has to be spacious and serene to provide some relief from the 88 bars of *ff* that have gone before; and since the words are "and sorrow and sighing shall flee away", nothing much can be done in the way of subtle chromaticism. So the tonality oscillates between the tonic and dominant in a simple hymn-like theme once repeated, sung with a very light and sometimes vanishing accompaniment; and the music settles down to its end with a typically Wesleyan plagal cadence.

Tonally, we have been hammering away at E major, except for the dramatic break at "And a highway", for nearly 240 bars. Indeed, there are moments when we are in real danger of overstatement of the obvious. It is the commanding quality of the themes, and the excellent texture of the fugue, that save us. After so much excitement, the last four pages are at least tolerable, and we can look without indignation on them because of their unusual and expressive part-writing. The spacing of the voices in the top line of page 26 of the score (letter O) is especially characteristic and the keen eye will not fail to observe the "octaves" at the point marked in Example 20.

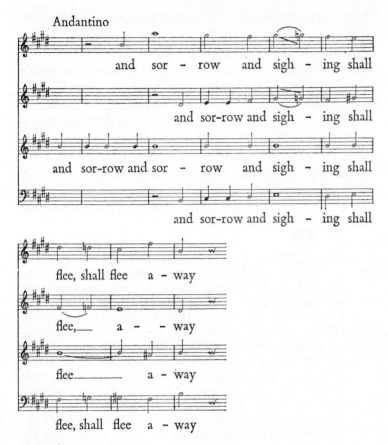

Example 20
From *The Wilderness*, by Samuel Sebastian Wesley

## "O LORD, THOU ART MY GOD"

Everything that was promised in these two anthems is
brought to fulfilment in "O Lord, thou art my God", Samuel
Sebastian's longest work. This five-movement verse-anthem
is of true cantata length, running twenty-two minutes in full
performance, observing the composer's metronome marks.

After a considerable organ introduction, it opens in E flat with a characteristically dignified movement for double choir—164 bars of $\frac{4}{4}$ at 96 crochets to the minute. Then comes a bass solo (B flat), then another movement, in D minor, for double choir. The fourth movement is for five-part chorus (B flat), and the last movement, again for double choir, is a prodigious working-out of fugal material, running 191 bars and taking eight minutes. Thus the outer movements are the longest in time, the inner ones taking two and three quarter, two and a half, and two and a quarter minutes respectively.

As an example of Samuel Sebastian's textual sensitiveness, this is a classic; it is good enough to justify our writing out the text in full.

1. O Lord, Thou art my God. I will exalt thee, I will praise Thy name. Thy counsels of old are faithfulness and truth; Thou has done wonderful things. Thou hast been a strength to the poor and needy in his distress. (Isaiah 25.1, 4]

2. For our heart shall rejoice in Him, because we have trusted in His holy name. Let Thy mercy, O Lord, be upon us, according as we have trusted in Thee. [Psalm 33.21–2]

3. He will swallow up death in victory, and the Lord God will wipe away tears from off all faces; and the rebuke of His people shall He take away from off all the earth; for the Lord hath spoken it. [Isaiah 25.8]

4. For this mortal must put on immortality. [I Corinthians 15.53.] Awake to righteousness, and sin not, for some have not the knowledge of God. [I Corinthians 15.34.] They that put their trust in Him shall understand the truth. [Wisdom 3.9.] We shall not all sleep, but we shall all be changed, in a moment, in the twinkling of an eye, at the last trumpet. [I Corinthians 15.51–2]

5. And in that day it shall be said, This, this is our God; we have waited for Him, and he will save us. We will be glad and rejoice in His salvation. [Isaiah 25.9]

The music retains a high standard almost all the way. Perhaps the section most often extracted as a separate anthem, the fourth movement, is the least convincing of the five; but the opening movement is a fine piece of construction, reflecting a wide emotional variety in the words, and including at least one moment of high dramatic distinction (Example 21).

Example 21
From "O Lord Thou art my God", by Samuel Sebastian Wesley

## "LET US LIFT UP OUR HEARTS"

Next in length, and equal in musical interest, is "Let us lift up our hearts", which, like the foregoing, divides into separate movements. The edition most often used today is that of Bairstow (1910), carefully and reverently compiled by one of Samuel Sebastian's most eminent disciples. This runs 436 bars in all, and fifteen minutes. Once again, there is a most interesting collocation of texts: the sources are Lamentations 3, verses 41 and 42; Isaiah 63, verses 16 and 19; Isaiah 64, verses 9, 1, 6

and 8; Psalm 71, verses 4, 5, 10 and 1; and finally, two verses of
Charles Wesley's hymn. "Thou Judge of quick and dead."
It is less symphonic in structure than "O Lord, thou art my
God", and more naturally falls into separate movements—and
for this reason is more often heard in sections nowadays. The
first movement is by far the longest, occupying 19 of the 29
pages in the modern edition. Its prevailing key is D minor,
giving way to D major three-quarters of the way through;
the first ten pages are for double choir and organ. This movement, and indeed the work as a whole, contains some of the
most passionate music that Samuel Sebastian ever put down.
There is more chromatic music here than anywhere else in his
work—as indeed the text would suggest. There are some fine
strong subjects supported on the decorative harmony, of which
two are Example 22. The most celebrated section of the work

Example 22
From "Let us lift up", by Samuel Sebastian Wesley

is the second movement, a bass solo, whose peroration is given at Example 22. But the fugue in the first movement at "O that thou wouldst rend the heavens", using the two subjects in Example 23 is worth anybody's study. As in *The Wilderness*, the second subject soon takes over and becomes more prominent than the first. The last movement is concerned with the two hymn-verses—the first in B minor, the second in D major with a characteristically quiet ending.

a Lento assai
   Tenor

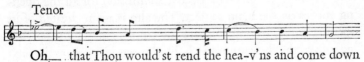

Oh,__ .that Thou would'st rend the hea-v'ns and come down

b   Lento assai
    Alto

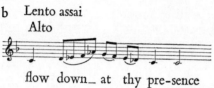

flow down_ at thy pre-sence

Example 23
From "Let us lift up", by Samuel Sebastian Wesley

## "ASCRIBE UNTO THE LORD"

"Ascribe unto the Lord" can be dated from Samuel Sebastian's Winchester period, between 1849 and 1865 (but of course before 1853), when he was at the height of his fame and executive powers. The text is taken from Psalms 96 and 115, and the general theme is the praise of God and the condemnation of idolatry. The prevailing key is G major. It opens with a massive unison song, in characteristic fashion, by the three lower voices; this soon expands into a four-part chorus on "Let the whole earth stand in awe of Him." The next movement is a gentle chorus for two trebles and two altos, "O worship the Lord in the beauty of holiness" (which is sometimes extracted and sung on its own). It has a good deal of eighteenth-century grace, but it leaves the hearer wondering whether the composer has any profounder points to make. He has. A sturdy E-minor fugue follows, on "As for the gods of the heathen"; this is very Handelian, and is like a maturer and sterner variation on the fugue in *The Wilderness*. Once again, there is a solemn triadic subject, and a counter-subject in florid form: but this time, the counter-subject waits with decent submission for all the opening entries on the main subject. The alto is again cheated of its opening entry, having to share the tenor's entry by supplying high notes that he cannot reach, but he gets his turn on the next

page with the first half of the subject. The second bass statement of the main subject combines it with the mood of the
counter-subject in a quite remarkable expression of ferocity
(Example 24). The fugue suddenly disperses itself into an

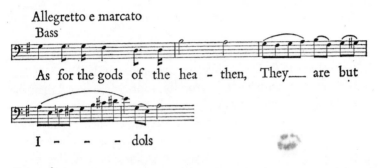

Allegretto e marcato

As for the gods of the hea - then, They___ are but
I - - - dols

Example 24
From "Ascribe unto the Lord", by Samuel Sebastian Wesley

accompanied dialogue between the voices, sometimes in unison,
sometimes two together in parts, with restless and ferocious
organ comments, to illustrate the Psalmist's laughter at the
impotence of the idols ("noses have they and smell not").
Then comes a page of "verse" singing for "They that make
them are like unto them"—B minor, followed by a sumptuous
chorale for "As for our God, He is in heaven", and then a fugue
on "The Lord hath been mindful of us". This fugue gives out
fairly quickly. Indeed, the first subject is stated only by the bass
and the soprano, the other voices providing mainly "fill-in"
material. The alto (who tends to get left out in Samuel Sebastian's fugues), gives out another subject—"Ye are the blessed
of the Lord"—very Mendelssohnian this time, and the tenor
and soprano answer him, but it is too much for the bass until
a later stage, when he sings it in unison with the tenor. He is
saving his energy, it turns out, for his contribution to a third
contrapuntal section which is going to demand of him a high
F sharp. Everything ends happily in a homophonic G major—

327 bars, ten minutes' performing time. On the whole, the composer seems to have slipped back a little from the standard of *The Wilderness* and "Let us lift up".

<br>

### SERVICE IN E

The *Service in E* must be regarded as one of his major works. It consists of *Te Deum*, *Jubilate*, *Magnificat* and *Nunc Dimittis*. The evening canticles are, naturally, more often heard than the morning pair, and they still provide a magnificent expression of praise for the kind of festive occasion when a *Magnificat* lasting six and a half minutes is not out of place. The style of the *Magnificat* is still that of the verse-anthem, and the whole conception is of brilliance and ceremonial dignity. They key-scheme is most interesting in its balance of colours. The movement analyses itself more or less as follows:

> v. 1. "My soul doth magnify the Lord": organ fanfare on the common chord followed by 31 bars of bright E major ¾, 120 crotchets to the minute.
> v. 2–3. "For He hath regarded . . .": B major, 35 bars ¾ at 108.
> v. 4. "For He that is mighty . . .": F minor leading to G minor, 30 bars ¾ at 108.
> v. 5. "And his mercy . . .": D major, 30 bars.
> vv. 6–8. "He hath shewed strength": D major, 53 bars.
> v. 9. "He remembering his mercy": E minor, 32 bars.
> *Gloria*: E major, 48 bars.

The predominance is towards the sharp keys, but the third section, in the flat keys, provides the needed touch of softness. One notices how, by 1845, the composer had achieved an assured touch in the handling of tonalities.

In good ceremonial style, he provides a different *Gloria* for each of the two evening canticles; but about the *Nunc Dimittis Gloria* there is a special and unique point, namely, that it is an abridged version of that provided for the *Jubilate*, and the com-

poser directs that it can be substituted for the longer one in the
morning at the choirmaster's discretion. The *Jubilate* Gloria
is, indeed, the longest setting of the doxology ever attempted
by an English cathedral composer, and its appropriateness to
the hundredth Psalm, as the only through-composed *Gloria*
which would be heard at Matins, is undeniable, if you have
time to sing it. More than this can be said of it, however, in its
*Jubilate* context; its surprise opening in D sharp major is
remarkable enough after the *Nunc Dimittis*, but after the B
major close of the *Jubilate* it is one of the most remarkable
moments in all English church music. (See Example 25).

Example 25
From *Jubilate in E*, by Samuel Sebastian Wesley

Of the *Te Deum* one can only say that, good though it is, it
is one more example of the probably universal truth that
nobody who wrote a first-rate *Magnificat* also wrote a first-rate
*Te Deum* in the same service. This hymn is notoriously difficult

Example 26
From *Te Deum in E*, by Samuel Sebastian Wesley

to make sense of in music (did even Stanford ever really bring it off?). Not but that there are many flashes of genius in Wesley's setting. It leads him into tonalities which he did not often explore (D flat and A flat), and there are very characteristic touches at the points indicated in Examples 24 a and b.

Example 27
From *Te Deum in E*, by Samuel Sebastian Wesley

### SHORTER ANTHEMS IN THE LEEDS PERIOD

Easily the best known of Samuel Sebastian's shorter anthems, apart from "Blessed be", is "Thou wilt keep him in perfect

peace". This is an almost perfect "cathedral sound", with its
serene five-part diatonic harmony and its unforgettable opening phrase. Yet again, the text is carefully and sensitively
selected: Isaiah 26 v. 3, Psalm 139 v. 2, I John 1 v. 5, Psalm 119
v. 175. (It is interesting in passing to note how C. Lee Williams
of Gloucester, a Wesley disciple, used exactly the same selection
of words for his simpler but vastly inferior setting.) The greatest
beauty of this anthem, apart from the evocative opening
soprano phrase which seems so exactly to describe the shape of
a spacious cathedral interior, is its use of diatonic discords, two
of which are illustrated at Example 28. (With them, we add

Example 28
a  From "Thou wilt keep him in perfect peace", by Samuel
Sebastian Wesley
b  ib.
c  From "The Lord is my shepherd", by Samuel Sebastian Wesley

another which is one of the few points of distinction in an otherwise uninteresting setting of Psalm 23, verses 1–4 and 6.)

An apt partner for "Thou wilt keep him" in the intimate style is "Wash me throughly"—a devout and contemplative setting of words from Psalm 51, which in its demand for sustained tone on long held notes calls for considerable choral skill. The famous dissonance in its second bar sets the general tone, and his particularly beautiful use of his favourite "common chord" phrase at the end (Example 15d) is one of his best inspirations.

Two anthems in the same key and in a style which seems to combine archaism with contemporary experiment are "Cast me not away" and "The Face of the Lord". Both are written on a semibreve-unit and could be sung unaccompanied. "Cast me not away" has 82 bars of beautiful six-part vocal writing, as serene as William Byrd could be in his quieter mood Only towards the end is there a touch of "modern" harmony (Example 29). "The Face of the Lord" (Example 30) is worth

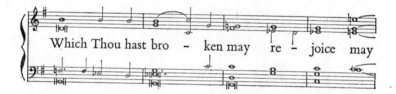

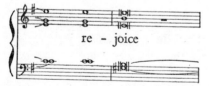

Example 29
From "Cast me not away", by Samuel Sebastian Wesley

quoting more extensively because it is hardly ever heard now. Its opening bars are a remarkable example of the way in which this composer at his best can "rescue" the harmony from becoming too early bogged down in the subdominant. Its opening again almost recalls Byrd or Tallis (whose work he was a good enough historian to know well). If we did not know what was coming, we might almost feel that the composition was to be in the mixolydian mode, so early do we hear that flattened F; but not so. Samuel Sebastian was always fascinated by the possibilities of placing tonalities boldly together, and

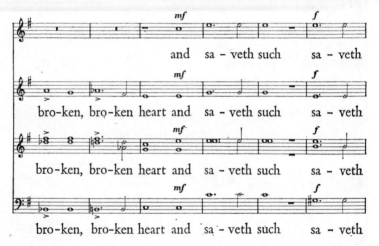

Example 30
From "The Face of the Lord", by Samuel Sebastian Wesley

especially (see below, p. 231) of the suggestiveness of F major
(or D minor) juxtaposed with B major, a tritonal musical crisis
which few composers before him (except Bach) had explored.

There are, inevitably, one or two points at which the twelve
anthems of 1853 fall below the best standards. It is difficult
to take "O give thanks" very seriously—a short three-move-
ment anthem consisting of the usual relatively weighty first
movement followed by a frisky soprano solo in a markedly
eighteenth-century style, and ending with a very ecclesiastical-
sounding last movement, "Blessed are they", which is sometimes heard as a separate anthem. The whole affair is in E flat
and it is interesting only because it brings into prominence
the composer's melodic "signature", which we have already
met in widely contrasted moods. He uses it twice in this
anthem (Example 15 e and f) and the other examples in the
series there given will indicate how often it appears and how
many different connotations he gives to it.

## OTHER CHORAL WORKS

There is no doubt that Samuel Sebastian's powers of composition in large forms waned after 1853. The best thing that came from his later years is "All go unto one place", a very agreeable piece about which there is a slight critical problem. E. H. Fellowes [p. 195] says of *Samuel* Wesley, "His funeral anthem 'All go unto one place', was written for the funeral of his brother Charles in 1834. It has wrongly been attributed to his son, Samuel Sebastian". The truth is that both composers[1] wrote settings of these words. Samuel Sebastian's setting was advertised in the *Musical Times* for early 1862, as a "Short Funeral Anthem, composed on the lamented death of His Royal Highness the Prince Consort, 'All go unto one place'".[2] Fellowes does not indicate whether he is ascribing *this* setting to Samuel; if he did so ascribe it, he was clearly in error. Nothing could be less characteristic of Samuel in 1834, or more so of Samuel Sebastian in 1861. Why, it contains one of the most dramatic and beautiful examples of the "Wesley signature" in the rising common-chord phrase on "Truly my hope is even in thee" (Example 15b). It reminds one strongly of a naïve tune, *Nativity*, by Lahee to the hymn "Come let us join our cheerful songs" (written originally for a Christmas hymn by Doddridge), but there is no chance that Lahee was inspired by Samuel Sebastian; his tune first appeared in 1855. The sudden modulation to B major in the second movement of the anthem is highly characteristic—time and time again Samuel Sebastian urges his music towards the mediant or submediant. But the beautiful coda contains something quite rare in his work, though common in that of the later Victorians—a melodic rising sixth in an emphatic position (Example 31).

One could hardly hope that Samuel Sebastian in his later days would be at his best when writing "occasional pieces". He clearly shows signs of discouragement at the non-perform-

[1] See Grove's *Dictionary of Music and Musicians*.
[2] See P. Scholes, *A Mirror of Music*, p. 858.

Example 31
From "All go unto one place", by Samuel Sebastian Wesley

ance of his larger works, and presumably for that reason turns
to smaller forms. But "Let us now praise famous men" is not
one of his happiest examples. At an early stage (Example 32),
he indicates his intention of reaching down from the Mendelssohn shelf whatever comes first to hand.

Example 32
From "Let us now praise", by Samuel Sebastian Wesley

"Praise the Lord, O my soul", written for the opening of the
new organ at Holy Trinity Church, Winchester, in 1861,
has a central section, with solo and chorus singing music
reminiscent of the standard of the Foundling Hospital hymns,

and some *bravura* manual work for the organist, designed to display the alertness of the instrument's pipes and action. The final section is the very well-known piece, "Lead me, Lord", and is easily the best thing in the anthem. On its own scale, it reaches perfection, but the rest is largely hack work.

The only secular choral work of Samuel Sebastian's that has survived in a modern edition is *The Praise of Music*, which was revived in 1960 by Hinrichsen in an edition by Stainton de B. Taylor. It was composed for the newly-founded Royal Albert Hall Choral Society of which, for the first few years from its inception (1871) Gounod was conductor. Apparently, it was something of a distinction to get a new contemporary work performed there at that time, since almost everything that was sung was composed or arranged by Gounod himself.[1] However, Wesley's eight-part unaccompanied choral piece, to words by Thomas Oliphant (1799–1879), will have appealed to Gounod, with its cheerful Hadynesque demeanour and its touches of undemanding but colourful harmony. The work was published in 1873, and is a harmless trifle, little more.

Today, Samuel Sebastian is known only by a handful of his pieces; he was at his best when he had a larger canvas to work on than ordinary liturgical occasions can accommodate. Therefore, it is easy today to remain unaware of the real gifts and courage of which his choral music shows evidence. There are flashes of genius, although the general level is just short of excellence. There are few problems that beset choral composers for the church to which Samuel Sebastian finds unique answers. Indeed, what he wrote was, despite his occasional harmonic and melodic originality, essentially conservative. The true verse-anthem died with him. Indeed, it died, to all intents and purposes, in 1853, but it died honourably. One does not feel, in hearing Samuel Sebastian's examples, that it was a played-out form. It died only because it was an essentially un-Tractarian form, and the new *ethos* in the Church of England, shunning the virtuosity inherent in the verse-anthem, froze it

[1] P. Scholes, *A Mirror of Music*, p. 32.

out of its services. His battle to keep the verse-anthem alive was all of a piece with his battle to defend unequal temperament and the G-pedal board on the organ. But what the verse-anthem could do was provide a context for asserting, in a lean time, professional musical standards. Samuel Sebastian cannot have often heard his best music well performed, but what later composers, like Parry and Stanford, could take for granted in choral and organistic custom, Wesley almost alone, made possible.

His influence was of that kind. The composer of later years who seems most clearly to inherit the approach to music that Samuel Sebastian had is Sir Edward Bairstow. In his time, Bairstow was an uncompromising upholder of professional standards in composition. His freedom with the choir, and especially with the organ, in his larger works is as reminiscent of Samuel Sebastian as was his capacity for lapsing into commonplace. If Harwood is Wesley's heir in organ music and hymns, Bairstow is probably the first in line in choral music. But that is to speak of direct influence. The indirect influence of Samuel Sebastian is incalculable.

In 1910, a memorial service was held at Westminster Abbey to celebrate the centenary of Samuel Sebastian's birth. This was the service-programme at 3 p.m. on 29 June in that year:

Psalm 84, to *Wesley in D* (*European Psalmist*, 702)
Canticles: *Wesley in E*
Anthems: O Lord my God
   Ascribe unto the Lord
   All go unto one place
   Cast me not away
   The Wilderness
   O Lord thou art my God
   Blessed be the God and Father
   Praise the Lord, O my soul
Hymn:
   "Brief life is here our portion" and "Jerusalem the golden" (eight verses in all) to *Aurelia*
Voluntary: *Introduction and Fugue in C sharp minor*

The organ recital at 6.30 the same day ran as follows:

| | | |
|---|---|---|
| *Andante in F* | played by | Edward Bairstow (York) |
| *Choral Song* | | Kendrick Pyne (Manchester) |
| *Air with variation in*<br>   *F sharp minor* | | Prendergast (Winchester) |
| *Andante in E flat* | | Brewer (Gloucester) |
| *Improvization on themes by*<br>   Samuel Sebastian Wesley | | Alcock (Salisbury) |
| *Andante Cantabile in G* | | Aylward (Chichester) |
| *Air, "Holsworthy Church Bells"* | | Sinclair (Hereford) |
| *National Anthem with Variations* | | Bridge (Westminster Abbey) |

# The Organ and the Wesleys

Samuel Sebastian stands at an historical watershed in English organ composition and design. He is the last of our considerable organ composers to write music almost entirely on the assumption that the instrument will have an incomplete pedalboard; and he is one of the first "modern" composers of what we now regard as true organ music.

To look at the organ music of his predecessors, including those in his own family, it is at once clear that to them the organ is essentially either a deviation from the clavichord or harpsichord family, or a kind of super-pianoforte. You cannot call any English organ music before about 1840 "true" organ music in the sense in which the music of J. S. Bach, or of our own composers after Parry, is "true" organ music. Indeed, there is a case (which I have argued in *Twentieth Century Church Music*) for saying that the first "true" organ music composer was Olivier Messaien. But that uses the term "true organ music" to mean music which positively could not be played on any instrument but the organ—music which makes full use of the distinctive quality of the organ, which is its unique capacity for sustaining sound at a constant volume for whatever duration of time the player prescribes. Using the term somewhat more broadly, to cover music which can be played only on either an organ with more than one manual or

7

on a pedal-harpsichord or pedal-piano similarly appointed, we can say that there was a great quantity of true organ music composed on the Continent from the time of Bach's predecessors; but there was none in England.

Samuel Sebastian would say that this was the result of a puritanical lack of interest in the possibilities of organ building; and historically he would be right. Compared with Continental instruments, English organs, and especially cathedral organs, were very poorly appointed indeed. It was not that the builders could not build complete organs: it was rather that the demand for them was nearly non-existent.

We have already referred to certain eighteenth-century developments in organ building, especially to the evolution of the Swell, which produced an effect so agreeable to John Wesley. Some excellent work was being done by Snetzler in the early years (for example, the Temple Church Organ of 1688), by Jordan, Byfield and, later on, Green. But the provision of a complete pedal-board, from low CCC to alto F, was, even half way through the nineteenth century, something which could not be counted on.

Sumner[1] tells us that the first pedal-board in an English cathedral was probably that of the organ at St Paul's, London, added to the organ in 1720. Renatus Harris had unsuccessfully suggested, in 1712, the erection of an organ at the west end of St Paul's, of full Continental proportions with a full and independent pedal organ. It looks as if the pedals added in 1720 were allowed soon to fall into disuse, and probably removed. It is quite clear that for another century and a half it was not normal for English organists to use pedals, even if they were provided. Two stories illustrate this: that of Spofforth, organist of Lichfield Cathedral, who told his builder that he could install a pedal organ of eight stops if he liked in the new organ but he, the organist, would never use them—that was in 1866. And Sir George Smart (now remembered only as the composer of the psalm tune *Wiltshire*) invited to try an organ at the

[1] See Sumner's, *The Organ*, pp. 173 ff.

Great Exhibition of 1851 with a full pedal-board, said that he had never in his life played on a gridiron, and did not (at seventy-five) propose to begin. There is also the well-known occasion when Mendelssohn, booked to give a recital at the Hanover Square Rooms, cancelled it because the organ was not fitted with "German Pedals"—which means a full pedal-board. The organ in Canterbury Cathedral in 1884 had one octave of short pedals, and, until the rebuild of 1890, the organ at Southwell Minster had no independent pedal pipes.

What an organist would normally have to work with, then, would be an instrument probably of two manuals, possibly of three; one manual might go only down to tenor C, but at least one would go to GGG. There would be a short pedal-board, if any pedal-board at all. The pedals would simply be a mechanism for playing the lowest manual notes; they would actuate no pipes of their own, and merely be connected to couplers that worked the bottom octave, or octave and a half, of the Great manual. Frequently, they were so short as to be playable only with the toe of the left shoe; indeed, if one wishes to get the feel of most cathedral organs in the days of the musical Wesleys, one has only to try to play one of the modern electronic entertainment-organs, which have revived the dreadful design of including an octave of "short" pedals to be played with the left toe only.

Two cathedral organs in England, Hereford and Westminster Abbey, had independent pedal pipes in 1810. (So Samuel Sebastian was lucky in his first cathedral appointment; good fortune which he celebrated in *The Wilderness*—see above, p. 152.)

It is interesting, therefore, to observe how reticent Samuel Sebastian is, in *A Few Words*, about the defects of English organs. The reason for this is probably that he had no personal experience of the Continental instruments, and that his curious conservatism in some matters prevented his raising much enthusiasm for modern organistic devices. (He is such a strange psychological mixture that such a judgment cannot be more than tentative.) All he does say about organs in that work is that there is no real need for a large organ in a cathedral, provided that the instrument is in decent order and adequate for the accompaniment of a choir.

It was outside the Church of England that organ-building flourished better. Samuel Wesley, in collaboration with Benjamin Jacob the resident organist, used the nonconformist Surrey Chapel organ for his first Bach recitals. The occasional "great house" would have a good organ; but the cathedrals offered the organ-builder no scope for his art until after 1851. It was, indeed, the Great Exhibition of that year which, improbably perhaps, gave considerable impetus to organ building in England. The Exhibition showed no fewer than fourteen instruments, eleven of them by English builders. The two which attracted most attention were Henry Willis's large instrument of three manuals and seventy stops, and Edmund Schultze's German instrument, a smaller organ with the characteristic "baroque" feature of similar but contrasting choruses on each manual. It was the Willis instrument (part of which went to Winchester in Samuel Sebastian's time) that set the style for later nineteenth-century English organ building. A direct result of the greatly increased interest in organ building which the Exhibition created was the foundation of the College (later the Royal College) of Organists. This was proposed in 1863 by Richard D. Limpus, Organist of St Michael's, Cornhill, accepted at a meeting in 1864, and inaugurated on 5 July, 1864 at the Freemasons' Hall; examinations began in 1866. It found its present buildings, a stone's throw from the site of the Great Exhibition, in 1904. One of its most important contributions to organ-history was made at a conference called by the College in 1881 to establish a standard pattern of keys and of pedal-boards on the English organ. The standard pedal-board is still referred to as the "R.C.O. pedal-board".

But most of this happened after Samuel Sebastian's death. He was too old, and too remote, to be invited to be an early examiner. Indeed, although he was regarded as one of the great recitalists of his day, he belonged obstinately to the "old school", and from certain things we know of him, would not have been at home in the post-1851 climate of organ playing at all.

For example, he was strongly in favour of the G compass for manuals and pedals. He wrote for it constantly, and on at least one occasion had a battle with Henry Willis I on that issue; for he was called in to advise on the design of the organ in St George's Hall, Liverpool, and played at its opening in 1854, having been a member of a deputation, with the resident organist W. T. Best and T. A. Walmisley, who examined the Willis organ at the Great Exhibition in connexion with the project. Samuel Sebastian wanted to insist that the pedal and manual compass should extend to G. Willis refused to build the organ on those terms, but eventually settled for an orthodox C pedal-board, and a manual compass to G.[1] His own organ at Gloucester, rebuilt in 1847, had Great and pedals to CCC, Swell to CC and Choir to GG, and of this he never complained. It was under Mendelssohn's influence that builders began to standardize the CC pedal-board, but this was never acceptable to Samuel Sebastian. Since the GGG pedal-board (which of course normally extended only two or two and a half octaves) made the playing of nearly all Bach's and Mendelssohn's music on the organ impossible; this throws an unexpected light on Samuel Sebastian's practice, as distinct from his precept, in organ playing. On the other hand, he is probably responsible for one technical improvement in the building of pedal-boards which has become standard practice. Henry Willis himself recorded[2] that Samuel Sebastian was greatly impressed with the new Continental concave pedal-board on the Schulze organ at the Exhibition, but at once suggested that the pedals should also be "spread out", i.e., radiating. Willis at once took up the suggestion.

With characteristic aesthetic inconsistency, Samuel Sebastian

[1] See *Musical Times*, July 1900.
[2] See *Musical Times*, May 1858.

was, to the end of his days, a defender of "unequal temperament" in organ tuning. Once again, he was out of step with
J. S. Bach, although in this case he had, in a sense, history on his
side, since all Bach's organ music was necessarily written against
a background of unequal temperament. What is really astonishing is that a composer who, in his own music, made such
adventurous harmonic explorations should have maintained so
obstinate an advocacy of unequal temperament; some of the
modulations in his anthems, and a good deal of his *Introduction
and Fugue in C sharp minor*, would have sounded hair-raising
when played on instruments so tuned. Kendrick Pyne of
Manchester, his old pupil, made this comment. Perhaps the
only modification of what it implies is the observation that,
with the single exception of that C-sharp minor organ piece,
Samuel Sebastian always chose keys very near "home" as the
tonics of his church music; but his work is highly chromatic,
and when one looks at this organ piece and the other music
written at Leeds—for example, the B-major section of the
*Jubilate in E*—his advocacy of the pre-Bach tuning of an organ
looks more like a pose than a practicality.

What kind of a recitalist was Samuel Sebastian? The answer
was, again, a recitalist of the old school. W. T. Best was virtually a pioneer of modern organ-virtuosity. A long line of great
players followed him, many of whom composed organ music
which exploited the performer's technical prowess without
making much demand on his musical genius—the great
Hollins, for example. But although in his later years, Samuel
Sebastian seems to have behaved like a dispirited and lazy
musician, in his Leeds days and earlier, people flocked to hear
him. The respect in which especially he showed himself to be
a musician of the old school was in that he was especially noted
as an improviser.

Concerning this improvisation business as an organist's
technique, it must be quite clearly stated that there was a
difference between the "improvisation" that would appear in
the programmes of either of the Wesleys, and that which is

cultivated still by French recitalists of the twentieth century. In the school of Marcel Dupré, improvisation has been developed to a very high art, and there are no organists in the world who practise it as he did and as his pupils do. Improvisation in the English school of the early nineteenth century was a different matter. It was cultivated for one special reason which does not at all press upon the modern French organists: that in the English situation there was precious little else to play. The great music of the pre-Bach school was not known. The music of J. S. Bach was unplayable on almost all English organs. Confined to the English school, a recitalist must needs play Greene, Stanley, and a Handel concerto if there is an orchestra present. A personal improvisation by the recitalist added a much needed touch of spice to an otherwise tedious programme of "Voluntaries". And to be candid, the fact that many people thought Samuel Sebastian and his father geniuses at improvising fugues, becomes a good deal less impressive when one examines the organ fugues which they succeeded in writing down. If such flatulence was possible in recollection and tranquillity, what sort of a fugue would be liable to emerge from an improvisation? One may safely suppose that the reputations of these players for improvisation may well have been somewhat inflated. The organ has long been the best of instruments for the purpose of deceiving a reasonably uncritical audience; this indeed is one of the evils which the construction of the organ room at the Royal College of Organists has been specifically designed to expose in aspirants to that institution's diplomas.

Like many indifferent players—which is a proper description of Samuel Sebastian in his later years—he was, it appears, an admirable conductor. The singing at the Three Choirs' Festival at Gloucester in 1874 was so bad as to draw an acid comment from the *Musical Times* reporter: "If the service of that evening were to be taken as any specimen of what the future Festivals are to be, we tremble for the poor widows and orphans for whose benefit they are carried on"; but the same journal

reported of the 1865 Festival, his first at Gloucester, that "the
perfect manner in which the whole of the instrumental portions
of the works were performed left us nothing to comment on".
The same report goes on to praise Samuel Sebastian for the
manner of his conducting the orchestra, mentioning—another
interesting sidelight on a custom which by this time was dis-
appearing, but which Samuel Sebastian, with his usual conservatism, kept up—that he did not conduct all the time, but
in certain passages laid down his baton, "becoming an attentive
and admiring auditor".[1] This contrast between a service in
1874 and an oratorio concert in 1865 indicates not only the
tragic decline in his powers in his last years, but probably also
the fact that the greater occasion tended to draw from him
better musicianship than the routine business of cathedral
music. No doubt, his relative failure to achieve quick results by
writing *A Few Words* produced in him a resigned attitude, and
it was only an occasion demanding special powers which
awakened him from this condition of lassitude.

Returning to the organ, a programme preserved by the
*Musical Times* of a recital given in St George's in the East,
London, on 26 June, 1852, indicates the manner of Samuel
Sebastian's work in his best days. It was a new organ, and this
is what the recitalist played:

| | |
|---|---|
| *Fugue, E flat* | Seb. Bach |
| *Andante* | Mozart |
| *Air* by Kozeluch, varied | S. S. Wesley |
| *Air*, varied (from *Organ Pieces*, 2nd set) | S. S. Wesley |
| *Instrumental Piece* | Spohr |
| *Prelude and Fugue* | Bach |
| *Air* | Mendelssohn |
| *Andante* | S. S. Wesley |
| Extemporaneous. | |

We omit the vocal and choral numbers in the programme. The
drawing up of the list is as perfunctory as programmes were in

[1] P. Scholes, *A Mirror of Music*, p. 379.

those days before the lack of specification was counted to a recitalist as illiteracy. Dr Scholes[1] suggested that the Spohr piece gets an intentionally evasive title because it was the recitalist's own arrangement of an air from Spohr's *Jessonda*, which a bishop had recently vetoed because he found something sinister in the secular sound of its full title. Scholes also suggests that the *Prelude and Fugue* by Bach were from the "48" rather than from the organ works, and possibly the first item also. Samuel Sebastian certainly did play pieces from the "48" on the organ, and with his large hand would have been able to play many of them quite effectively on manuals only. The other unspecified identities we can only guess at, but in any case there was clearly a good deal of "arranged" music in the programme, apart from Samuel Sebastian's own pieces. The "*Air* varied" may have been the F-sharp minor variations, which still occasionally turn up in recital programmes.

As a composer for the organ, Samuel Sebastian shows a quite remarkable versatility. That is the kindest way to put it. Perhaps it would be equally fair to say that he regarded the organ as his best medium for "occasional" pieces. What is beyond doubt is that he did none of his best work, and some of his worst, on this instrument; and in this, he resembles many other composers. Once again, the psychological difficulties of the organ as a musical instrument have to be brought in evidence. The reason for the existence (now, we may be glad to know, only in libraries and historical collections) of such a quantity of fantastically vulgar organ music is simply that organ solos, as distinct from organ pieces related to Christian worship, have, in Britain, been composed on the assumption that the people who came to hear them would be people of more or less frivolous musical appreciation. This was a social judgment which the composers could not escape. Organ recitals were usually given in churches, and very often on occasions of local significance, such as the opening of new organs or patronal festivals. They were designed by the church authorities to attract to the

---

[1] *A Mirror of Music*, p. 593.

church as many people as possible who would help with the church's support. They were very rarely such purely musical occasions as celebrity organ recitals now are in this country. The greater part of the audience would be to only a modest degree musical. The recitalist might have severe taste himself, but he would not be invited again, or elsewhere, if he bored the patrons of the church, and the subscribers to the new organ, with music of too austere a kind.

The greatest practitioner of the ear-catching technique in organ-composition must have been Alfred Hollins (1865–1945) of Edinburgh; and Hollins lived in the days of the fully-developed organ. He was in demand as a recitalist and an opener of new organs all over the country, and he had a most winning and dexterous technique. As a blind organist—a member of a long line of distinguished blind recitalists—he excited all the greater wonder. His programme always contained one or two orchestral arrangements (the overture to *William Tell* electrified the audience at the opening of a new organ in Brighton in 1921), and a piece or two of his own. In emotional range, his own compositions covered what ground exists between the ponderously sentimental and the lusciously sentimental; but he was one of the best of the recitalist-composers of his generation, and indeed one or two of his pieces are even now heard occasionally. (Parry and Stanford were, precisely, not "recitalist-composers".) Anybody can see why he composed as he did. It was, to a large extent, the same with Samuel Sebastian in his day.

All Samuel Sebastian's organ music is written for an organ with a G pedal-board, and most of it on two staves. Easily the most serious and the finest of his pieces is the *Introduction and Fugue in C sharp minor*, which is still deservedly well known. This must have been written for something near to our own orthodox organ, and it is, unusually in his case, "true organ music". It consists of a massive fugue, 137 bars long, five minutes' duration, preceded by a stately and sombre introduction of 44 bars. The music is tightly-knit, a prominent four-note theme in the introduction being taken up in the subject of the fugue. (Example 33.)

Example 33
From *Introduction and Fugue in C sharp minor*, by Samuel Sebastian Wesley

(We have already referred to Samuel Sebastian's large hands; bars 3 and 4 of the original score of this introduction confirm that.) And it is especially to be noted that here, as very rarely, he writes an "organistic" fugue subject, with the result that the pedal voice can take its full part in the working out of the fugue. It turns out to be a very orthodox fugue, employing all those standard devices which Bach used so rarely, but which other classic contrapuntists delighted in, including augmentation (bars 53 ff.) inversion (bar 65), and the combination of direct and inverted statements (there and bar 121). His rather disastrous propensity (shared with his father) for writing "false entries" is not much in evidence here (there is one at bar 111). It is an entirely unexceptionable piece, and in Henry Ley's edition of 1952 is still gratefully accepted by recitalists.

But he never reached that height again in organ music. One of his better known pieces today is still the *Choral Song*, sometimes called *Choral Song and Fugue*, because its second and longer section has some of the appearances of a fugue. This is much nearer the normal form. The *Choral Song* is a cheerful, emotionally arid 4 + 4-bar march in C major, with one of the composer's most classic "false modulations" in the middle.

(You really believe that the C-major thumps are going to give way to some relief in F major; but what happens is a swift and exasperating return to the tonic long before it was due.) Then consider the subject of the "fugue". Nothing could more completely expose its composer's conviction that the organ is a super-piano. There will be no hope of playing that subject on the pedals. The contrapuntal interest, then, will be confined to the manuals. Three voices enter with the fugue-subject (Example 10c), but after the first sixteen bars or so, it is a waste of time looking for them. The piece turns quickly into an "invention"—almost a *perpetuum mobile* in semiquavers, with the interest shifting from counterpoint to tonality. There is a considerable section in B minor on the third page (of Gordon Phillips's edition, Hinrichsen Ltd), which climbs further out into C sharp minor; indeed, 30 bars (of a total of 85) are in B minor or sharp of that key. An abrupt enharmonic modulation, pivoting on D sharp—E flat sends us into E flat major, then in the next bar we are in E flat minor, and in the next in G flat. A scramble through sharps and flats brings us out on a resounding chord of C sharp major, from which we are catapulted back to C through a dominant-seventh held for six beats (Example 34), and the rest is a fifteen-bar cadence bringing the whole piece home to C.

The technique throughout is pianistic, and the tonality reminiscent of what he did much better in his anthems. The first subject is unorganistic: the second (which occupies the whole of the "sharp" middle section), is easily arranged to accommodate pedals, so that in Walter Emery's edition (Novello, 1950), it looks much more like an organ piece than it really is.

The most attractive of his small-scale pieces is perhaps the *Andante in G* (ed. Stainton de B. Taylor, Hinrichsen). This is unashamedly sentimental, exploiting the piquancies of the gentler organ stops, and using the colours of modulation with considerable discretion. It is, you might say, good pre-Hollins. The *Larghetto in F sharp minor* (ed. Chambers, Novello) is also very pleasant and discreet. The variation which follows its

Example 34
From *Choral Song*, by Samuel Sebastian Wesley

opening statement gives the player a chance to show how cleanly he can play repeated notes and how quickly the pipes will speak. The middle section contains several "pathetic" clichés, and returns to the main theme through a pleasing and characteristic enharmonic modulation; but here, once again, the ear is deceived by the composer. Only 4 bars are in A major, then we are back in the home key long before we really wanted to be.

This indeed is Samuel Sebastian's besetting sin, as we have seen in some of the anthems; at least, it is a sin when it is unsuccessful. He does not always show himself a master of background-modulation, of a true shift of tonality sustained through a large section, and moving rhythmically from key to key. Sometimes, when concentration falls off in composition, he wanders, playing with keys as if they were a new toy (which in a sense of course they were). This happens in the second movement of the *Choral Song*; sometimes he makes a tentative effort and withdraws quickly, coming in rapidly out of the cold with the journey hardly begun. So his modulation devices are sometimes matters of mere foreground-play, and the whole effect is key-tied. Words often distract the ear from this and make it tolerable, as they almost do in "Love one another" from "Blessed be the God and Father". Occasionally, however, he is capable of turning this foreground-play into a witty conceit. This happens in that otherwise rather commonplace piece, the *Andante in E flat*. On the first return of the exasperating main subject, there is an intrusive chord (Example 35a) which arouses all our worst suspicions; but at the return after the "development", there is a more complex modulation which ends with the same progression (Example

Example 35
From *Andante in E flat*, by Samuel Sebastian Wesley

35b). It is still foreground-stuff, but here the musical pun is forgivable. The only trouble with this piece is its general air of musical platitude.

The *Andante in E minor* (Hinrichsen's series, book 13) is a pleasanter piece. It says nothing that was not better said in "Wash me throughly", but it is at least coherent, unpretentious and serene.

Samuel Sebastian's organ music is scattered about in modern collections, and most of what is now playable is published either in three-stave editions or in the scholarly collections of Hinrichsen's edition, which have valuable historical and biographical prefaces and preserve the two-stave form. A good deal of the "occasional" material is now forgotten and can only be consulted in the major libraries.

A word might, however, be added about that curiosity, his variations on the *National Anthem*. This piece was composed in his juvenile days; it was performed (not necessarily for the first time) at Samuel Wesley's famous recital in St Mary Redcliffe, Bristol, in 1829, when the new organ there was being opened. At that recital, the son assisted the father and performed this piece. Example 36 shows the opening of one of its more fantastic variations. It appears in the 1910 centenary recital (p. 176).

What causes the reader to pause is not so much the wild vulgarity of the piece itself, but the fact that it appeared in an album of organ music, called *Coronation Album*, published by Novello to celebrate the Coronation year, 1901. The rest of the contents of this book give a handy compendium of the excesses to which organ composers allowed themselves to be tempted in the first generation of the English "big organ" fashion. In themselves, the variations are beyond musical criticism and rationality. The historical fact is that it was only during Victoria's reign that the *National Anthem* settled down behind its hagiological myth. It would now be considered poorish taste to offer variations on it at any organ recital; the music is too threadbare to produce great variations at the hands of anybody less gifted

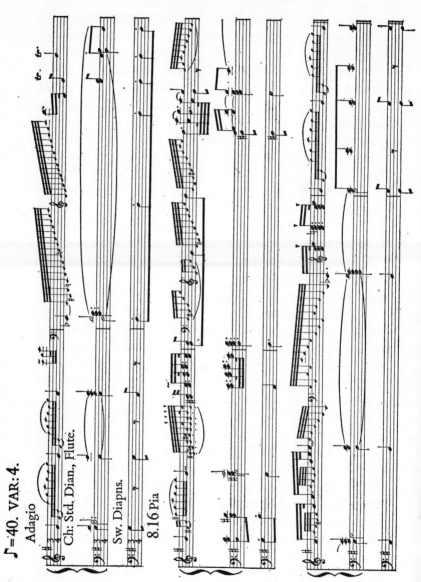

Example 36
From *The National Anthem*, by Samuel Sebastian Wesley (before 1829)

than the composer of the variations on the Diabelli Waltz; and
its associations are now such as to place it beyond serious
musical thought. But in 1828 (or thereabouts), neither the
monarch nor the *National Anthem* aroused such sensitive feelings. Indeed, by that time, neither the tune nor the words had
found an official and invariable form—as one can learn in
detail from Percy Scholes's monograph on the subject. The
really remarkable thing is that it should have been revived by a
serious publishing house in 1901 and played in Westminster
Abbey in 1910, by which time the *National Anthem* had become
a much more venerated national possession. Its preservation is
one more example of the latitude in taste which public opinion
permitted to organists at the turn of our own century.

Samuel Sebastian, hardly did himself justice on the organ.
He was not without influence, in this department as in that of
the hymn tune. As we shall see when we come to discuss his
hymns, he left a considerable musical legacy to Basil Harwood,
another composer whose music was virtually confined to
church forms and who made a small but enduring contribution
to the organ repertory. There are passages in his C sharp minor
organ sonata (the choice of key may not have been an accident)
and in, for example, *Communion* from the Op. 58 set of organ
preludes, which suggest that they are what Samuel Sebastian
would have written, had he been fifty years younger. Parry,
too, might well have acknowledged a debt to Samuel Sebastian,
especially in his larger organ works, and certainly Charles
Wood exemplified in his music the ideals that Wesley followed
when he was at his best.

Of prior influence on Wesley himself, it is not easy to make
any assessment. The other works, when we come to them, will
show a much greater influence of Mendelssohn than of J. S.
Bach. But we shall find that we are unable to be at all definite;
and this is because of those circumstances which surrounded
him, and which especially appear in his organ work. The
limitations were so severe, his own temperament was so easily
discouraged, that although many influences must have been

present to him in his deep musical learning, those to which he could respond covered a limited field. If he had been more influenced by his beloved Gabrieli, or by his father's beloved Bach, the circumstances of cathedral music and the limitations of the English organ would have left him helpless to express the ideals of either, unless he had approached music with a greater sense of dedication and objectivity than his nature permitted.

# 12

# Samuel Sebastian Wesley
# and the English Hymn Tune

The English hymn tune during the Victorian era was easily the most interesting of England's contributions to music at that time. It was the only genuinely English musical form available. All other music in England was Continental in sympathy and ethos. It was cosmopolitan, "common market" music. English folk-song had largely gone underground, and nothing corresponded to the remarkable contribution which English composers of the Tudor period, working within a European framework, made to polyphony. There is something recognizable, and you might say recognizably English, about Byrd when he is laid alongside Lassus or Palestrina, but there is nothing English about the Wesleys when their music is laid alongside that of their Continental contemporaries, and it is fanciful to suggest that there is.

But here, in the hymn tune, is a musical form which nobody else particularly wanted on the Continent, since nothing on the Continent corresponded to English Dissent, or to the Church of England. To the Victorian age of music, this was a godsend. Here, if nowhere else, Englishmen could be English; their dependence on Continental music must necessarily be at several removes. The reason for this is the historical fact that although there was a common market in the arts, there most certainly was none in religion. England had been "going it alone" ever since Henry VIII had set the English Reformation in motion. The most popular argument against the Pope was that he was a foreign prince. Wilkie Collins's Roman Catholic priests correspond exactly to the international spies and double agents of Len Deighton and John le Carré. Any association between Continental Protestants and their British counterparts has been the effect of the twentieth-century Ecumenical movement.

The very insularity which made England a possible refuge for Roman Catholic priests escaping from the French Revolution protected the country from the influences of Continental religion, and to a large extent from those of Continental religious music. Influences of French, German and Italian opera came into English church music through the oratorio and the extended anthem, as Professor Hutchings has recently shown (in *English Church Music of the Nineteenth Century*, 1967). Before it got to the hymn tune it had to go through a further process of, as it were, "screening". English religion was fiercely nationalistic where its secular music was generously cosmopolitan. The three great Reformations each contributed to this: that of the sixteenth century, by cutting England off from Continental Catholic influence; John Wesley's and the Tractarian movement, both by instituting reforms of ideas and machinery which were designed specifically for the revival of English religion. Tractarians who became Roman Catholics missed the central purpose of their movement, which was to arouse in England a religion appropriate to England's peculiar and secular prestige and responsibility.

It was the common market in the arts that was the exception. In other matters, England was self-consciously isolated. No other culture has succeeded in producing a true imitation of the English industrial town, the English parish church, the English public school, or the English public house, all of which, in the forms familiar to us still, are Victorian inventions or transformations.

Nor has anybody succeeded in producing a true imitation of the English hymn tune. This too is something which, although it existed before the nineteenth century, was transformed by Victorian culture. Before about 1840, we still talk either of "psalm tunes" or of "Methodist hymns". Thereafter, it is, with an affectionate or a patronizing air according to one's temperament, simply "hymns".

To speak of a "Victorian hymn tune" is to set off in any remotely musical mind the strains of John Bacchus Dykes's tune to "The King of Love" [EH 490: M 76]. There is nothing more centrally Victorian in all English religion than those words set to that tune. Probably, without the least consciousness that he was doing anything of the kind, that folk-genius Dykes gathered up there everything that this kind of Victorian music has to say. It is a good enough piece of music to be called by Vaughan Williams himself a "beautiful tune"; this he did in the 1906 Preface to the *English Hymnal*, regretting that copyright barriers made it unavailable to him for his book; and there was at that time no more ferocious critic of the Victorian musical manner than Ralph Vaughan Williams, except perhaps his literary editor, Percy Dearmer. It is beautiful indeed; cunning in its simplicity, inerrant in its choice of melodic texture and intervals. The way the second line is nearly, but not quite, repeated in the fourth, yet without any sense of setting a trap for the unwary, is in itself a stroke of inspiration. (You can "miss the boat" in the third line of "Holy, Holy, Holy": people do get the last note wrong, but nobody wants to go wrong in *Dominus Regit Me*; and the musical reason for this is too evident to need stating here.) The sheer friendliness of the tune depends primarily on its choice of key and its use of the major-sixth between the low dominant and the mediant of that key in its background structure—a device which Dykes loved, but never again brought off with so little sense of mawkishness.

Finally, the tune does exactly what the words do with Psalm 23. Sir Henry Baker writes, not a pastoral paraphrase like

George Herbert's or an eighteenth-century country-house paraphrase like Addison's, but an English parish-church paraphrase.
"The Lord is my shepherd" becomes, "The King of *love* my
shepherd is": quite different from Herbert's "The God of
love". Later on, he introduces the Tractarian "chalice" to
represent "Thou preparest a table before me". This is the purest
Anglican Herefordshire, and the tune comes flying across the
country from Anglican Durham to meet it. It may not be
everybody's taste, but its objective beauty is simply undeniable.
If the beautiful is in some sense, as St Thomas Aquinas said,
"*id quod visum placet*", then you can only assail the proposition
that this is beautiful by asking a moral question about the
pleasure it gives.

Our purpose here is not to add to the mountain of execration
that has fallen on Victorian hymn tunes. Take a hundred
assorted hymn tunes from the period 1861–1900, and there will
be a good case against ninety-seven of them. Much the same
would be true of modern commercial pop-songs; ninety-seven
of every hundred ought not to have been written. The reason
would be the same; producing both kinds of music is, or was,
too easy for aesthetic safety. A vast demand and a new ease of
distribution made publishers ready to take anything that looked
as if it would get by. All this is well enough known, and elsewhere I have myself written about it. The point to be made
here is simply this; that in the Victorian age, for the first time,
composers looked at their work in hymn tunes with a conscious
desire to make it beautiful.

It is obvious that this was to impose on themselves an almost
impossible artistic limitation. You cannot get far in any kind
of artistic creation if you are primarily hoping to make your
work of art beautiful—pleasurable to the viewer or hearer.
Indeed, history in music has proved, I think conclusively, that
it is wise to confine yourself, if that is your primary aim, to
music of the length of the double Anglican chant. In a hymn
tune you may be successful, but even twenty-eight syllables
may prove to be more than you can manage. Too much self-

consciousness about *effect* is fatal to any art-form on any but the most minute and epigrammatic scale. And it is in the hymn tune that we see this most satisfactorily. We have already said that the eighteenth-century composers were never afraid of being thought dull. Compare with that the assiduous, and sometimes anxious, and even frantic, desire of the Victorian hymn-tune writer to be sure that at every beat there will be something to catch the listener's attention. You cannot, in the romantic and sophisticated days of Victoria, hope to do this simply by writing a fine melody and adding an adequate bass. There must be not only plenty of passing interest in the melody, but also experiment with the new technique of confronting monotonous melody with a moving bass and chromatic inner parts, and of decorating it with incidental and episodic chro-maticisms. Just as in architecture, empty space is intolerable without some kind of decoration, so in music, silence and repose are emotionally taboo. All must be *picturesque*.

When a composer is full of these compulsions and deliber-ately fines down his product so that the emotional power is properly disciplined, the result is excellent, and beautiful in a way in which Victorian art can be uniquely beautiful. This is the virtue of Dyke's "King of love" tune. It says enough, but not too much. It is the virtue of more other Victorian hymns than some musicians care to admit. But all the same, it is, among current Victorian church music, too rarely encountered.

The truth about Samuel Sebastian Wesley is, I think, that he is a clearing-house for every possible kind of Victorian experi-ment. He was, by heredity and by personal exertion, the best-educated English church musician of his day. He had a larger vocabulary than any other in which to express himself. Where others had to make do either with repetitions of eighteenth-century clichés or with the adoption of nineteenth-century styles unaccompanied by any certain knowledge of their real history, Samuel Sebastian knew perfectly well of the connexion between nineteenth-century chromaticism and the counter-point of J. S. Bach. Possibly he knew it better, and grafted it into his own music with more assurance than anybody in England, or than anybody alive except Mendelssohn. Not that he was infallible. He was no Bach; he was not even a Mendelssohn. The movements when he strikes the authentic note are few; but the difference between his music, especially his hymns, and those of anybody else round him was that he showed any knowledge at all of history and of Continental music.

This means that whereas in his anthems it is just possible to detect a "Wesley style", even if, as we have said, it is hazardous, the only indication in an unknown nineteenth-century hymn tune that it was by Samuel Sebastian would be some eccentricity. If you were able to say, "How on earth would the composer expect anybody to sing that?" of a nineteenth-century hymn tune, the chances are high that it would be by Samuel Sebastian; but the proposition cannot be simply converted. Only a minority of his tunes are in the least eccentric or curious. Most of them are strictly lyrical, and many of them strictly commonplace.

But the curiosities in his tunes are the result of the pressure of musical influences, of which most of his contemporaries took no notice. The one English Victorian church composer in whom we can see the influence of an eminent European musician, and in respect of whom we can check that influence historically, is Arthur Sullivan. The profound impression made upon him by his visit to Vienna with Grove in 1866, and by being a witness there to the discovery of some of Schubert's music, is clearly testified in his secular music, and if his church music had not been corrupted by sentimental notions of the church's dignity, he would have mediated Schubert to the singing congregation. As it is, only faint and usually incongruous traces of the Viennese style appear in his church music—for example, in his tune *Angel Voices* and in his setting of "We therefore pray Thee, help Thy servants" in the *Festival Te Deum*. Mendelssohn, Spohr and Gounod, all of whom were at their best in secular music, are normally blamed for their influence on our minor Victorians, but usually this is a generalization unsupported by any particularly tangible evidence. The trouble with our worse Victorians was that either they simply did not hear much fine music from Europe, or, if they did, they were oppressed by the idea that music on that scale could not be used for church; it was at once too demanding and too frivolous. Two notions collided with disastrous results; that the church must not be asked to do too much intellectual work, and that this was because its mind was set on higher things. Consequently, very bad music was represented as very good music, because it was unintellectual and emotionally restricted. Musically, the result was that the composers were psychologically inhibited from admitting the influences that worked on them. That is, they could not help being vulnerable to the influences, but they dared not analyse or control them.

That was true of many, but it was not true of Samuel Sebastian Wesley. He did know what he was doing. His thoroughly disagreeable social temperament was a symptom of an impatient, independent and thoroughly unsentimental mind. He was never a great enough artist to guard against the dangers in which this temperament placed him. Therefore, as we have seen, he was capable of being slapdash, tedious and uncritical of his own work, but he was never the plaything of aesthetic forces as his lesser contemporaries so often were.

If we look first at a handful of his hymn tunes, all of which have to some extent survived in religious use, we shall see what a chameleon he could be. Take *Aurelia* [EH 489: M 701], by far his best known, indeed his most notorious, tune. This is one of the tunes that are inevitable victims of satirical parody. Several sets of very secular words have been written for it. How much do we know about it?

We happen to know, as we know of hardly any others among his tunes, in what circumstances it was written. Dr Kendrick Pyne recalled (in *English Church Music*, V. 1, January 1935, pp. 5 ff.):

I was in his drawing room in the Close, Winchester, as a lad of thirteen, with Mrs Wesley, my mother and Mrs Stewart (the mother of the distinguished General Stewart who fell in Egypt); we were all discussing a dish of strawberries when Dr Wesley came rushing up from below with a scrap of MS. in his hand, a psalm tune just that instant finished. Placing it on the instrument, he said, "I think this will be popular". My mother was the first ever to sing it to the words "Jerusalem the golden". The company liked it, and Mrs Wesley on the spot christened it *Aurelia*.

[*English Church Music*, v. 1, January, pp. 5 ff.]

This dates the tune precisely, if we can rely on the vivid memory of the very aged Kendrick Pyne who wrote the anecdote down nearly sixty years after its subject's death.

So it comes from Wesley's mature period—perhaps the period after most of his liveliest work was done. What else can be said about it? Experience has shown how tenacious it is, especially since its association with two very popular hymns, "From Greenland's icy mountains" and "The church's one foundation". In some ways it is admirable—easy to learn, easily remembered, and universally "singable". What has made it notorious? The answer is, its use of a musical device which invariably loses its effect when it is too often repeated. This is the suspension which occurs in this tune at the end of every odd line. It seems to fall so naturally in this tune that one wonders whether it is not forced on it by the metre, until one looks at earlier examples in the same metre like *St Theodulph* [EH 622: M 92]; but it is this falling cadence in the melody, which no revision of the harmony can disguise, which gives the tune its depressing and threadbare quality. And this most certainly was the legacy of Mendelssohn.

But observe that whereas most English musicians knew Mendelssohn only through his music—and probably mostly through his church music—the Wesley family knew him personally, and Samuel Sebastian knew his music intimately. He knew that his music at its best was full of fire and grace, and that its less noble qualities were perversions of qualities which other composers had brought to greatness. It is his misfortune that *Aurelia* is his best-known composition. The fact is that he made a great deal more of Mendelssohn, and knew more of composers other than Mendelssohn, than his contemporaries did.

Observe secondly the tune *Wigan*. If you did not know who had written it, and if it had only been written in equal notes throughout, with minims at the point marked in Example 37, to whom would you ascribe it? I should quite surely have said, "School of Crüger, arranged and harmonized by J. S. Bach, and subsequently simplified". To reharmonize it in the style of Bach would be a perfectly legitimate student-exercise.

Thirdly, consider *Hereford*. Here is a tune which has had a different history from the other two. Whereas *Aurelia* achieved

WIGAN                                                                [430]

Example 37

popularity at once and retained it, and *Wigan* has been locked up with a rather unmeritable hymn which is the only one in its metre and therefore has had very few hearings, *Hereford*, hardly ever heard for fifty years after its composition, is at present a tune very nearly as popular as *Crimond*. This was due to its being set to "O Thou who camest from above", a well-known hymn by Samuel Sebastian's grandfather, by Sir Sydney Nicholson in his Second Supplement (1916) to *Hymns Ancient and Modern*, and to its later being made much of in BBC religious broadcasts under the influence of Sir Walford Davies.

*Hereford* is, like *Wigan*, a perfect piece of musical construction; also like *Wigan*, its melodic line is a judicious blend of stepwise melody with occasional significant leaps. Its mood, however, is that of the gentle part-song; its inner parts are as melodious as its treble part. Every line, like four of the eight lines of *Aurelia*, ends with a suspension, but this time a pure suspension with a moving treble over a held bass. The style is, in fact, eighteenth century, and to be more precise, it is Handel. The sequential tendencies in the melody and harmony of the last two lines give the secret away. Handel himself knew better than to use sequence in any of his three hymn tunes, but the eighteenth-century Englishmen often drove it to exhaustion. Here it is not a blemish, but it is an "author's signature". We find it all over Wesley's hymn tunes.

### THE EUROPEAN PSALMIST

Samuel Sebastian's testament to hymnology is his collection, *The European Psalmist*, published, in 1872, jointly by Novello, Boosey and Hamilton, three London music publishers. This is a collection of 733 pieces on 558 pages; the first 615 pieces are hymn tunes; nos. 616–23 are settings of the Sanctus; 624–35 are single chants; and 636–722 double chants. Then follow 11 short anthems:

723 : "O deliver me", by Samuel Wesley, extended by Samuel Sebastian Wesley.

724 : "I will arise", by Samuel Sebastian Wesley.

725 : "O remember not", by Samuel Wesley [16 August, 1821].

726 : "Might I in thy sight appear", by Samuel Wesley [1827, but see above, p. 86].

727 : "Who is the trembling sinner", by Samuel Wesley [1821].

728 : *Benedicite in D*, by Samuel Sebastian Wesley.

729 : "Blessed is the man", by Samuel Sebastian Wesley.

730–3 : *Chant Service in G*, by Samuel Sebastian Wesley, *Te Deum, Jubilate, Magnificat* and *Nunc Dimittis*.

The hymn tunes come from all manner of sources. Only 143 of them are the composition of Samuel Sebastian, but many more are arranged by him. His purpose in this labour of love, which took him many years to complete and whose publication was made possible by a subscription list of about 500 names including those of Sir Henry Baker, Joseph Barnby and Henry Willis I the organ builder, was to collect all the hymn tunes which had not appeared in hymn books printed by 1872, or which he had himself composed (whether or not these were published), and which he felt worth preserving. His range of exploration was for those days remarkable. It went much farther than did *The Psalmist*.

The form of the collection shows how tenaciously it took hold on him. For the first three hundred numbers or so, it seems to have a certain coherence: a group of long-metre tunes is followed by a group of common-metre tunes, and after those come the short-metre tunes, bringing us to no. 269. Then comes a significant group of German tunes, interrupted occasionally by tunes of Wesley's own and occasional contributions from other sources. Up to about 400, the contents are predominantly German, including many Bach arrangements accurately transcribed; then the organization seems to become somewhat less predictable. Already, a long metre tune, *Winscott*, has been slipped in at 370 (we shall return to it), and after 400 the Samuel Sebastian tunes become much more frequent. While there is still a great deal of German material, original tunes, arrangements of older tunes, and original versions of older tunes seem to be added just as he discovered them. It is certainly impossible to guess dates for the Wesley tunes from their position in this book; the excellent *Harewood*, published in 1839, appears as no. 410; its nearest Wesley neighbour is no. 401, *Wrestling Jacob*, which certainly did not appear before 1872.

He shows no knowledge of or interest in the Genevan tradition, although there are many English psalm tunes in his collection. Neither does he include much by Gibbons (*Angels Song* is there, in the corrupt $\frac{3}{2}$ version, and so is *Song* 13, also rhythmically devitalized), or anything by Henry Lawes. Tallis's canon appears in the eighteenth-century form (Example 38). It is quite clear that the German tradition meant everything

EVENING HYMN                                               [23]

Example 38

to him, and the English and sixteenth-century traditions nothing at all. But the German tradition, to him, meant the post-Bach tradition, for he never includes old chorales in their pre-Bach rhythmical form.

Subject to these limitations, he shows great zeal for the preservation of everything he knew which had quality. We owe to him the rediscovery of a delightful short metre tune called *Egham* [CP 616], by the seventeenth-century composer John Turner. Another of his arrangements, which merits special study, we shall come to in a moment.

A few of his tunes considered in detail will show his strange and versatile treatment of the form. We can suitably begin with *Mara* (Example 39), a tune which has disappeared from

MARA                                                                    [554]

Example 39

present-day use largely because the words with which it was associated are no longer sung and their metre is unusual. Here is the "E-flat" Wesley of *Aurelia*, but with a good deal more character. The two points especially to be noted are these: first, the sequential pattern in the third phrase; and second, the care he has taken with his cadences. From a study of his complete hymn tunes, it is clear that he saw at an early stage the great challenge that the hymn-tune form offers to the composer. Paradoxically, in so abbreviated a musical form, the

great danger is that the finished composition will lose momentum and architectural integrity because its cadences are out of
balance with each other. The best tunes show a true balance,
the worst ones, a lack of balance. It is partly a matter of the
handling of keys, partly a matter of the distribution of harmonies, and especially of the inversion of pivotal chords.
Referring back to *Aurelia* for a moment, observe how much
worse the tune would have been had its composer not been a
master of cadences. One could represent its cadences thus,
taking first the cadences at the ends of the four long phrases:

|   |   |   |   |
|---|---|---|---|
| 1. perfect, tonic | (bass) | 5–1 |
| 2. perfect, dominant | | 2–1 |
| 3. perfect, subdominant | | 5–1 |
| 4. perfect, tonic | | 5–1 |

That is commonplace enough, but now add the cadences at the
ends of the short phrases, and the pattern becomes this:

|   | modulating | to bass E flat |
|---|---|---|
| 1a. imperfect, tonic | 1–5 | 1–5 |
| 1b. perfect, tonic | 5–1 | 5–1 |
| 2a. interrupted, tonic minor | 5–6 | 3–4 |
| 2b. perfect, dominant, | 2–1 | 6–5 |
| 3a. plagal, tonic | 4–3 | 4–3 |
| 3b. perfect, subd. minor | 7–1 | 1 sharp–2 |
| 4a. imperfect, tonic | 1–4 | 1–4 |
| 4b. perfect, tonic | 5–1 | 5–1 |

This is the secret of construction, and the smaller the scale of
the piece, the greater the danger of its being neglected. In a
short tune the simplest form is 5–1, 1–5, 5–1, 5–1, which is
what we have in *Hereford*, and unless the tune has a good deal
of inner interest to compensate, that unsophisticated form can
lead to dullness and heaviness. It was one of the characteristics
of the earliest English psalm tunes, when written to four lines
of fourteen syllables, that their cadences tended to cause the
tune to fall apart in the middle. *Old 137th* is a good example

[EH 404]; either half of the tune makes a self-sufficient four-phrase tune. *Old 132nd* was so obviously two tunes running consecutively that, at quite an early stage, the first half came to be used by itself, and this we still know as *St Flavian* [EH 161: M 43]. That fine old tune, *French* (or *Dundee*: EH 428: M 625] has an unusual cadence-pattern in Ravenscroft's version:

|  | modulating | to bass E flat |
|---|---|---|
| 1. subdominant tritone | 2–1 | 5–4 |
| 2. tonic perfect | 5–1 | 5–1 |
| 3. dominant perfect | 5–1 | 2–5 |
| 4. tonic perfect | 5–1 | 5–1 |

Were it not for the placing of the climax note in the third phrase, this would be a dull tune. Such tunes as *Newington* (or *St Stephen* [EH 337: M 56]) and *Stracathro* [EH 445: M 102] repay examination, and decisions on whether each overcomes the disability of the perfect tonic cadence at the half-way point will probably vary from one judge to another.

Samuel Sebastian, however, was quite clear that cadential balance was a necessity, and in the great majority of his tunes it is evident that he worked to a cadential framework, not from a melodic episode. Back, then, to *Mara*; here is the cadential pattern:

| 1. perfect tonic | 4–3 | 4–3 |
|---|---|---|
| 2. perfect dominant | 7^–1 | 4^–5 |
| 3. plagal tonic | 4–3 | 4–3 |
| 4. perfect tonic minor | 5–1 | 3–6 |
| 5. perfect dominant | 5–1 | 2–5 |
| 6. perfect tonic | 5–1 | 5–1 |

This introduces the first of Wesley's "author's signs" which one encounters in his hymn tunes: the decisive modulation to the relative minor. The motive for this is cadential variety and balance, and the effect is the infusion of a strong relative-minor tonality into the tune.

Associated with this, and equally frequent in Wesley, is the

8

modulation to the mediant minor—a progression of which John Stainer in the next generation was particularly fond. The most remarkable example of this, with an unusually rapid modulation to follow, is *Gweedore* (Example 40), a tune which, after long neglect, has found its place in several modern hymnals [AMR 397: HCS 193]. The cadential scheme here is as follows:

|  | modulating | to bass D |
|---|---|---|
| 1. imperfect tonic | 4–3 | 4–3 |
| 2. perfect tonic | 5–1 | 5–1 |
| 3. perfect mediant minor | 5–1 | 7–3 |
| 4. perfect subdominant | 5–1 | 1–4 |
| 5. imperfect tonic | 1–5 | 1–5 |
| 6. perfect tonic | 5–1 | 5–1 |

GWEEDORE [530]

Example 40

The effect is remarkable. There are (a) an unusually early tonic 5–1; (b) the violent modulation from F sharp minor to G major, and (c) the complete absence of a perfect-dominant cadence.

*Cornwall*, a very happy tune [AM 195] to "O love divine", one of his grandfather's hymns, combines the mediant minor modulation at the half-way point with a typical sequential movement in the fifth phrase, and again, the absence of a straight dominant cadence. A dramatic development on this device is the modulation to the mediant major, as in *Seraphim* (Example 41). This, we have already noticed in dealing with his anthems.

*Winscott* (Example 42) has a curious story; one needs to have the two versions of *Winscott* and the tune *Kerry* (Example 43) alongside one another for comparison.

Example 41
From *Seraphim* (1875)

*Winscott* and *Kerry* are both settings of Keble's "Sun of my soul". If we may presume that the earlier appearance of *Winscott* in *The European Psalmist* is the earlier version, then both it and the rather more colourful *Kerry* use the same device —a sudden modulation to the relative minor combined with a dramatic rise in the melody—to express the last line. Wesley must have had in mind especially the words "we lose ourselves in heaven above". There is no telling why he wrote the second version of *Winscott*. It is of course tame and conventional compared with the first, and it is sad, but hardly surprising, that on the whole it is the second which hymnal editors have preferred. There are two examples of these "second thoughts" in *The European Psalmist*, and the other is even more surprising. This is the tune *Orisons* (Example 45), possibly Samuel Sebastians' most remarkable experiment. The words "Abide with me",

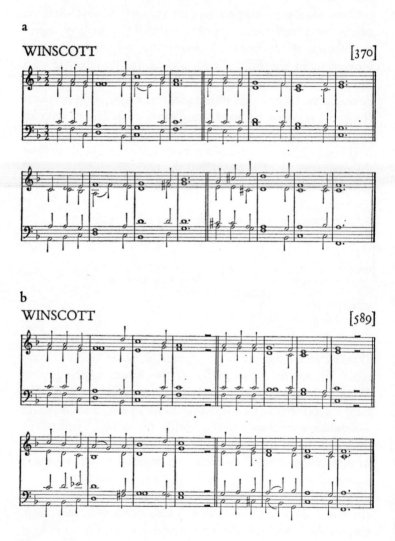

a

WINSCOTT                                                                                [370]

b

WINSCOTT                                                                                [589]

Example 42

KERRY                                                                    [500]

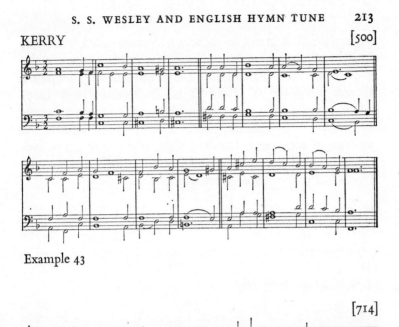

Example 43

[714]

Example 44

to which it is set, were, even by 1872, comparatively new. They were written probably in 1847, and their author would, when Samuel Sebastian was compiling his book, have been dead not much longer than Dean Alington or G. W. Briggs have been in 1968. His words made an immediate appeal to hymn singers, and their popularity was assured by their inclusion with Monk's tune in the first (1861) edition of *Hymns Ancient and Modern*. But Monk's tune *Eventide* was, in the 'sixties, neither the earliest tune written for the words nor by any general consent the inevitable one. Of hymn books published in that decade, Chope's *Congregational Hymn and Tune Book* (enlarged edition, 1862) set the hymn to a tune called *St Saviour*, by R. F. Smith, specially composed for the book; while the *Bristol Tune Book* (first edition, 1863), Steggall's *Hymns for the Church of England* (1865) and Turle's *Psalms and Hymns* (1867) all set it to the *Old 124th*: only the last of these three preserves that tune in its five-phrase version, requiring a repetition of the last line of each verse. It seems, then, that Monk's tune was competing chiefly with the excellent but usually bowdlerized Genevan tune for partnership with these words.

a

ORISONS                                                                          [539]

A-bide with me . . .

b
ORISONS    [540]

'Abide with me'

Example 45

It is clear that they appealed strongly to Samuel Sebastian, for he provides three different settings of them in *The European Psalmist*. One is an arrangement of a tune which he misascribes to Michael Wise and calls *Reliance* (EP 356: preserved at AMS 696). The true source of this tune is "W.L.'s *Collection of Tunes*, 1719" (see Frost, *Historical Companion*, p. 603), but Samuel Sebastian got it from *Harmonia Perfecta*, 1730. It is a demure and blameless tune, but not so distinguished as to prevent him from making an attempt himself at setting the words.

He made two attempts, one of which is *Orisons*. Which came first, we cannot possibly know; all that is evident is that the other one, *Refuge* (EP 580) is a commonplace E-flat tune maintaining the same restricted compass as *Reliance* (a fifth, with only one note rising to the sixth degree).

It seems reasonable to suppose that the version standing first in the source represents his original thoughts, and that the one standing second was a more congregational revision. The second version survived into the *Oxford Hymnal* (1908) and, surprisingly to historians, in *Congregational Praise* (1951). In both versions the tune is a profoundly personal utterance. Its melodic range is in the first version a minor sixth, in the second, a perfect fifth. If *Hereford* is a part-song, and *Wigan* a chorale, what musical form is this? The first version suggests a recitative in a cantata or oratorio (it is the only unison hymn tune that Samuel Sebastian ever wrote); the second, quite irresistibly, a string quartet playing in the style of the slow movement of Schubert's "Death and the Maiden". Only strings could do justice to those repeated chords. It seems that Samuel Sebastian was overcome by the personal poignancy of the words, and set them quite unequivocally as a solo. The other version in four parts simply reduces the harmonic demands which the earlier one would have made on people trying to sing it in four parts.

### WESLEY AND DYKES

In providing these settings for "Abide with me" Samuel Sebastian was striving after a good setting for words he admired, and whose current settings did not satisfy him. It appears indeed that few of what he would have called the "modern" composers gave him any satisfaction. *The European Psalmist* not only does not include more than a very few tunes by contemporaries, it includes very few of their names in its subscribers' list. And the one name whose absence stirs the imagination above all others is that of J. B. Dykes. In the 'sixties, Dykes was easily the leading composer in the new style—the part-song style derived from opera and popular ballad. Samuel Sebastian had no use whatever for this except when it was convenient to him to employ it in his own work.

There is no evidence that he and Dykes ever met. His life, apart from the sojourn at Leeds, was spent in the south-west of England within a hundred miles of the Wesleys' almost ancestral city of Bristol. Dykes lived in Durham, Wesley knew Sir Henry Baker, and got a subscription out of him; but Monk did not subscribe.

Looking over some of the tunes in the later part of *The European Psalmist*, the eye is sometimes caught by the words of a familiar hymn inscribed between the staves; and gradually it begins to appear that Samuel Sebastian was making a dead set at Dykes. For quite often the words are words which have been made familiar by Dykes's settings of them in the first two editions of *Hymns Ancient and Modern* (1861 and '68). Closer examination confirms this. In the first edition of *Hymns Ancient and Modern* there are seven tunes of Dykes, of which six have become universally popular despite all attempts to dislodge some of them. They are:

*Hollingside*, to "Jesu, lover of my soul"
*Horbury*, to "Nearer, my God to Thee"
*Nicaea*, to "Holy, Holy, Holy"
*Melita*, to "Eternal Father strong to save"
*St Aelred*, to "Fierce raged the tempest"
*St Cuthbert*, to "Our blest Redeemer"

The seventh is *Dies irae*, to "Day of wrath", an anthem-like setting which fortunately falls outside our terms of reference and criticism. Now in the later part of *The European Psalmist*, there are tunes to five of those six—the exception being "Eternal Father"—and there is also a tune to "Day of Wrath". Since Samuel Sebastian scattered his original tunes all over his book, but provides a large block of new tunes near the end, the supposition that he wrote the later ones at a late stage is at least plausible. If he did, then his disapproval of Dykes obviously follows. We can go on to observe that he provides

settings for several more hymns which Dykes set in 1868—
namely, "Lead, kindly light", "Fierce raged the tempest",
"Hark, hark, my soul", "O Paradise, O Paradise", and "Sun
of my soul". We have to note that Dykes's tunes to the last
two of these are alternatives in 1868; and we must also say that
the Samuel Sebastian tune to "Jesu lover of my soul" is an
arrangement (from Spohr, surprisingly enough). But we may
reasonably guess that Dykes seemed to call for special treatment
by the choleric maestro at Gloucester. See Examples 46–52.

Not only Dykes, of course: Monk himself came under
censure. We have referred to "Abide with me". There were
also "Christian, seek not yet repose", "God of mercy, God of

COMMUNION                                                    [524]

'Nearer, my God, to thee'

Example 46

TRINITY [454]

'Holy, Holy, Holy'

Example 47

WHITBY [610]

'Fierce raged the tempest'

Example 48

DOVER                                          [423]
'Our blest Redeemer'

Example 49

REFUGE                                         [580]
'Abide with me'

Example 50

PATMOS                                         [569]
'Lead, kindly light'

Example 51

## SUPPLICATION [586]

'Lord of our life and God of our salvation'

Example 52

grace", "God who madest earth and heaven" and "Lord, in this Thy mercies' day", all of which appeared in 1861, and all of which Samuel Sebastian re-set in his collection.

Samuel Sebastian would of course set only those words which appealed to him, and seems to have left alone hymns which had already had good tunes before his contemporaries tackled them. So when you set aside seasonal and occasional hymns in which he would have had little interest, and hymns with serviceable earlier tunes, and when you then note how many hymns in the later part of *The European Psalmist* are referred to *Hymns Ancient and Modern*, you cannot escape the conclusion that Vaughan Williams himself hardly took less satisfaction in it than did Samuel Sebastian.

The reason for this hardly needs stating if we look back over what we have already said. To Samuel Sebastian, the musicians of *Hymns Ancient and Modern* (and indeed of all the hymnals that appeared in the 'sixties) were hardly better than ignorant provincials. They wrote nothing but hymns. Monk and Dykes were professional hymn-tune writers, nothing more. Neither could have explored even the fairly limited field of music which Samuel Sebastian made his own. To him, their tunes were tedious and unenterprising.

But he hardly ever won. In popular esteem, hardly any of his tunes stood a chance against Monk and Dykes, or later Sullivan and Stainer. (He wrote a tune to "Onward Christian soldiers", 585 in *The European Psalmist*, a total disaster of a tune which required the repetition of the chorus and then the repetition of its last two lines, in every verse: as surely a non-starter as Sullivan's *St Gertrude* was a winner.) His single contribution to *Hymns Ancient and Modern* before his death was *Aurelia*, which appeared in the 1868 edition. Certain other tunes of his have achieved limited popularity since his death, but that is the only one in the accepted canon of "Everyman's hymn tunes", to which Monk has contributed several, and Dykes such a remarkable number.

The point is that Samuel Sebastian, as nobody before him

but as so many after him, usually packed too much music into his tunes. They were, in many instances, untidily packed. Often, when he wrote a really good tune, by musicians' standards, it made its appeal long after his death to musicians who in turn failed to capture the attention of the hymn-singing public as a whole. The best example of this is Basil Harwood (1859–1950), that very faithful musician of the Church of England, whose contribution to the history of church music has turned out to be so limited in comparison with his labour and output. Harwood (for whom see *The Music of Christian Hymnody*, pp. 135f.) wrote many hymn tunes, almost all of which are too full of subtlety to stand up to the demands of congregational singing. The two of his which are well known correspond almost exactly to Wesley's *Aurelia* and *Harewood*. They are *Thornbury*, which is now universally sung to "Thy hand, O God, has guided" [EH 545] and *Luckington*, often sung to "Let all the world in every corner sing" [M 5]. It is roughly true to say that people who know *Aurelia* know *Thornbury*, and the smaller number who know *Harewood* know *Luckington*.

Again, Harwood edited the *Oxford Hymn Book* in 1908, primarily for the rarefied and pedantic demands of college chapels. It is a book of great literary distinction, and its music pages are packed with Samuel Sebastian Wesley. On page after page you come across a tune of surprising sensitiveness and musicianly wit, and you hardly know whether it is by Wesley or by Harwood: it certainly could not be any other composer. But the *Oxford Hymn Book* has had a brief and precarious life, and the parochialization of the college chapels in their ethos of worship has edged it away towards the periphery of hymnology.

That is the kind of thing that has always happened to Samuel Sebastian's hymn tunes. A selection appears here, another selection there. The *Moravian Liturgy and Hymns* of 1914 included a great deal of his work, but the incentive towards this would have come from the Germanic associations both of the Moravian community and of Wesley's idiom. Even the name of Wesley will have had some influence there. Otherwise, the Wesley tunes are, with the exceptions noted, in the outer circles of public hymnody. Allowance must be made for the unfortunate fact that he enjoyed setting his grandfather's hymns to tunes which, on the whole, Methodists did not take to. This meant the writing of many tunes in metres which only Charles Wesley could use successfully, tunes useless for any other purpose, and tunes composed by a musician who disliked few things less than the Methodist idiom of his time.

To write a good hymn tune, a composer must have an especially assured touch in the handling of emotion. The twentieth century is teaching us this. Reaction against cheap nineteenth-century emotion has produced a crop of very learned and tedious tunes which people have simply refused to sing. What the Victorians taught us was that emotion is nothing to be ashamed of; what we had to recover from was the conviction that every kind of emotion was fit for public exposure in music. But the really successful hymn writer knows not only how to restrain his expression of emotion, but exactly when to open the ports and put it on.

There are only two devices for expressing and arousing emotion available to the hymn-tune writer; harmony (which should also be counterpoint) and melody. Rhythmical devices for drama are impossible in a composition that has to be performed several times in quick succession. Samuel Sebastian lived at the time when the new harmonic vocabulary was fully developed, but still relatively newly developed; and where he is most chromatic, he is also thoroughly contrapuntal. The movement of the voice parts for example in the first phrase of *Atonement* (Example 53a), when compared with those in the fourth phrase of Dykes's *Lux benigna* (Example 53b) is thoroughly musicianly.

The juxtaposition of keys, to which we have already referred, is an intellectual rather than an emotional device; his tunes which employ it make special demands on the singer rather

Example 53
a  From *Atonement*, by Samuel Sebastian Wesley
b  From *Lux Benigna*, by John Dykes

than conceding anything to his emotional outreach. Therefore, on the whole, when Samuel Sebastian uses chromatic harmony, he underpins it with good counterpoint and the result is a satisfactory piece of music. But what of melody? Melody is as effective an arouser of emotions as harmony, and is much older. It is not really the harmony of Dykes's famous *"Liebes-träume*-type" tunes that gives them their emotional effect, but their melody (on which, see *The Music of Christian Hymnody*, pp. 264, 266). The harmony merely conforms; altering it produces musical confusion.

Nothing could be further from Samuel Sebastian's taste than the *"Liebesträume"* style. Indeed, in his melodic invention,

KENSINGTON [1st half]                    [446]

Example 54
From *The European Psalmist*, 446

austerity often becomes surliness, when it does not slip into platitude. A particularly vexatious example of melodic failure is *Kensington* (Example 54).

One feels that he rarely indulges himself melodically when writing hymns—although *Hereford* [AM 329] may well be a conspicuous exception to that. What he cannot resist occasionally is the tell-tale "arpeggio" phrase which we noticed in his anthems (compare Example 55 with Example 15). It is just as much an "author's signature" in the hymns as in the anthems.

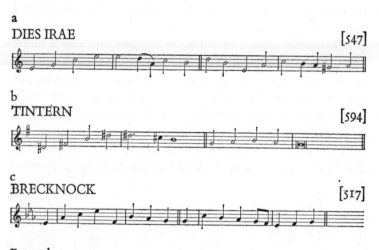

a
DIES IRAE                                    [547]

b
TINTERN                                      [594]

c
BRECKNOCK                                    [517]

Example 55
Samuel Sebastian's "signature" again (see also Example 15), from *The European Psalmist*

Virtually nobody else uses it quite as he does—to lift a tune off the ground after a somewhat sticky beginning. (Melodies founded on the common chord are familiar enough in the nineteenth century.) The major-key tunes of the Welsh composers often show this tendency, such as *St Denio*, *Ffigysbren* and *Gwalchmai*, and Smart's *Regent Square* is a good example in the English style. But the Welsh are usually content with the triad, and both they and the English often use zig-zag motion. Steggall's *Christ Church* [EH 411: M 653] is one of the few English tunes to make use of the full and uninterrupted ascent of the common chord. As we saw in the anthems, this device in Samuel Sebastian is always associated with some special emotional tension in the words he is setting.

Samuel Sebastian's settings of his grandfather's hymns are, of course, prominent in his collection. He referred for the words to the 1831 edition of *Wesley's Hymns* (that is, the second revision of the original book, and the collection on which the 1874 revision was to be based). A reference to Appendix I will indicate what his contribution was to Wesleyan praise; close examination will reveal one or two places where he brought his severe musical criticism to bear on traditional Wesleyan hymnody: for example, in his provision of a tune designed to dislodge *Helmsley* [EH 7: M 264] from its association with "Lo, He comes". One or two of his best efforts appear in this list, notably *Bolton* and *Cornwall*. But in the case of *Cornwall*, and in that of *Hereford*, although both tunes are at the present time associated with hymns of Charles Wesley, the associations are not original; *Hereford* goes originally with the middle section of a metrical version of Psalm 103, and *Cornwall* with a much more virile and majectic hymn than "O Love divine, how sweet thou art", its present association. The composer probably did not see either tune in the devotionally contemplative light which their modern collocations throw on them.

The greater number of the tunes in *The European Psalmist* are taken from other sources than the composer's inventiveness. Many are harmonized by him. Among these is Handel's *Gopsal*, which he altered considerable—nowadays, one wonders why. These arrangements repay study by the specialist, but there is only one of them to which we must finally draw attention here. This is the remarkable tune *Eltham*, which he found in *Harmonia Perfecta*, a book which he must have especially treasured. That collection was published in 1730 by

Nathaniel Gawthorne for the use of the congregation at the King's Weigh House Chapel, London. Among much else that is interesting, there is this *Eltham*, set to Isaac Watts's paraphrase of I Corinthians 13, beginning, "Had I the tongues of Greeks and Jews" (Example 56).

ELTHAM                                    Harmonia Perfecta, 1730

Example 56 a

The tune is, musically, a collector's piece. Hymnal editors have been shy of it. It was virtually lost to sight between 1730 and the day when Samuel Sebastian rediscovered it. Then his harmonization of it lay in *The European Psalmist* until the editors of *Hymns Ancient and Modern* included it in their revision of 1904 (no. 322). In this version, it has never appeared since, and the suppression of the 1904 *Hymns Ancient and Modern* caused it to be almost forgotten again. It was included in the *Irish Church Hymnal* of 1919 (but omitted from the 1960 revision), *Congregational Praise* included it in 1951, and the *Anglican Hymnal* set it, in the same harmonization, to the same words, in 1965.

But it had not in earlier days escaped the notice of Sir Hubert Parry, who, in 1914, published as one of his *Three Chorale-Fantasias* for organ a prelude on it, entitled "When I survey the wondrous cross", which J. A. Fuller-Maitland described (in *The Music of Parry and Stanford*, 1934) as "a worthy companion to the 8th *Prelude* of Bach's '48'". The organ piece is as rarely heard, probably, as the hymn tune, but it is perhaps Parry's most perfect composition for the instrument.

However, it is structurally a very remarkable tune. The melody (which earlier we compared with *Invitation*, p. 36) is built up on the striding theme announced by its first four notes: this phrase appears twice more in the melody and once in the bass. Further, its second, third and fourth lines all finish with another four-note phrase sounded each time at a different pitch. Now the third phrase of any four-line long-metre tune is usually the test of its composer's faculties for construction and continuity. But in this particular case, there are special problems. The highest note of the tune appears at the beginning of this line; the rest of it is concerned with the business of getting the tonality from that of the dominant to the subdominant. Given eight notes, this need not be too difficult; you can take the orthodox route via the tonic. But the anonymous composer of this tune has made everything difficult for himself by using up his last four notes in a decisive subdominant cadence phrase, and by insisting on keeping his first four notes in the dominant key; so the two tonalities are brought face to face with each other, and there is no way of negotiating the gap between the two tonalities without producing an effect of hidden octaves—that is, of acute discomfort. The composer originally achieved his end by that subtle imitation of phrase (a) in the bass part, making his fourth chord a modulating chord. But this was at the expense of writing a very athletic bass, dropping a ninth in three notes, and of introducing a modulation on the fourth chord which the melody does not in itself imply.

The problem, then, is how to organize the harmony so that there is no uncomfortable false relation, and no sense of "hidden octaves". In the two subsidiary examples given we note how Kitson, in the *Irish Hymnal*, was content simply to invert the parts so as to keep the original bass, while Eric Thiman, in *Congregational Praise*, rewrote the harmony to give a smooth bass line, but produced a modified false relation between the treble leading note on chord 2 and the bass note in chord 4 (in this case, D sharp against D). Not a word could be said in criticism of two such eminent masters of harmony; yet it is this sense of false relation which makes ordinary singers think of a tune as "difficult" or "wayward".

All this evidently occurred to Samuel Sebastian. Harmonizing the tune in F sharp minor, he decided that there is no

ELTHAM                                                    S.S.W. [68]

Example 56 b

Kitson

Example 56 c

Thiman

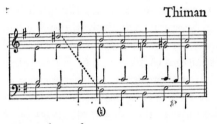

Example 56 d

possibility of a modulation via the tonic from the C sharp major at the end of the preceding line. We are still in C sharp major until the B-minor tonality faces us. So he takes a short cut, and the fourth and fifth chords in this line produce a progression which is absolutely unknown in the whole of hymnody—at least so far as published tunes go—until the time of Vaughan Williams. The chords of C sharp major and E minor are juxtaposed without compromise; we are moving, as it were, from four sharps to two sharps via one sharp, not via three. It is about the only progression that is not to be found in Bach (this is no doubt because Bach did not have this kind of angular tune to harmonize, and had he had it, he would have found a way through by using passing notes).

Even in secular music one searches long before finding this progression in the nineteenth century, and when one does find it, it is used for some other musical purpose. The passage from the fourth to the fifth phrases of Vaughan Williams's *Down Ampney* [EH 152: M 273, 1906] has something of the same flavour, and the late romantics, such as Rachmaninoff, were much given to experimenting with progressions leading direct from one chord to another with no implied linking note (for example, the C-sharp-minor to F major progression at the end of the eighteenth variation in the Rachmaninoff-Paganini *Variations*).

The secret of making an issue of false relation rather than using devious means to avoid it was one which Samuel Sebastian seems to have stumbled on here, but which he never used elsewhere. I hazard the guess that, although it has no parallel in Bach, Samuel Sebastian had Bach in mind when he wrote it. It is, as it were, in the bold spirit of Bach. And, like Bach's remarkable solutions of harmonic problems posed by the tunes he arranged, it is thoroughly congregational; a sharp shock, substituted for an uneasy evasion, is exactly what congregations can take most easily—that is the secret of *Down Ampney*. Therefore, it is remarkable that those few modern editors who have used this tune have not taken over Samuel Sebastian's harmonization of it. The compass is wide, and that third line begins very high: it is an uncompromising piece of work. But in this version it becomes entirely viable.

It would be idle to pretend that Samuel Sebastian's judgment was always as shrewd as this. Some of his arrangements would strike an educated modern reader as hazardous, or even ham-fisted. Some of his original tunes are remarkably dull, and he shows little sense of how to rearrange for modern use any tune much older than *Eltham*. Some of his tunes are prickly and positively unpleasant. But where they are disagreeable to the ear, they represent that principle of dissent in him which made him sometimes an uncompanionable person, but none the less a brave and effective opponent of that supine conformity in which English church music was doing its best to suffocate itself.

# 13

# *A Postscript and a Conclusion*

The only musical form in which Samuel Wesley and his son
Samuel Sebastian composed and to which we have as yet made
no reference is the Anglican chant. Since this essay appears in
a series of books dealing with English church music, and it is
improbable that any of my learned and distinguished colleagues
will find space in which to deal with this especially nineteenth-
century subject, a word or two about it here will perhaps not
be out of place.

Both Samuel and his son contributed to the literature of
Anglican psalmody, and both happen to have written chants
which are still very well known. One of the accidents that make
it so difficult to write about Anglican chants is the fact that they,
are not named. I once suggested, not meaning any frivolity,
that they should be rounded up and given some of the less
impossible-sounding names from the Old Testament. Not
Jezebel, perhaps, or Ehud, but Elijah, Melchizedek, and Ruth
would surely have sounded well enough. As it is, we must
speak of *Attwood in D*, and then our reader can, in these days
of transposition down, hardly know whether we mean *Attwood
in E* which we happen to know in D, or *Attwood in C*, which
has, in modern psalters, been transposed down from D. It is
all very perplexing and inconvenient.

None the less, this is a perfectly serious subject, with which it
is not in the least out of place to deal in a study of church music.

The Anglican chant is a natural development from the plainsong tone, demanded by the evolution of music from rhythmic plainsong towards metrical melody. The "Gregorian tones", now so familiar, but in the days of the Wesleys virtually only known to Catholics, provide an entirely satisfactory variety of very simple tunes for singing to the psalms. The eight intonations with their various endings provide, with the addition of *Tonus Peregrinus*, a repertory of forty-two tunes, of which in the church tradition preserved in the English *Manual of Plainsong* (edited most recently by J. H. Arnold, 1952) about thirty are in use for the psalms and canticles.

It is beside the point here to argue the merits of Anglican chants over against this traditional repertory of plainsong. Some deplore the fact that the Anglican chant was ever invented, but it was invented, and we are still living with it. Its immediate source is the descant to the plainsong tone which choirs came to employ in the days of polyphony. Composers like Tallis and Byrd composed varied settings for choral use, normally to be sung to every other verse. Perhaps the most celebrated of all such settings is the fantastic *Miserere* of Allegri, for so long a closely-guarded secret in the Pope's Chapel, illicitly noted down by Mozart, and now generally published and known—but quite unsingable by any choir which does not possess a solo treble who can find and sustain a high C. Allegri's descant is a double decoration of Tone II Ending I, always associated with Psalm 51, which gives a fairly normal choral setting for the second, and a nine-part florid setting for the fourth verse of each four-verse group.

The honour of having composed the first piece in Anglican chant form must go to William Byrd (1543–1623), who wrote a continuous, non-plainsong setting of Psalm 114 that is today often heard in cathedrals. It is a five-part piece, setting two verses at a time, with reciting note and mediations exactly as they appear in later chants.

This was, it seems, the only double chant in print for about a century after its publication. All plainsong tones are, of course, "single"; they set one verse at a time. The double chant was not taken up again until the eighteenth century had begun. How it came to be is a mystery. People say (but nobody can prove historically) that it occurred to a cathedral organist to run two single chants together and thus provide variety. If this happened at all, it will have happened in the days of the Restoration, for even "composed" single chants did not appear until then. Pelham Humfrey's famous two-note tune to Psalm 150 was certainly one of the earliest to be written, and Humfrey's dates are 1647–74. However this may have been, among the first double chants are *Robinson in E flat* (Sibthorp, *Anglican Chant Book*, 14) and *Flintoft in F (or G) minor* (Sibthorp, 46). Robinson (1682–1762) was organist of Westminster Abbey, and Flintoft, who probably devised his chant out of an old long psalm tune from Allison's *Psalter* of 1599, was a canon of the same Abbey and died in 1727.

During the eighteenth century, a good many chants were added to the repertory, as the dates in Sibthorp's excellent index show. The demand was natural. Puritan opinion reacted against plainsong for political reasons. Where psalms were not sung to Anglican chants they had to be read. And music was well settled into the metrical form. We must suppose that the singing of these chants would have been, throughout the eighteenth and nineteenth centuries, such as to make the hair rise on any R.C.S.M. Commissioner's head: "speech rhythm" appeared only in the earlier twentieth century with Walford Davies (1869–1941). Anglican chants were flexible hymn tunes, but only part of them was flexible at all. This must have been so, because composers began to think of them as short metrical pieces, and to introduce dotted notes into the mediation, and flourishes into the reciting notes. Many famous chants have nowadays, bowing to the demands of speech rhythm, to omit these metrical comments, and sometimes they suffer considerably as music because of this. The omission of a dotted passing note is not necessarily the omission of a disposable ornament.

Not only did composers treat the chant as a metrical form and expect their choirs to sing it so: they treated it as an opportunity to express such shades of emotion as the psalms seemed to call for. During the Romantic age (to which as we have seen the Wesleys on the whole contributed little), chants became highly chromatic and harmonically convoluted. Chants were also made out of famous melodies in the classics. Living memory preserves one by Stainer, based on the slow movement of Beethoven's eighth piano Sonata (op. 13), and another devised by Goss out of the *Andante* from the same composer's seventh Symphony.

The ingenuity of composers in packing music into fourteen bars has turned out to be unlimited. And while this has obviously led to some forms of excess which strike the modern ear as comical, it has also uncovered unexpected gifts in minor composers. Barnby, for example, who can hardly be said to have put together even a hymn tune which stood up for more than two generations, wrote two or three Anglican chants which are perfect miniatures (Sibthorp 73 and 150, for example —in E and A minor), and Stainer at least once reached the top flight, in his chant in E minor (Example 57).

Stainer

Example 57

The composition of Anglican chants has not been halted by the twentieth-century reaction towards plainsong. Nor have such devices as that of Josef Gélineau seriously threatened it. There is a bewildering variety of psalters, musically edited with all degrees of sensitiveness, for congregational use, but it can generally be said that there is a reasonable repertory of well known chants which the ordinary parish-church congregation can stumble through. It is rare for any addition to be made to these. But in the cathedrals, the psalms are sung to all manner of tunes; there are one or two where you cannot attend evensong on any evening of the month without hearing a chant that is new to you unless you are very well-read in the repertory. And whereas a hundred years ago, before the publication (1885) of the *Cathedral Psalter*, it was normal for all the psalms for the morning or evening to be sung to the same chant, and then often a single chant (a practice against which, as we have seen, Samuel Sebastian Wesley protested), nowadays the changing of chants once or even more often within the course of a psalm is a quite normal custom among cathedral choirs. In some circles, the form of the chant is altered by the omission of a bar in one or more of its parts, to fit the rhythm of a particular psalm: Dr Thalben-Ball's *Temple Psalter* and the *Broadcast Psalter* both experiment in this way, sometimes with good effect.

The Wesleys' contribution to the literature was made at just about the half way point of its development. We have already seen that Samuel senior was capable of writing chants which presupposed a wide range in the treble voice, and clearly were intended only for choral singing. Probably neither of the composers ever heard a chant of his performed congregationally. But the testimony of Sibthorp is that they left a useful handful that have come into congregational use. He has three from Samuel, in E flat (originally F), no. 254, in F minor (originally A minor), 93, and the very well known one in G, 119, which we reproduce in Example 58a. Samuel Sebastian contributes four to the same collection, two of which are double chants, in D minor (194) and another in F (75). One or two others are at Examples 58b and c. What Sibthorp missed, or despised, was Samuel Sebastian's very evocative chant in F sharp minor from *The European Psalmist*.

a                                                S. Wesley [707]

b                                                S. S. Wesley [702]

c                                                S. S. Wesley [710]

Example 58
Chants from *The European Psalmist*

## CONCLUSION

It remains only to gather up our judgments of the Wesleys
and try to present them coherently. In the end, it still remains
important that they were Wesleys. The fact that they came
from this strange, highly-strung, brilliant and wayward family
affected their careers and their music profoundly. In Charles
junior, the conflict between the evangelical Puritanism of his
parents and the musical culture they came to favour was enough
almost to extinguish his creative talent. His brother Samuel

may have been a disappointing composer, but no disappoint-
ment felt by any onlooker can match a hundredth part of that
which informed his own life, which never achieved enough
spiritual or intellectual momentum to become the origin of
continuously creative work. Samuel Sebastian, strangely born,
eminently gifted, evinces in his music more than a trace of his
stormy temperament and restless career. Once again, he comes
early to his best work, and it vanishes into insignificance well
before the end. This is to judge them only as composers; so
much else that Samuel and Sebastian achieved has turned out to
be historically important. Both, in their way, had the fighting
spirit of John plus the aesthetic talent of Charles the elder.
Both were deservedly famous as organists. Both battled against
different forms of philistinism.

So the Wesley generations gather up in themselves the
characteristics of their time, and reflect them, as it were, by
contrast: very much as John and Charles his brother reacted
against the religious dimness of the English eighteenth century,
so Samuel and his son reacted against the musical dimness of
the nineteenth. But whereas John left a great structure of piety,
and Charles the elder a great structure of hymnody, the two
church musicians were dragged down into the stream of music
history, and lived, not as the great seniors had done, above it,
but wholly within it. Charles, the musician, let it sweep him
along. The other two swam against the tide as long as they
could. And now perhaps the ordinary church-goer knows
nothing of their music except an Anglican chant, one of
Samuel Sebastian's least meritable hymn tunes, and two or
three of his less magnificent anthems. The story has a dying
fall, but it was worth telling, even thus imperfectly. There is
always something to be said for men who keep the genius of a
great name alive in unexpected ways. And I think that there
were many at the time who would have been capable of saying
to those two doughty dissenters in religion and music, Samuel
and Samuel Sebastian—and saying with affection tempering
exasperation—"I fancy you will be a Methodist".

OLDHAM

Example 59
*Oldham*, from *The Psalmist*, in an older style

NEWCASTLE

Example 60
*Newcastle*, arranged from Handel's Minuet from *Berenice*

9

CHRISTCHURCH

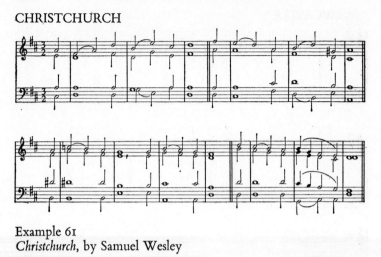

Example 61
*Christchurch,* by Samuel Wesley

PHILIPPI

Example 62
*Philippi,* by Samuel Wesley

SYRACUSE

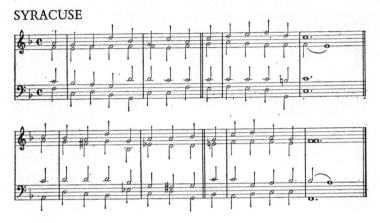

Example 63
*Syracuse,* by Samuel Wesley

WALWORTH

Example 64
*Walworth,* by Samuel Wesley

WEYMOUTH

Example 65
*Weymouth,* by Samuel Wesley

PHILADELPHIA

Example 66
*Philadelphia*, taken from "a Gregorian tone", by Samuel Wesley

# APPENDIX I

| Name | Source | EH | AMR | AMS |
|------|--------|-----|-----|-----|
| AURELIA | K64 | 400 | 255 | 215 |
| ALLELUIA | P72 | | 399 | 316 |
| ALMSGIVING | H72 | | 204 | 273 |
| ASHBURTON | K64 | | | |
| BRECKNOCK | P72 | | 468 | 777 |
| BUDE | P72 | | | |
| COLCHESTER | P72 | | 90 | 720 |
| COMMUNION | P72 | | | 277 |
| CORNWALL | P72 | | 195 | |
| EPIPHANY | K64 | | | 643 |
| ENGEDI | P72 | | 184 | 492 |
| FAITH | K64 | | | |
| GRÂCE DIEU | P72 | | | |
| GROSVENOR | P72 | | | 717 |
| GWEEDORE | P72 | | 394 | |
| HAREWOOD | H39 | | 243 | 239 |
| HAWARDEN | P72 | 496 | | |
| HEREFORD | P72 | | 329 | 698 |
| HORNSEA | P72 | A28 | | 499 |
| HOUGHTON LE SPRING | K64(1860) | | | 318 |
| MEMORIA | H72 | | | |
| MORNING | P72 | | | |
| ORISONS | P72 | | | |
| PATMOS | P72 | | | |
| RADFORD | C74 | | | |
| ST MICHAEL NEW | P72 | 244 | | 752 |
| SERAPHIM | S75 | | | 550 |
| WETHERBY | P72 | | | |
| WESTON | P72 | | | |
| WIGAN | P72 | | 212 | 212 |
| WIMBLEDON | K64 | | | |
| WINSCOTT (a) | P72 | | | |
| (b) | | | | |
| WRESTLING JACOB | P72 | | 343 | 774 |

[1] Explanation of symbols, p. 249.

| CP | M | B | CH | BBC | HCS |
|----|----|----|----|-----|-----|
| 254 | 701 | 263 | 205 | 184 | 174 |
|  | 267 | 168 | 138 |  |  |
|  |  |  | 392 |  |  |
|  |  |  | 515 |  |  |
| 496 | 605 | 349 | 332 |  |  |
| 428 |  | 65 |  |  |  |
|  |  |  |  | 87 |  |
|  | 365 |  |  |  |  |
|  |  |  | 536 |  |  |
|  |  |  |  | 199 | 208 |
| 431 | 702 | 267 | 458 | 258 | 179 |
|  |  | 353 | 336 |  |  |
| 438 |  | 519 |  | 362 |  |
|  | 773 |  | 322 |  |  |
|  |  |  | 374 |  |  |
| 622 |  |  |  |  |  |
|  |  |  | 568 |  |  |
|  | 667 |  | 289 |  |  |
| 225 | 217 |  | 513 |  | 170 |
|  |  |  | 452 |  |  |
|  |  |  | 539 |  |  |
| 556 |  |  |  |  |  |
|  |  |  | 338 |  |  |
|  | 339 | 767 | 416 |  |  |

# APPENDIX IA

HYMN TUNES BY SAMUEL SEBASTIAN WESLEY APPEARING
IN THREE ENGLISH HYMNALS PUBLISHED 1904–14
(excluding those named in Appendix I)[2]

| Name | Source | AMH | OH | MOR |
|---|---|---|---|---|
| ACHILL | P72 | | | 162 |
| ARRAN | K64 | | 58 | 178 |
| ATONEMENT | P72 | | 127 | |
| BATH NEW | K64 | | 178 | 205 |
| BEDMINSTER | P72 | | 317 | 282 |
| BOLTON | P72 | 494 | 261 | |
| BRIXTON | P72 | | 223 | |
| CALVARY | P72 | | | 778 |
| CELESTIA | P72 | | | 438 |
| CLEVEDON | P72 | | 41 | |
| DIES IRAE | P72 | | 42 | |
| EPWORTH | P72 | | 216 | 204 |
| ELLINGHAM | K64 | | 25 | |
| EXCELSIOR | P72 | | | 346 |
| GILEAD | P72 | | | 54 |
| GILBOA | P72 | | 22 | 372 |
| GLASTONBURY | P72 | | 141 | |
| HAMPTON | H39 | 141 | | |
| HAVERHILL | P72 | | | 742 |
| HAWKRIDGE | P72 | | | 378 |
| HYMNARY 613 | H72 | 444 | | |
| KENSINGTON | P72 | | 299 | |
| KILKHAMPTON | P72 | | | 262 |
| LEINTWARDINE | P72 | | | 375 |
| MARA | P72 | | | 234 |
| MARTYRS | P72 | | 105 | |
| MORNING | P72 | | 3 | |
| PROVIDENCE | P72 | | 146 | |
| REFUGE | P72 | | 144 | |
| SENNEN | P72 | | | 279 |
| STORNOWAY | K64 | 178 | | |
| TIME | P72 | | 32 | |
| WHITBY | P72 | | | 93 |

[2] Explanation of symbols, p. 249.

# Symbols Used in Appendix
# I and Ia

AMR: *Hymns Ancient and Modern*, Revised Edition, 1950
AMS: *Hymns Ancient and Modern*, Standard Edition, 1922
B: *Baptist Hymn Book*, 1962
BBC: *BBC Hymn Book*, 1951
CP: *Congregational Praise*, 1951
EH: *English Hymnal*, 1933
HCS: *Hymns for Church and School*, 1964
M: *Methodist Hymn Book*, 1933

(Sources)

K39: C. D. Hackett, *National Psalmist*, 1839
H64: C. Kemble and S.S.W., *A Selection of Psalms and Hymns*, 1864
P72: *The European Psalmist*, 1872
C74: *Church Hymns with Tunes*, 1874
S75: *The Song of Praise*, 1875

# APPENDIX II

Three of the hymns composed by Charles Wesley, this excellent poet and able divine, were set to music by the celebrated George Friedrich Handel, a copy of whose settings is now before me. The music (full sized) was published in 1826, by Samuel Wesley, son of the above, with the following title page:

The Fitzwilliam Music

Never Published

Three Hymns

The words by the late Rev. Charles Wesley, A.M., of Christ Church College, Oxon; and set to music by George Friederich Handel, faithfully transcribed from his Autobiography in the Library of the Fitzwilliam Museum, Cambridge, by Samuel Wesley, and now very respectfully presented to the Wesleyan Society at large, etc. The hymns are:

    I. "The Invitation"

        Sinners, obey the Gospel word—
        Haste to the supper of my Lord, etc.

    II. "Desiring to Love"

        O, Love divine, how sweet thou art—
        When shall I find my longing heart
        All taken up by thee?

    III. "On the Resurrection"

        Rejoice, the Lord is King,
        Your Lord and King adore,
        Mortals, give thanks and sing
        And triumph evermore.

The form of the music is that of an air with accompaniment for the Pianoforte or Organ. The first and third will be found in Mercer's Hymn Book, arranged in short score for four verses; the one being called "Cannons" and the other, "Handel's 148th".[1] The harmonies

---

[1] The hymn book referred to is *Church Psalter and Hymn Book*, 1858, edited by William Mercer. Both tunes are used three times in the book. That which we now call *Gopsal* is amended in its melody, and *Cannons* in its rhythm.

of both, and the melody of the latter are slightly altered. The compiler of Mercer's Hymns appears to have obtained them from Havergal's Collection.[1]

The best account of these original tunes of Handel's set to Wesley's hymn is that given in the *Methodist Magazine* (XLIX, 1826, p. 817) by Samuel, the son of the Rev. Charles Wesley, which is as follows:

"I take the liberty of addressing you upon a subject which appears likely to prove both of interest and utility, especially to the Wesleyan Connection. Having been honoured by the University of Cambridge with a grace, authorizing me to transcribe and publish any portions of the very valuable musical manuscript in the Library of the Fitzwilliam Museum—of which privilege I have lately and assiduously availed myself—I was very agreeably surprised at meeting with the three hymn tunes (most noble melodies), composed by our great Handel (in his own handwriting), and set to words of my good father—stanzas well known for many long years by the veteran members of the Society. You well know, Sir, that the order of verse in the first hymn is four lines of eight syllables in each strophe, that of the second hymn six lines in each strophe—four of eight syllables and the other two of six; and that of the third, six lines also in each strophe, the former consisting of six syllables, the two latter of eight. The said melodies therefore are correctly applicable to every hymn in any of these three metres; and consequently will be a valuable acquisition in all congregations where similar metres are in use. The style of the music is alike simple, solemn, and easy of execution to all who can sing or play a plain psalm tune; it were therefore a culpable neglect to withhold from publicity articles so appropriate to the purpose of choral congregational devotion.

"With a full persuasion of this, I have resolved to print forthwith these combined relics of a real poet and a great musician, hoping that what will probably appear to giddy thinkers, a mere furtuitous coincidence (but which I firmly believe to be the result of a much higher causality) will be ultimately effective of much good, by the union of what delights the ear with that which benefits the soul. The plates are already engraven, and the three hymns will be inscribed to the Wesleyan Society. I wish the whole Society may be convinced that I never felt so truly gratified from my knowledge of music, as when I discovered this most unexpected coincidence;

---

[1] No. Havergal's *Old Church Psalmody* prints a differently altered version of *Gopsal*—that which survived (if anyone cares to look it up) in the *Congregational Hymnary* (1916), no. 137 ii.

and I cannot anticipate a greater musical gratification (no, not even at the York or Birmingham Festivals!) than that of hearing chanted by a thousand voices, and in strains of Handel—'Rejoice! the Lord is King!'

"That the son of Charles, and the nephew of John Wesley, happened to be the first individual who discovered this manuscript after a lapse of seventy or eighty years, is certainly a circumstance of no common curiosity; and if the statement I have made be considered of sufficient consequence to engage your attention to a publication—slight only in price—I cannot reasonably doubt that abundance of good, to the best of causes will accrue."

The circumstances which in all probability led Handel to set Mr Wesley's hymns to music are this stated by Miss Wesley:

"Mr Rich was the proprietor of the Covent Garden Theatre, which he offered to Handel to perform his oratorios in, when he had incurred the displeasure of the opera party. Mrs Rich was one of the first who attended the West Street Chapel, and was impressed with deep seriousness by the preaching of my dear father, who became her intimate friend; upon which she gave up the stage entirely, and suffered much reproach from her husband, who insisted on her appearing again upon it. She said if she did appear on the stage again it would be to bear her public testimony against it. Handel taught Mr Rich's daughters; and it was thus that my father and mother used to hear his fine performances. By the intimacy of Mr and Mrs Rich with Handel, he was doubtless led to set to music these hymns of my father, which are now, with the tunes annexed to then, in the collection at Cambridge, whence Mr Samuel Wesley has permission to copy and print them. My brother Charles was born a little before Handel's death."

This account of the discovery of these three tunes supplies a useful gloss on something we said in Chapter 3. The three Handel tunes were written as "airs with accompaniment". The two which came into general currency (*Desiring to Love* always lagged behind the others) suffered at once from the prevailing tendency, at the time when they were published, to write all hymn tunes in four parts. Samuel's cheerful assertion that *Cannons* would do for any long metre hymn at once encouraged editors to alter its rhythm, so that the characteristic trochees at the beginnings of the first and second lines became more commonplace imabuses. Right down to the 1904-edition of *Hymns Ancient and Modern* this alteration was made. *Gopsal* suffered much worse; the difficult angles in the melody were variously ironed out, and the awkward corners cut; the accompaniment was left out altogether, and the pause at the end of line 5 was crushed into a regular $\frac{4}{4}$ rhythm. The results, as one goes through hymn books right down to and including the *Cambridge Hymnal* of 1967 are all spurious, even though later recensions come much nearer to Handel's score than did the earlier ones. Even Samuel Sebastian included a thoroughly corrupt text in the *European Psalmist*, and this was all Samuel's fault. The one exception at present to this generalization is *Hymns for Church and School*, in which the tune is set out for unison voices, and the accompaniment has been skilfully realized by one of the music-editors of that book, Mr John Wilson. By referring to no. 117 in that book, the reader can see not only what the famous interpolated notes in the score of *Hymns Ancient and Modern* from 1875 onwards really meant, but also a plausible reconstruction of the postlude which Handel designed to follow the last verse. Whatever other realizations of Handel's figured bass at these two points editors may authorize, or accompanists may perform, there is no excuse now for ignorance of the original text. Samuel may have unearthed the tunes in 1826, but it was 1864 before *Gopsal* ever received anything like an authentic performance. We must add in justice that Dr F. B. Westbrook, in his appendix to *The Music of the Methodist Hymn Book*, put in a strong plea for the restoration of the proper cadential phrase in the melody of the fifth line, a point which even the Oxford Press editors in the *English Hymnal* and derivative books had overlooked.

# APPENDIX III

Extract from a letter (MS.Clar.Dep.c.378) from Christian Iganatius Latrobe to Joseph Foster Barham, M.P.

18 April, 1808

... Tomorrow I am going to introduce Mr. Samuel Wesley to Mr. Greville to play upon his new organ. I wish you were there to hear him. He is the man for me, combining all the grandeur of old harmonies with the sprightliness and fancy of a most vivid and luxuriant musical imagination, and unquestionably the most perfect extempore performer in this country (which is not saying much), but as Solomon says, anywhere abroad. I hope the organ will be in tune. Mr. Novello plays very prettily on the pianoforte, but there is nothing soul-elevating in his ideas, and on the organ, as you say, he is apt to play violin concertos. In *our* church we get better acquainted with the true organ style, by the majestic old tunes in use among us, but from the recluse mode of our education, we are generally poor sheepish creatures, and not able to perform to advantage in large parties, being utterly deficient in that modest assurance, for which the present generation, and especially the younger part of it, is so eminently distinguished.

On Easter Sunday I went to St. Pauls to hear Sam. Wesley's Responses to the Litany, which are very good and have much singularity about them showing his genius; but they sung a parcel of the most clumsy services, published by Boyce (but not his). I never heard worse (a noise, praetereaque nihil). However, to introduce good music into our Cathedrals is as difficult, as to raise the building itself. A Bishop preached, I believe, for I did not hear him, but only saw him wagging his head and sending forth from under his beehive-wig certain sounds, harsh and undulating, among which I discovered however this most astonishing piece of news, that if we cultivate virtue we shall go to heaven, and if we delight in vice, we must go into what the Germans call Das ewige Daneben. Meanwhile, I must confess, I was contemplating the organ, having got into the organ loft for the first time in my life. It has 28 stops and no more; two octaves of pedals in the German style; 3 rows of keys, the middle, or great organ going down to double double G. It is a most clumsy, inelegant structure, and as you know, with its square compartments, looks more like a press bedstead than an organ.

Everything is horribly dirty and I suppose neither broom nor brush has been seen in that gallery since the days of Sir Christopher Wren. Having taken an accurate survey of the organ and its appurtenances, and looked over the score of S. Wesley's Responses which lay there, I left his Lordship of Lincoln to direct his motley audience how to follow after virtue and eschew evil, and steered my course homeward.

# APPENDIX IV

A summary of the works of the musical Wesleys
(For the details, see Grove's *Dictionary of Music and Musicians*)

CHARLES WESLEY
6 Concertos for organ or harpsichord. op. 1 (about 1778)
5 String quartets (about 1778)
Concerto Grosso, 1784
Music for *Caractacus*
A few anthems
Organ works


SAMUEL WESLEY
4 Masses (mostly transcriptions)
30 Motets
*Morning service in F*
*Te Deum, Sanctus, Kyrie, Nunc Dimittis* and *Burial Service*
*Jubilate*
*Sanctus in F*
9 Anthems
Psalm and hymn tunes, computed at 600 in all
7 Large choral works, including oratorios, *Ruth* (1774), *The Death of Abel*, and *Ode on St Cecilia's Day*
Glees for 3 and 4 voices (26)
4 Symphonies, and one unfinished symphony
4 Overtures (one unfinished)
March for wind band
11 Concertos for organ and orchestra
11 Pieces for string quartet and other chamber combinations
8 Lessons for piano
3 Piano sonatas op. 3
4 Piano sonatas and 2 duets, op. 5
*Sonata with Fugue* (subject by Salomon)
2 Sonatinas
25 Rondos for piano
14 other piano works
Sonata for three pianos
3 Grand duets for organ
*Concerto in D* for organ, 1800
About 50 organ pieces
25 Songs
4 Vocal duets

SAMUEL SEBASTIAN WESLEY
26 Anthems and church solos
*Full Service in E*
3 Other services (chant) and one *Gloria*
*The European Psalmist*
*The Psalter Pointed for Chanting*
Chants and hymn tunes
2 Secular choral works
3 Glees
2 Piano works
Some 12 organ works
6 Songs

On Samuel Wesley's *Original Hymn Tunes*, 1828

Original Hymn Tunes
Adapted to every Metre in the Collection
by
The Rev. JOHN WESLEY, A.M.
late Fellow of Lincoln College, Oxford
Newly composed and arranged for
FOUR VOICES
with a separate accompaniment
for the
ORGAN OR PIANO FORTE
by
SAMUEL WESLEY

London, Published for the Author, 16 Euston Street, Euston Square and sold at the Conference Office, 14 City Road and 66 Paternoster Row.
Messrs Mayhew & Co., 17 Old Bond Street, & Willis, 55 St James's Street.

Some account of this book, now very rare (but a copy with the author's signature is in the possession of Sir John Dykes Bower, who kindly lent it to me) may be of interest to hymnologists, besides furnishing a sidelight on one or two aspects of Samuel's later techniques of composition.

THE PREFACE [transcribed]

That Variety of Versification and of Cadence constitutes two brilliant charms in Poetry is acknowledged as an experimental Truth; and surely these Means of mental Gratification cannot be more worthily or laudably employed, than when the Subjects of the Poesy are sacred and devotional.

It appears, however, that a sufficient Variety of both has not been generally cultivated in the Psalmody of the Established Church; The old Version of the English singing Psalms, composed by THOMAS STERNHOLD, JOHN HOPKINS, and others of the same Date, extends only to six Metres; and it is needless to animadvert on the homeliness of their Versification, which has been long justly branded as pure Doggerel.

[The following paragraph appears as a footnote at this point]
Take the following Specimen from the 50th Psalm 5th ver. (4th line):

> Eat I the flesh
>     of great Bulls and Bullocks?
> Or drink the Blood
>     of Goats or of the Flocks?
> Offer to God
>     Praise and hearty Thanksgiving,
> And pay thy Vows
>     unto God everliving.

Nevertheless there occurs one Verse (the 10th) of the 18th Psalm, as happily expressed, that our Poet DRYDEN is reported to have wished himself the Author of it.

> On Cherub, and on Cherubims[1]
>     Full royally he rode;
> And on the Wings of mighty Winds
>     Came flying all abroad.

[end of footnote]

What is termed the new Version, by TATE and BRADY, has also six Metres, and contains some hundred of Lines, more approximating towards Poetry than the other, but yet every good Judge of it will frankly own, that the Majority of the Verses is poor, flat, and prosaic.

[here follows a quotation from John Wesley's famous *Preface* of 1779]
It occurred to my mind long ago that a Set of Tunes appropriate to all the several Metres (which amount to twenty-six in this excellent and valuable Collection) has hitherto been wanting.

The late CHARLES FREDERICK LAMPE, a Native of Germany, and an accomplished Musician, at the Solicitation of my Father, the Revd. CHARLES WESLEY "the greater part" of the Hymns "was composed by the Revd. C. Wesley": see Preface p. IV Note). who had an extensive regard for him (see the Set of Funeral Hymns, in which will be found a very beautiful one "On the death of Mr C. F. Lampe" . . .) furnished an admirable Set of Tunes, fitted to several

---

[1] This is Tautology, because the Order of Angels is in both Words the same.—Cherubim is the plural of Cherub, so that Cherubims is wholly wrong.

of the Metres, and which in the Author's Time were in high Estimation and general Use.

Probably a Portion of them may yet be occsaionally sung in some of the various Congregations; but I rather believe, that the greater Part of them has grown into Disuse, and very inferior Strains substituted and practised in their Stead.

To all those who feel a conscientious Interest in promoting and extending the Exercise of "Psalms, Hymns and spiritual Songs, singing and making Melody in their Heart to the LORD" (Ephesians Chap. V. Ver. 19), regarding it as a Union of Duty with Delight, the following Volume is now respectfully presented; and I have endeavoured to form the several Melodies in the most commodious Method I could devise for general Utility.

In the Time of LAMPE, (the excellent Composer before mentioned) it was not a customary Practice for an English Congregation to sing Psalms or Hymns in separate Parts, but almost always in Unison only: Since which, the Cultivation of the Harmony united with the Melody has been gradually increasing: I have accordingly set the latter in four parts, suiting the several Divisions of the human Voice; viz: Treble, high Tenor, lower Tenor and Base; and have employed only the G and F Clefts throughout, which are universally known to all who can read music; excluding altogether the C Clefs, which are less so.

It is proper to observe that although just Harmony conjoined with pure Melody will be always manifestly preferable in Richness of Effect to Melody alone; yet if a Melody be composed of such Intervals as are naturally gratifying, even to an uncultivated Ear, the general Effect of such Melody will always be pleasing and attractive, when uttered only by a single Voice, and may be increased by a multiplied Unison of Voices to an incalculable Extent of simple Grandeur (II Chronicles. Ch. V. Ver 13.14).

When the late JOSEPH HAYDN—one of the brightest luminaries in our musical Hemisphere—happened to be present in St Paul's Cathedral, during the Service annually performed at the Meeting of the several Charity Schools, he was heard to declare, that he had "never witnessed Effects of the simple sublime in Music, equal to those of a vast Multitude of Voices singing together in Unison."

It is proper to apprize those Students who are accustomed to accompany their own Voices singly, that the Harmony produced by four Voices, is in this Collection, condensed into the two separate staves of the Organ Part; so that when only the upper Part—i.e. the Treble—is sung, and all the rest played—in the Arrangement for

the Organ—the Tune will be as truly—though not so effectively—
performed, as if it were sung by four Voices, in the Score that
stands in the Page above the Accompaniment.

In Conclusion, let me be permitted to observe, that in the following Collection of original Melodies, there will be found neither a
fastidious Affectation of Novelty, nor a pedantic Display of Science;
no Attempt to seduce Attention from the Expression of the Melody
by chromatic or eccentric Harmony: the primary and grand Aim
has been to produce universal Utility in the Advancement and Encouragement of devotional Singing in a Stile perfectly easy to all
who can attain the Intervals of a common Psalm Tune.

That good Poetry is enhanced by a judicious Application of
musical Measures, long and daily Experience continually demon-
strates; and I have been conscientiously seculous in endeavouring to
render every Strain appropriate to the energetic Beauties by which
these Hymns are characterized throughout; to steer equally clear of
insipid Monotony and of secular Levity; and to render the Work
an acceptable Present to all who promote and cherish Hermony in
the Heart; who are zealous to increase and establish "Peace on
Earth, good Will towards Men, and who are preparing to enter the
heavenly "ZION, with Songs, and everlasting Joy upon their Heads."
(Isaiah Chapr. XXXV. Ver. 10.)

NOTE: a few footnotes are here incorporated in the text in parentheses, and
the two scriptural quotations are written out in full in footnotes.

### THE CONTENTS

The book contains 38 tunes in the 26 metres (as he calculates it:
examination suggests that the number is in fact 27) mentioned in the
*Preface*. There are four tunes in common metre, five in long metre,
three in 87.87 D, and two in each of 10.10.11.11 and 7.6.7.6.7.7.7.6.

Certain stylistic points at once strike the reader.

1. *Wide compass*. Despite what Samuel has said about the possibility of singing the tunes in unison when required, their melodies
frequently have a wide compass. Only four of them stay within the
octave, seven more have a compass of a ninth, 15 have a compass of
a tenth, nine go to an eleventh, and three go as far as a twelfth—
which is the compass of the original version of *Miles Lane*, but
would be regarded as impracticably wide for a modern congrega-

tion. (It might be added, however, that it is the compass of "The Star-Spangled Banner", and that no patriotic American has ever been heard to complain of this.)

2. *Unison effects.* In view of the same observation in the *Preface*, it is interesting to observe in nine of these tunes the deliberate use of emphatic unison effects. The tune to "Ye servants of God"—a very good one indeed—ends with unisonal treatment of the last five melody notes, and in other tunes whole lines are left without harmony. At this period this is most unusual: the classic nineteenth-century example (outside Wales) is *Christ Church* [EH 411] whose composer, Steggall, was clearly an admirer of the Wesleys.

3. *Scales and arpeggios.* An oratorio-like use of long uninterrupted melodic scales, rising or descending, is another characteristic of these tunes. There are rising scales of an octave or more in two, and descending scales of similar length in five.

The use of the notes of the common chord in direct and un-interrupted succession, which is such a feature of Samuel Sebastian's anthems, is a very conspicuous feature of these hymn tunes. The device appears in no fewer than nine—almost one in four.

4. *Repeat.* Although the style of the tunes is much more open and simple than the late eighteenth-century evangelical style, Samuel is not above including a repeating section, almost always a simple re-peat of the words of the final line of the verse with an expansive finish to the melody.

The style of the tunes might well be compared with that of Bach's tunes in the Schemelli collection of 1736; Wesley's are as English as Bach's are Continental—that would be expected. But in the same way, Wesley seems to be looking for a lyric and ample melodic expression, and when he says that the tunes would go well in unison, he is justified in that they are almost always thoroughly well-proportioned and graceful melodies.

They have passed right out of English use—if indeed they were ever in it. Although Samuel had the current Wesleyan hymn book open before him (that is, the edition of 1780 with the supplement published in 1800, a fact we deduce from the fact that he refers to hymn numbers up to 558, and it was the 1800 supplement that brought the numbers to 560), subsequent music editions of this book ignored him as completely as hymn books since have done, excepting that of the Moravians. His one "famous" tune—*Doncaster*—is not in this collection. The reason for this neglect—which there is now no hope of repairing—is that musical taste in congregational hymns had already begun to change before Wesley put pen to paper in this project. The two roads for a composer to follow had already been marked out as the "popular" (which brought us such trivia as the still celebrated *Sagina* and *Diadem*) and the undemonstrative, which Novello advocated in *The Psalmist*, and which the new Anglican hymnody encouraged. No place was left for these expansive lyrics, but as historical curiosities they occupy a quite unique place in the history of hymnody, as the considered and far from trivial work of one of England's most influential musicians.

# SELECTIVE BIBLIOGRAPHY

### PRIMARY SOURCES

John Wesley: *Journal* (8 volumes, ed. Curnock, 1909. Epworth Press).

Charles Wesley: *Journal* (2 volumes, ed. Thomas Jackson, 1849. Methodist Book Room).

Samuel Wesley: *Autobiography*, in manuscript (B.M. Add. Mss 27,593: substantially transcribed in Winters: see below).
*Bach Letters*, edited by Eliza Wesley, 1875, reprinted by Hinrichsen (facsimile).

Samuel Sebastian Wesley: *A Few Words on Cathedral Music*, 1849, reprinted by Hinrichsen (facsimile).

### SECONDARY SOURCES

Martin Schmidt: *John Wesley, A Theological Biography* (Epworth 1962).

F. C. Gill: *Charles Wesley, the First Methodist* (Lutterworth, 1964).

W. Winters: *An Account of the Remarkable Musical Talents of Several Members of The Wesley Family*, published by F. Davis, 1 Chapter House Court, Paternoster Row, London: also to be had of the Author, Church Yard, Waltham Abbey, 1874 (now very scarce).

I. T. Lightwood: *Samuel Wesley* (Epworth, 1937; now out of print).

### ARTICLES OF PRIMARY INTEREST

Biographical article on the occasion of the centenary celebrations at Winchester of the birth of Samuel Sebastian Wesley, 1910: *The Hampshire Gazette and General Advertizer for the West of England.*

Kendrick Pyne: article in *English Church Music*, vol. V no. 1, 1935.

Thomas Armstrong: *The Wesleys, Evangelists and Musicians*, in *Organ and Choral Aspects and Prospects*, Hinrichsen, 1958, pp. 95 ff.

Gordon Phillips: *The Wesleys*—introductory articles on Charles, Samuel and Samuel Sebastian in *Tallis to Wesley* (organ music), vol. V, Hinrichsen edition 1757a, 1960.

Gordon Phillips: Samuel Wesley: notes postscripted to Vol. VII of the same series (above), Hinrichsen edition 1766, 1957.

Peter F. Williams: *The Three Wesleys*: introductory notes to Vol. XXIV of the same series (above), Hinrichsen edition 1757b, 1961.

Max Hinrichsen: *Wesley and Mendelssohn in England*: introductory notes to *Sameul Wesley and Dr Mendelssohn* (organ music), Hinrichsen edition 1744b, 1962.

Gerald Finzi: Introductory notes to Charles Wesley, *Concerto no. 4*, Hinrichsen edition 290, 1956.

NOTE: The Hinrichsen edition of extracts from the corpus of Wesley music includes references to other works on the Wesleys: but two of these were never published—namely, G. W. Spink, *Samuel Sebastian Wesley's Cathedral Pilgrimage* and a symposium by S. de B. Taylor and others called *The Curious Case of Samuel Wesley.*

### OTHER BOOKS

J. A. La Trobe: *The Music of the Church, Considered in its Various Branches, Congregational and Choral,* 1831.

P. Scholes: *A Mirror of Music* (*The Musical Times,* 1844–1944), 2 vols., Novello and O.U.P., 1947.

H. Watkins Shaw: *The History of the Three Choirs Festival.*

N. Medici and R. Hughes: *A Mozart Pilgrimage* (Travels of Vincent and Mary Novello), Novello, 1955.

W. L. Sumner, *The Organ,* Macdonald, 1952.

NOTE: Peter F. Williams's important book on the Organ, published 1967, should be consulted, but it was published too late to be used in this work.

### UNPUBLISHED THESIS

A. J. Hiebert: *The Anthems and Services of Samuel Sebastian Wesley* (1810–76). Deposited at George Peabody College, Nashville, Tenn., U.S.A. Microfilm and Xerox copies available through University Microfilms, Inc., Ann Arbor, Michigan, U.S.A. Reference number for microfilm is 66-10,701.

# Index to the Principal Members of the Wesley Family

## JOHN WESLEY (1703–91)

Pronunciation of the Wesley name, 2; Distinguished relatives, 3–4, Ancestors, 4; Personal qualities, 5; views on music, ch. II; Meetings with or references to—Avison, 7; Pepusch, 8; visit to Llanelly, 9; Neath, 9; views on polyphony, 9–10; Thomas Arne, 10; Handel, 11, 23; Bristol cathedral, 10; on the organ, 10–11; Manchester, 10, Exeter, 10; Macclesfield, 11–12; Louth, 12; Builth, 12; Leominster, 13; Newcastle under Lyme, 13; J. F. Lampe, 14; waning of interest in music, 14; "On the Power of Music", 15–21; Scottish visits, 15; Music and emotion, 22–3; his puritanism, 23; views on Scottish tunes, 24; easily bored, 25; his "conversion", 26; further material on his attitude to music, 49.

## CHARLES WESLEY I (1707–88)

His unlikeness to John, 28; views on music, 29, 49; his hymns, 29–42; a faithful anglican, 32, 52; his two sons, 43–57; his puritanism, 48–50; on his sons' being musicians, 49–52; his defence of music-making, 62–3.

## CHARLES WESLEY II (1757–1834)

His early life, 43–8; disadvantages of the Wesley name, 58–9; appointments, 58; early genius, comments on, 59–61; love affair, 63; shiftlessness, 63; Chapel Royal appointment vetoed by family, 63–4; "an obstinate Handelian", 78, 93.
*String quartets*, 76–7
*Concerto C major*, 77
*Organ Voluntaries*, 77–8
*Organ fugues*, 96

## SAMUEL WESLEY (1766–1837)

BIOGRAPHICAL

His father's account of him, 53–7; a prodigy, 53n; Composes *Ruth*, 54; Boyce's commendation, 54; young organist, 55; *Eight Lessons for Harpsichord* (1777), 56; religion, 65–7; views on the R.C. church, 67; the Snow Hill accident, 68–70; his temperament, 65, 69, 71; marriage, 71; influence of Madan, 72–3; Sarah Suter, 74; birth of Sam. Sebastian, 74; Bach letters, 89–98; Surrey Chapel, 90–1; influence of Bach, 98; meeting with Mendelssohn, 99–101; last years, 99; praised by S.S.W., 130; a misascribed anthem, 172; letter about him from C.I. La Trobe, 253; hymn tunes, 240–5, 258–263

WORKS

*Mass de Spiritu sancto*, 67
*In Exitu Israel*, 67, 70, 80–3
*Exultate Deo*, 70, 83
*Omnia Vanitas*, 80, 83–4
*Later anthems*, 84–6
*Might I in thy sight appear*, 86, 91, 205
*Organ Voluntaries, op. 6*, 95
*Organ fugues*, 96
*Twelve Short Pieces*, 96–7
*Voluntary in C for 4 hands*, 98
*Fugue in G*, 98
*Introductory Movement in E*, 98
*Chants*, 99–100
*Fugue in B minor* ("Mendelssohn"), 100–1
*O deliver me*, 205
*O remember not*, 205
*Who is the trembling sinner?*, 205

## SAMUEL SEBASTIAN WESLEY (1810–76)

BIOGRAPHICAL

Birth, 74, 102; Chapel Royal, 102; visit to Brighton, 102; early organ posts, 103; Hereford, 103; conducts *Cosi fan Tutte*, 103; Hereford, 103; first appearance at Three Choirs Festival, 103; Gloucester, 107, 122, 183–4; Exeter, 103–4; Oxford degrees, 104; unsuccessful applications for Edinburgh university chair, 104; and that of London, 104; Leeds Parish Church, 104; Winchester, 105–7; interest in fishing, 106; Organist: 105, 108, 150, 152, 173, 177–192; Temperament, 106; Death, 107; professional standards, 108, 111; *A Few Words*, 84, 105, 127–137; S.S.W. and J. B. Dykes, 216–21.

WORKS

*The European Psalmist*, 76, 99, 106, 107, 204ff
*Choral Song* (organ), 96, 105, 187–8
*Blessed be the God and Father*, 103, 141–8, 149
*The Wilderness*, 102, 152–7
*Variations in F sharp minor* (organ), 105,
*Service in E*, 105, 131, 164–6
*Ascribe unto the Lord*, 106, 143, 162–4
*All go unto one place*, 106, 149, 172
*Praise the Lord*, 107, 173
*Man that is born of woman*, 107
*Wash me throughly*, 148, 149
*Let us lift up*, 149, 159–62
*O give thanks unto the Lord*, 149, 171
*O Lord thou art my God*, 157–9
*Thou wilt keep him in perfect peace*, 166–7
*The Lord is my Shepherd*, 167–8
*Cast me not away*, 168
*The face of the Lord*, 168–9
*Let us now praise famous men*, 173
*Lead me, Lord*, 174
*The Praise of Music*, 174
*Introduction and Fugue in C sharp minor* (organ), 175, 186–7
*Andante in G* (organ), 188
*Andante in E flat* (organ), 190
*Andante in E minor* (organ), 190
*I will arise*, 205
*Benedicite in D*, 205
*Blessed is the man*, 205
*Discovery of Handel's hymn tunes*, 250–53
*Original hymn tunes*, 201–27

# General Index

HYMN TUNES are printed in SMALL CAPITALS

Abel, K. F., 55
Addison, J., 31, 198
Aldrich, H., 26
Amati family, 20-1
AMESBURY, 37-8
Anglican chants, 99-100, 117, 233-8
Arne, T., 7, 10, 46
Arnold, J. H., 234
Arnold, S., 46, 47, 53
Attwood, T., 102, 124, 130
Avison, C., 6-7
Aylsbury, Lord, 55
Aylward, T. E., 108

Bach family, 3
Bach, J. C., 53n
Bach, J. S., 37, 55, 70, 75, 91ff, 140,
   181-2, 199
Bairstow, Sir E., 159, 175
Baker, F., 30
Baker, Sir H., 197, 205, 217
Barham, J. F., 254
Barnby, J., 205
Barrington, D., 53, 61
Barrington, Lord, 55
Barry, Canon (fl. 1865), 122
Battishill, J., 47
Beard, J., 44, 45
Beethoven, L. van, 64, 119, 122, 124,
   133, 140, 236
BERKSHIRE, 58
Berlioz, H., 125
Best, W, T., 98, 181, 182
Bevan, M., 27

Bishop, Sir H., 104
Blom, E., 3
Boswell, J., 1
Boyce, W., 7, 47, 48, 54, 67, 89, 98,
   130
Brahms, J., 125, 140
Bridge, Sir F., 26-7
Broderip, J., 43
Bromfield, W., 46, 47
Burney, C., 91, 94
Butts, T., 25
Byfield (organ builder), 178
Byrd, W., 7, 84, 135, 234

Cardew, C., 22
Carter, S., 121
Chambers, H. A., 188
Chappell, publisher, 94
Charlotte, Queen, 45n
Chesterfield, Lord, 45
Chope, R. R., 213
Colley, R., 3
Corelli, G., 45, 48
Cowley, Baron, 3
Cowper, W., 62
Cramer, W., 55
Croft, W., 26, 139
Crotch, W., 56-7, 61

Davies, H. Walford, 235
DIADEM, 41
DOWN AMPNEY, 231
Dryden, T., 16, 21

Dudley, Lord (fl. 1770) 55
Dudley, Lord (fl. 1865) 123
Dupré, M., 183
Dvořák, A., 125
Dykes, J. B., 140, 197, 216–21
Dykes-Bower, Sir J., 26, 258

Eardley-Wilmot family, 54
Economics of church music, 131–4
Edinburgh, chair of music at, 104, 130
Elgar, Sir E., 125, 140
Elman, M., 59
ELTHAM, 35–6, 227–32
Emery, W., 188
EPWORTH, 58
Evangelicalism, 51, 61–3, 111
EVENTIDE, 213
Exhibition, the Great, 1851, 107, 179, 181

Fellowes, E. H., 149, 172
Finzi, G., 76
Fischer, J., 56
Fitzhead (Somerset), 110
Fletcher, J. W., 63
Flute, 20
Folk Music, 121
Forkel, G., 92
Francillon, P., 12
FRENCH, 209
Freylinghausen, J. A., 35
Frost, M., 215
Fuller-Maitland, J. A., 229

Gabrieli, G., 135, 136
Gainsborough, M., 56
Garrett, G., 108
Gawthorne, N., 228
Geiringer, 3
Geminiani, 47, 48
Genius, pattern of early, 59–60
George III, King, 64
Giardini, F., 46, 61
Gibbons, O., 84, 135, 206

Gill, F. C., 50, 62n
Gladstone, F. E., 108
GOPSAL, 227, 249–52
Goss, J., 236
Gounod, C., 174, 200
Granville family, 45, 46
Grant, L., 15
Greene, M., 44n, 183
Gregory, J., 17, 22
Guarneri family, 20

Hackett, M., 134
Hampden, Lord, 123
Handel, G. F., 34–7, 45, 47, 48, 52, 53, 55, 64, 77–9, 81–3, 93, 119, 122, 139, 183, 249
Harris, Renatus, 178
Harwood, B., 175, 193, 223
Havergal, W. H., 250
Haydn, F. J., 37, 60, 79, 83, 119, 122
Heifetz, J., 60
Helmore, T., 136
HELMSLEY, 227
Henry, Matthew, 32
Herbert, G., 198
Heylyn, P., 129
Hill, R., 90
Hinrichsen, M., 98
Hodsall, publisher, 97
Hollins, A., 182, 186
Hook, W. F., 104
Horn, K. F., 92
Hotham family, 45
Hume, D., 51
Humfrey, P., 235
Hutchings, A. J. B., 138, 196
Hymn tune, the English, 196–9
Hymns Ancient and Modern, 107, 217
Hymns for the People Called Methodists, 15
Hymns, Methodist, style of, 37

Insularity in music, 138
INVITATION, 35–6
Isaak, H., 135

Jackson, W., 14
Jacob, B., 90, 97
John XXII, Pope, 7
Johnson, Dr S., 1
Jordan, organ builder, 11, 178
Josquin des Pres, 135
*Judas Maccabaeus*, 13-4

Keeble, J., 46
Kelway, J., 45, 47, 53
Kemble, H., 157
Kendall, H., 12
King's Weigh House Chapel, 35
Kitson, C. H., 230
Kollmann, A., 89-90, 97

La Feillée, 67
La Trobe, C. I., 254
La Trobe, J. A., 111-9, 126
Lampe, J. F., 14, 35
Landseer, 131
Law, W., 8
Lawes, H., 40, 206
Lee Williams, C., 167
Leo, X, Pope, 6
Lightwood, J. W., vii-ix, 66, 68, 70, 71-5
Limpus, R. D., 180
Linley, T., 44n, 54
Lock Hospital, 10, 41, 58, 64, 72
Loosemore, organ builder, 11
Lovelace, A. C., 27
LUCKINGTON, 223
LUX BENIGNA, 224-5

Maclardie, A., 11
Madan, M., 7, 10, 41, 44, 45n, 46, 54, 62, 72-3
Maryborough, Baron, 3-4
Mechlin *Graduale* (1848), 136
Nendelssohn-Bartholdy, F., 95, 98-101, 124, 139, 145-6, 179, 181, 200, 202
Menuhin, Y., 60

Mercer, W., 250
Nessiaen, O., 20, 177
Methodist music, 34-42
Milton, J., 49
Monk, W. H., 213, 217, 218
Mornington, Lord, 3
Mozart, W. A., 52, 60, 119, 124, 133, 184

National Anthem, 53n, 56, 191-2
Nature, philosophy of, 8
NEWINGTON, 209
Nicholson, Sir S., 204
Novello, V., 59, 75, 87, 99, 119-21, 126, 253

OLD 124th, 214
OLD 132nd, 209
OLD 137th, 208
Oliphant, T., 174
ORGAN
    John Wesley and, 10ff
    music and design, 95, 117-8
    pedal board, 175, 178-9, 181
    recitals, 176, 184-6

Palestrina, G. P. da, 133-4, 135
Parry, C. H. H., 229
Patrick, M., 24
Patronage, 79
Pepusch, J. C., 7-9, 17, 34
Philips, G., ix, 77, 97, 188
Pierson, H., 104
Pinto, G. F., 89, 90
Plainsong, 136
Plato, 20
Portuguese Embassy, 66-7, 70
Poston, E., 121
Purcell, H., 26, 31, 45, 119
Puritanism, 4, 5, 23, 48-50, 113, 129, 139
Pyne, K., 102, 108, 182, 201-2

Rachmaninoff, S., 232
RELIANCE, 215

Rich, J., 45, 252
Rippon, J., 120n
Rogers, "Mr" (of Bristol), 44, 45
Roman Catholicism in the 18th cent.,
    66
Royal College of Organists, 180
Royal School of Church Music, 133

St Martin's in the Fields, 12, 45n
*St Matthew Passion*, 95, 124
St Paul's (London), 26–7
Salomon Concerts, 90
Savage, S. M., 47
Scarlatti, D., 45, 47, 48
Schemelli Song Book, 37
Schobert, J., 55
Scholes, P., 49, 53n, 69, 172n, 184n,
    185, 192
Schubert, F., 200, 216
Schütz, H., 135
Shaw, H. Watkins, 103n, 172
Sibthorp, R. E., 235–7
Smart, Sir G., 178
Smart, H., 124, 226
Smith, J. C., 44, 47n
Smith, R. F., 214
Snow Hill, 68–70
Spark, W., 108
Spencer, K., 94
Spohr, L., 124, 184, 185, 200
Stainer, J., 107, 140, 210, 236
Stanley, J., 44, 47, 77, 183
Steggall, C., 139, 214, 227, 262
Stradivari, A., 20
STRACATHRO, 209
Sullivan, Sir A., 200
Sumner, W. L., 11, 12n, 178
Surrey Chapel, 87, 90, 180
Swell organ, 11

Tallis, T., 7, 135, 206
Taylor, S. de B., ix, 174, 188
Telemann, 89
Thalben-Ball, G. T., 237
Thiman, E. H., 230–1

THORNBURY, 223
Three Choirs Festival, 103, 121–6,
    183–4
Timotheus, legend of, 18, 21
Turle, J., 214
Turner, J., 206

Vaughan Williams, R., 2, 138, 197,
    231
Vento, M., 46, 55
Violin, 20
Virgil, 22
Voluntary, organ, 78

Walmisley, T. A., 150, 181
Watts, I., 30–2, 228
Webbe, S., 67
Weelkes, T., 135
Wellesley family, 3
Wellington, Duke of, 3
Welsh hymns, 226–7
WESLEY
    for the five principal Wesleys
    see separate index beginning on
    page 266
Wesley, Bartholomew, 4
Wesley, Charlotte L., 71, 73, 74
Wesley, Charles III, 73
Wesley, Eliza, 75, 90
Wesley, Emma Frances, 73
Wesley, John W., 73
Wesley, Robert Glenn, 75
Wesley, Samuel (senior), 4
Wesley Sarah ("Sally"), 29, 50, 71
Wesley, Sarah (Suter), 74–5, 102
Westbrook, F. B., 253
Whitfeld, J. Clarke, 103
Williams, P. ix, 77, 97, 98
Willis, Henry, 107, 180, 181, 205
Wilson, J. W., 253
Winters, W., viii, 68, 70
*Wir glauben All'* (Bach), 95
Wise, M., 215
Worgan, J., 44, 47
Wynne, W. W., 55